Double Agent Balloon

In loving memory of my late wife and soulmate
Evelyn Jean Tremain
(1952–2022)

Double Agent Balloon

Dickie Metcalfe's Espionage Career for MI5 and the Nazis

DAVID TREMAIN

Pen & Sword
MILITARY

AN IMPRINT OF PEN & SWORD BOOKS LTD.
YORKSHIRE – PHILADELPHIA

First published in Great Britain in 2023 by
PEN AND SWORD MILITARY
An imprint of
Pen & Sword Books Limited
Yorkshire – Philadelphia

Copyright © David Tremain, 2023

ISBN 978 1 39906 109 4

The right of David Tremain to be identified as Author
of this work has been asserted by him in accordance with the Copyright,
Designs and Patents Act 1988.

A CIP catalogue record for this book is available from the British Library.

All rights reserved. No part of this book may be reproduced or transmitted in
any form or by any means, electronic or mechanical including photocopying,
recording or by any information storage and retrieval system, without permission
from the Publisher in writing.

Typeset in Times New Roman 10/12 by
SJmagic DESIGN SERVICES, India.
Printed and bound in the UK by CPI Group (UK) Ltd.

Pen & Sword Books Limited incorporates the imprints of Atlas, Archaeology,
Aviation, Discovery, Family History, Fiction, History, Maritime, Military, Military
Classics, Politics, Select, Transport, True Crime, Air World, Frontline Publishing,
Leo Cooper, Remember When, Seaforth Publishing, The Praetorian Press,
Wharncliffe Local History, Wharncliffe Transport, Wharncliffe True Crime and
White Owl.

For a complete list of Pen & Sword titles please contact
PEN & SWORD BOOKS LIMITED
47 Church Street, Barnsley, South Yorkshire S70 2AS, United Kingdom
E-mail: enquiries@pen-and-sword.co.uk
Website: www.pen-and-sword.co.uk

Or
PEN AND SWORD BOOKS
1950 Lawrence Rd, Havertown, PA 19083, USA
E-mail: Uspen-and-sword@casematepublishers.com
Website: www.penandswordbooks.com

Contents

Author's Note   vii
Acknowledgements   viii
Abbreviations   ix
Dramatis Personae   xii
Foreword, by Nigel West   xiv
Introduction   xvi

Chapter 1   Arms and the Man   1
Chapter 2   'The man's keen!'   13
Chapter 3   Going Dutch   16
Chapter 4   BALLOON's Report on Holland   22
Chapter 5   The Air Ministry Leaks   25
Chapter 6   'A man of intelligence and resource'   28
Chapter 7   A Network Evolves   34
Chapter 8   Plan MIDAS   46
Chapter 9   BALLOON's Reports   60
Chapter 10 Plan STENCH   76
Chapter 11 The 'mythical Christmas card'   78
Chapter 12 'Gardiner is all right'   81
Chapter 13 The Scandinavian Connection   84
Chapter 14 'A sub-machine gun of outstanding design'   89
Chapter 15 A thorn in BALLOON's side   103
Chapter 16 The Grand, Cliveley and Postnikow Affair   105
Chapter 17 'It is clear that B is in debt'   108
Chapter 18 Correspondence   113

Chapter 19	The BALLOON Traffic (Part 1)	120
Chapter 20	The TRIBAGE Organisation	140
Chapter 21	The BALLOON Traffic (Part 2)	144
Chapter 22	'Plan A'	151
Chapter 23	'I regard this as very naughty of BALLOON'	155
Chapter 24	Cover Addresses	158
Chapter 25	Going nowhere	166
Chapter 26	'He continues to provide such information …'	186
Chapter 27	'A man of intelligence and resource'	193
Epilogue		195
Afterword		200
Bibliography		202
Notes		206
Index		239

Author's Note

Unless otherwise specified in the Notes, all quotes and extracts have been taken from files at the National Archives at Kew (TNA). When quoting from these files some minor formatting changes have occasionally been made to ensure the text flows better, and accents added to French and German words where they were missed out in the original text because the typewriters of the time lacked those keys; otherwise, no changes have been made to the original punctuation or spelling. The terms 'MI6' and 'SIS' are frequently used interchangeably to mean the British Secret Intelligence Service. Unless it is specifically used in a quote or a bibliographic reference, the term 'SIS' will be used in this book. Codenames or aliases are prefixed using the symbol @. Some names have been redacted from the original documents, but where possible these have been identified and inserted in square brackets, thus: [John Smith].

Acknowledgements

All files in the National Archives are © Crown Copyright and are reproduced with permission under the terms of the Open Government Licence. Quotes from *Hansard* contain Parliamentary information licensed under the Open Parliament Licence v3.0.

Every attempt has been made to seek and obtain permission for copyright material used in this book. In certain cases this has not been possible. However, if we have inadvertently used copyright material without permission/acknowledgements we apologise and we will make the necessary correction at the first opportunity. The author and publisher would like to gratefully acknowledge the following for their assistance or for permission to reproduce copyright material:

Malcolm Atkin; Barry Attoe, Postal Museum; Charles Beck; Olivier Blanc-Brude; Hannah Dale, Cheltenham College Archives; Getty Images; Henry Hemming; Alan 'Fred' Judge, Military Intelligence Museum, Chicksands; Ian Kelly (Militaria); Michaela Keyserlingk; Steven Kippax; Raymond Lutz; Paul McCue; John Tepper Marlin; Royal Armouries, Leeds; Peter C. Smith for permission to use a map from his book *Into the Minefields*; and Nigel West for the Foreword.

I would also like to thank Claire Hopkins, Lucy May, Richard Doherty, and all the team at Pen & Sword for making this book possible. Finally, to the team of dedicated care-givers at Forest Valley Terrace I want to extend a heartfelt very special thank-you for the excellent care they provided to my wife Evelyn. You exemplify all the best things that your job requires – patience, warmth, compassion, empathy – and I admire each and every one of you in more ways than I can ever express. The world needs more people like you.

Abbreviations

AA	Anti-aircraft
ACASI	Assistant Chief of the Air Staff (Intelligence)
ACIGS	Assistant Chief of Imperial General Staff
ADA	Assistant Director, 'A' Branch (MI5)
ADC	Aide-de-camp
ADNI	Assistant Director Naval Intelligence
AEG	Allgemeine Elektricitäts-Gesellschaft AG (English: "General electricity company")
AFDC	Air Force Department Constabulary; Air Force Development Centre
AGF	Anglo-German Fellowship
AOA	Air Officer i/c Administration (RAF)
AOC	Air Officer Commanding (RAF)
APM	Assistant Provost Marshal
ARP	Air Raid Precautions
A/T	Anti-tank
ATS	Auxiliary Transport Service
BAOR	British Army of the Rhine
BOAC	British Overseas Airways Corporation
BRCS	British Red Cross Society
BSA	Birmingham Small Arms Company, Enfield
BSS	Bayswater Security Section (SOE)
BUF	British Union of Fascists (later shortened to British Union)
CCG (BE)	Control Commission Germany (British Element) (post-war)
CDRD	Chemical Defence Research Department, Porton Down
C-in-C	Commander-in-Chief
CIA	Chief Inspector of Arms
CID	Criminal Investigation Department
CIGS	Chief of Imperial General Staff (British Army)
CISA	Chief Inspector of Small Arms
CIU	Central Interpretation Unit, RAF Medmenham
CO	Commanding Officer
CPR	Combined Planning Research Office
CRO	Criminal Records Office
CSWBL	Central Security War Black List

CX	SIS reports
DAF	Deutsche Arbeitsfront (German Labour Front)
DofI (S)	Director of Intelligence (Security), Air Ministry
DDI (S)	Deputy Director of Intelligence (Security), Air Ministry
DDW	Deputy Director of Weapons (War Office)
DMI	Director(ate) of Military Intelligence
DNI	Director(ate) of Naval Intelligence
DNO	Director(ate) of Naval Ordnance
DOT	Department of Overseas Trade
DSR	Director(ate) of Scientific Research
FBI	Federal Bureau of Investigation (USA)
FPS	Future (Operational) Planning Section (also FOPS)
GLU	General Look-Up
GOC-in-C	General Officer Commanding-in-Chief
GPO	General Post Office
GRU	Soviet/Russian military intelligence
GSO2	General Staff Officer 2 (Major)
HDE	Home Defence Executive
HMG	His Majesty's Government
HO	Home Office
HOW	Home Office Warrant
IARHC	Inter-Allied Rhineland High Commission
IB	Investigation Branch (GPO); Intelligence Branch
IO	Immigration Officer
IP	International Police (Portugal)
IPI	Indian Political Intelligence
IRBd	Information & Records Branch, Imperial Censorship
ISOS	Intelligence Service Oliver Strachey/Illicit Services Oliver Strachey (Abwehr hand cypher intercepts)
ISRB	Inter-Services Research Bureau (cover name for SOE)
ISSB	Inter-Services Security Board
JIC	Joint Intelligence Committee
KO	Kriegsorganisation (War Organisation – Abwehr in Allied and neutral countries)
LCS	London Controlling Section
LU	Look-up
MAP	Ministry of Aircraft Production
MEW	Ministry of Economic Warfare
MGB	Motor Gun Boat
MGO	Master-General of the Ordnance
MI1c	Former designation for MI6
MI5	Security Service
MI6	*q.v.* SIS
MI10	Directorate of War Office responsible for weapons and technical analysis
MI11	Directorate of War Office responsible for field security

ABBREVIATIONS

MI(R)	Sabotage and guerilla operations (forerunner of SOE)
MOL	Ministry of Labour
MOS	Ministry of Supply
MOT	Ministry of Overseas Trade
MS	Military Secretary's Office (War Office)
MTB	Motor Torpedo Boat
MTC	Motor Transport Corps
NID	Naval Intelligence Division
NSDAP	Nationalsozialistische Deutsche Arbeiterpartie (National Socialist German Workers' Party – Nazi Party)
OGPU	Soviet intelligence (1922-34)
OKW	Oberkommando der Wehrmacht (High Command of the German Army)
OMGUS	Office of Military Government United States
PCO	Passport Control Officer
PID	Political Intelligence Department (Foreign Office)
PUS	Permanent Under-Secretary
RAC	Royal Automobile Club
RAD	Reichsleitung des Arbeitsdienstes (Management of the Labour Service)
RAE	Royal Aircraft Establishment
RAF	Royal Air Force
RAFVR	Royal Air Force Volunteer Reserve
RAMC	Royal Army Medical Corps
RAOC	Royal Army Ordnance Corps
RCMP	Royal Canadian Mounted Police
RE	Royal Engineers
REME	Royal Electrical & Mechanical Engineers
RMO	Royal Marine Office
RNVR	Royal Navy Volunteer Reserve
Room 055	War Office liaison with MI5
RSHA	Reichssicherheitshauptsamt (Reich Main Security Office)
RSLO	Regional Security Liaison Officer (MI5)
RSS	Radio Security Service, MI8c (MI6)
SD	Sicherheitsdienst (SS intelligence)
SIME	Security Intelligence Middle East
SIS	Secret Intelligence Service *q.v.* MI6
SO2	Forerunner of SOE
SOE	Special Operations Executive
SOI	Staff Officer Intelligence (RN)
STD	Soviet Trade Delegation
VAD	Voluntary Aid Detachment
VCIGS	Vice Chief of the Imperial General Staff
WAAF	Women's Auxiliary Air Force
WO	War Office
XX	Double Cross Committee

Dramatis Personae

MI5
Brig. H.I. 'Harry' Allen, Director, C & D Divisions
Hugh Astor B1a
Milicent Bagot B4b
Susan Barton B1a
John Bingham B5b
Roland Bird B3a
F/Lt Charles Cholmondeley B1a; member of the Twenty Committee
Maj. Edward Cussen SLB2
Alan Grogan B3d
Brig. Oswald Allen 'Jasper' Harker A/Director (1940-41); Deputy Director General (1941-46)
Christopher Harmer B1a
Tomás Harris B1g
C.P. (Cyril) Harvey B1a
Maj. Gen. Sir Vernon Kell Director General (1909-40)
Maj. Maxwell Knight B5b
Maj. Gilbert Lennox Room 055, War Office, MI5 liaison
Capt. Guy Liddell ADB1, B Division
W.E. 'Billy' Luke B1a
John Marriott B1a; secretary of the Twenty Committee
Maj. J.C. (John) Masterman B1a; chairman of the Twenty Committee
Cyril Mills B1a
Desmond Orr Room 055, War Office, MI5 liaison
Brig. Sir David Petrie, Director General (1941-46)
Lt Col Thomas Argyll 'Tar' Robertson B1a
Victor, Lord Rothschild B1c
Dick Goldsmith White ADB, Assistant Director, B Division
D.H. Whyte B2a
D. Ian Wilson B1a
Kenneth Younger ADE, Assistant Director, E Division
William 'Bill' Younger B5b, cousin to Kenneth Younger

MI6/SIS
Felix Cowgill Head, Section V

DRAMATIS PERSONAE

Maj. Frank Foley Section V
Capt. M. Lloyd Section Vx
Sir Stewart Menzies 'C', Chief of SIS (1939-52)
Ian 'Tim' Milne Section Vd
H.A.R. 'Kim' Philby Section Vd
Col Valentine Vivian VCSS, Vice Chief of SIS

Double Cross Agents
ARTIST Johann 'Johnny' Jebsen,
BALLOON Christopher 'Dicky' Metcalfe (German: IVAN II)
CARELESS Clarc Korab
DREADNOUGHT Ivo Popov
G.W. Gwilym Williams
GELATINE Friedl Gartner (German: YVONNE)
METEOR Eugn Šoštarić
TATE Wulf Schmidt
TRICYCLE; SKOOT Dušan 'Duško' Miloradoff Popov (German: IVAN I)
VELOCIPEDE Unidentified
THE WORM Stefan Zeis

Foreword
by Nigel West

In 1970 the American historian Ladislas Farago was trawling through captured German records at the National Archives' warehouse in Suitland, Maryland, when he stumbled across a military footlocker packed with microfiche films. Upon examination these turned out to be a collection of files seized from the Abwehr's headquarters in Hamburg. This particular *Abstelle* had played an important part in the espionage war because the port, a pre-war centre of transatlantic shipping and maritime trade with England and Farago uncovered a veritable treasure-trove of intelligence records that, sensationally, suggested that German spies had operated undetected across the United Kingdom throughout the conflict. Indeed, one enterprising agent, designated A-3725, had parachuted into Cambridgeshire in September 1940 and had been in almost daily wireless contact with the Abwehr's receiving station at Wohldorf right up to the German surrender. Based on his discovery, Farago wrote *The Game of the Foxes*[1] which he submitted to his publishers who warned him that a former British intelligence officer, Sir John Masterman, was negotiating the publication of a book, *The Double Cross System of the War of 1939-45*[2] which was alleged to be based on an MI5 report drafted immediately after the hostilities. Reportedly, Masterman had a very different perspective on German wartime espionage, and was claiming that every enemy agent in the UK had been captured or turned. Shocked by this revelation, Farago used his extensive publishing contacts to acquire a copy of Masterman's manuscript, which prompted a hasty re-assessment of his own draft, and a substantial last-minute rewrite. Far from being a loyal Nazi, A-3725 was better known to MI5 as the double agent TATE. Indeed, all his radio messages to his Abwehr controllers had been transmitted under MI5's supervision.Masterman's authoritative version of events effectively transformed our understanding of wartime espionage and gave a compelling account of how a handful of British case officers had manipulated a large group of enemy spies and fed them, and their Abwehr contacts, a carefully fabricated diet of 'chicken-feed' with the intention of exposing other, as yet undiscovered, assets and of mounting deception schemes to mislead Axis analysts about Allied strategic intentions.

> Not only have double agents been run on a long-time basis, but they have been run so extensively that we can think not in terms of a

FOREWORD

few isolated cases, but in terms of a double agent system. In fact by virtue of this system *we actively ran and controlled the German espionage system in this country*. This is at first blush a staggering claim and one which in the nature of things could not be advanced until late in the history of the war. Even after we felt sure that it was in fact justified we took the greatest care not to assert it lest the bubble of premature confidence should be pricked by unexpected events. Nevertheless it is true, and was true for the greater part of the war.[3]

By the time Masterman had made his disclosures, several of MI5's double agents had written accounts of their exploits, among them Christopher Draper in *The Mad Major*;[4] Eddie Chapman in *The Real Eddie Chapman Story*;[5] Lily Sergueiev in *Secret Service Rendered*;[6] and Roman Garby-Czerniawski in *The Big Network*.[7] Taken in isolation, none of these titles even hinted at a large-scale, co-ordinated effort to recruit and manage double agents, as none were aware of the others, but the release of Masterman's detailed account prompted Duško Popov (TRICYCLE)[8]; John Moe (MUTT);[9] Juan Pujol (GARBO);[10] and Ib Ruiis (COBWEB)[11] to describe their contributions. Other authors were also inspired to undertake biographies of SNOW[12]; CELERY;[13] SUMMER;[14] TATE;[15], FIDO;[16] CHEESE;[17] and ZIGZAG.[18] Over the past ten years, with the help of an enlightened policy of declassification, much of the history of the Second World War has been revised to take account of signals intelligence, strategic deception, and the other components of clandestine counter-intelligence.

The great challenge, of course, in double-agent operations is to persuade the relevant military authorities to sacrifice sufficient authentic information to retain the enemy's interest so that they are dissuaded from infiltrating yet more spies. A failure to find a suitable mechanism to channel material to an adversary will inevitably result in the exploitation of other sources, and the abandonment of developing conduits. It was not until December 1940, and the arrival in London of a Yugoslav, self-confessed Abwehr agent with instructions to build an independent spy ring, that the Security Service and the three branches of the armed forces agreed to collaborate to extract maximum advantage from the opportunity to mislead the enemy, capture genuine spies, milk the Axis of resources and study their methodology and tradecraft. The supervising inter-agency committee, technically a sub-committee of the all-powerful Chiefs of Staff Committee, met for the first time in January 1941. It was into this Yugoslav spy ring in London that BALLOON was inserted.

© Nigel West
www.nigelwest.co

Introduction

'Dicky' Metcalfe did not look like a secret agent. Indeed, his codename, BALLOON, stemmed from his rotund appearance. His story is multi-faceted, spanning the years before the Second World War until just after it ended: a less-than-stellar Army career; his attempts to have his commission reinstated; his recruitment by MI5 as a double-cross agent; his involvement in the development of a new sub-machine gun for British forces, and various arms deals.

As double-cross agent BALLOON his contribution to the war effort is less well-known than the more celebrated double agent 'Duško' Popov (TRICYCLE), whose vicarious lifestyle has often been compared to that of James Bond, and frequently been touted as one of many models for Ian Fleming's famous secret agent. His visit to the casino in Estoril, Portugal in July 1941 may have inspired Fleming's scene in *Casino Royale* based on his own visit there, but in Popov's autobiography he says:

> I'm told that Fleming said he based his character James Bond to some degree on me and my experiences. As for me, I rather doubt that a Bond in the flesh would have survived more than forty-eight hours as an espionage agent. Fleming and I did rub shoulders in Lisbon, and a few weeks before I took the clipper for the States he did follow me about. Perhaps he developed what happened that night into a Bond adventure.[1]

While the Hon. Ewen Montagu commented in the Foreword, 'At the same time, he exhibited a basic common sense that James Bond never displayed'[2] His career as a double-cross agent has been well-documented in a couple of recent books, and his autobiography,[3] so will only be mentioned here where it involves BALLOON.

Together with double agent GELATINE (Friedl Gartner) they formed the TRIBAGE organisation (from the first few letters of their codenames). In keeping with properly compartmented spycraft, she and BALLOON would never meet or be aware of each other's existence; only TRICYCLE and their MI5 case officers had met them all.

INTRODUCTION

Throughout his career as a double-cross agent BALLOON kept MI5 supplied with titbits of information from his circle of friends and contacts. Since the development of the sub-machine gun occurred concurrently with his role as a double agent, it is sometimes necessary to jump forward or step back in time to relate both. Exactly how successful he was in the eyes of his British and German masters will be explored as his story unfolds.

David Tremain
Ottawa, 2023

Chapter 1

Arms and the Man

Always known by his family as 'Dicky', Christopher Le Strange Metcalfe was born on 23 May 1907 at Sandal Magna, a suburb of Wakefield, Yorkshire, the only son of Lieutenant Colonel Herbert Charles Metcalfe DSO and Bar (1864-1940) and Dorothea Maude Metcalfe *née* Knight (1870-1954). He had two sisters, Violet Beatrice Armine (1899-1981), formerly Mrs Young, and Daphne Geraldine Dorothea (1904-79).

Before the First World War Herbert had served as Chief Constable of West Suffolk (1902-05) and Chief Constable of Somerset (1908). Much of his early Army career had been spent serving in the Northamptonshire Regiment in Hong Kong, Malaya (Penang), and Ireland (The Curragh). During the First World War he served in a training role before being sent to France and Flanders in 1917; in 1918 he was attached to the 21st Battalion Middlesex Regiment; from 2 November 1918 to 29 May 1919 he commanded the 3rd Battalion Northamptonshire Regiment. Later, he again served as Chief Constable of Somerset (1931-39) before retiring in 1939. He died on 19 January 1940.[1]

Unlike his father, who was educated at Oakham School, Dicky was sent to Cheltenham College in 1921, but only stayed until 1924. An entry in the College Register for 1921 shows that he was in Lower 5b Military.[2] In 1925 he passed out of the Royal Military College, Sandhurst[3] and was commissioned into The Loyal Regiment (North Lancashire) as a second lieutenant on 30 August 1926; on 30 August 1929 he was promoted to lieutenant.[4]

But then at some point his Army career took an about-turn, beginning with being convicted and fined for driving an unlicensed and uninsured car, incurring the 'severe displeasure of the Army Council ... [and] placed under the keen supervision of his superior officers in the Army', even though he had carried out his military duties satisfactorily. Consequently, any further chances of promotion were blocked. Then in December 1934, while serving at Tidworth, a garrison town in Wiltshire, he was tried by general court martial on 15/16 December 1934 and convicted of two of the six charges of

> 'conduct to the prejudice of good order and Military discipline,' in that he, at Tidworth on or about the 25th of May 1934, was concerned in the holding out as genuine by 2/Lt R.A. Pulliblank to Captain M. Thorn, President of the Mess Committee of the

Officers' Mess, 2nd Battalion, The Loyal Regiment, of a certain false receipt purporting to be for the sum of £15 in respect of the purchase of a horse; and that on or about the same date he produced to Captain Thorn, who was President of the Mess Committee of the Officers' Mess, another false receipt purporting to be the receipt of this same W.S. Wood, dated 12th May 1934, for the sum of £40.19.6 in respect, among other items, of the purchase of a horse. Burnett-Stuart had written to Colonel Underwood to ask whether he [Metcalfe] should not be given another chance. To this Colonel Underwood demurred.[5]

He was sentenced to 'take rank and precedence in his Corps and in the Army as if his appointment as Lieutenant bore the date 30th August 1932'. On 6 April 1935 he was forced to resign his commission, something he did under protest. His attempts to re-apply for a commission in the Army in November 1939, and the Administrative and Special Duties Branch of the RAFVR in September 1940, were rejected because of his Army record.

William 'Billy' Luke of MI5's B1a commented on 5 March 1935 that he had been

> very much struck by [Metcalfe's] address and demeanour. He looked me straight in the eye and gave his story with moderation. His allegations against his late Commanding Officer were obviously given with reluctance. The impression I got ... in an interview of nearly an hour was that while his instability in his private affairs probably cannot be questioned, the excellence of his professional conduct is quite borne out by his bearing and address.[6]

An interview conducted by the Master General of the Ordnance (MGO), Lieutenant General Sir Hugh Jamieson Elles, dated 5 March 1935, provides further information on Metcalfe, who had given him a draft petition to the King 'setting forth the main grounds of his arguments':

1. He feels that Colonel Underwood, if he had considered that he was not worthy to continue to hold a commission, might have taken steps to get rid of him after the incident in 1932 when he incurred the grave displeasure of the Army Council.
2. He states that about September 1932 he had run into debt, and appealed to his Father for assistance. His Father paid off his debts, which were entirely a matter within his family and did not concern his professional status. His Father then interviewed Colonel Underwood, and Lieutenant [Metcalfe] urges that Colonel Underwood's impressions that he was extravagant and irresponsible in the matter of debts originated entirely from this

private incident – which in his view was finished and done with – and it is only from that time that Colonel Underwood has always referred to his financial instability.

3. That in August 1934 he received an adverse report, coming on the top of a very favourable report of February of that year (the interim report). Lieutenant [Metcalfe] received this report while on leave in Scotland, and demurred to initialling it and asked to see the Brigade and Divisional Commanders. He states that when he saw the Brigade and Divisional Commanders they had already written their comments on Colonel Underwood's report before having heard his plea. He admits that he had an interview with both these formation Commanders, but suggests that they had both made up their minds beforehand.

He states that the cause of this adverse report was the fact that he had failed to pay –
  (a) A bill for £6 for hay; and
  (b) A bill for £60 for garage.
He was summoned by his Commanding Officer in respect of these two bills and ordered to pay them: he paid the £6 bill at once and the £60 in two instalments within 3 months.

4. Lieutenant [Metcalfe] states, as indeed is set forth in the draft petition, that Colonel Underwood, throughout his service under him, showed him animosity which was patent to all his brother officers, and that he had openly said that he would get rid of Lieutenant Metcalfe before he (Colonel Underwood) gave up command. He contrasts this treatment with that he received from his two previous Colonels – Walter Hill and Green.[8] He also contrasts Colonel Underwood's attitude towards him with that which he showed to other officers of the Battalion who had erred equally with himself.

5. He states that, owing to Colonel Underwood's attitude towards him, he applied three times for extra-regimental duty. In 1932 and 1933 he applied for service in Iraq and in Trans-Jordan, and towards the end of 1933 for secondment to the Royal Air Force. In each case his application was not recommended.

6. He states that after his court-martial in December of 1934 he wrote an apology to the C.in C., Southern Command, on which Sir John Burnett-Stuart[9] wrote to his Father to the effect that he (Metcalfe) had written him a straightforward and manly letter – or words to that effect. Further, that Sir John Burnett-Stewart had written to Colonel Underwood to ask whether he [Metcalfe] should not be given another chance. To this Colonel Underwood demurred.[10]

Dicky was also a good boxer and horseman, as well as riding point-to-point, hunting, and motor racing. He had begun motor racing at Brooklands in 1929 in a Morgan-JAP, a sport he continued until 1979, and was a regular racer at Silverstone and Goodwood tracks, where he was 'immortalised in motor sport history as winner of Goodwood's period race in Lola Mk1 BR-32 on July 2nd, 1966'. From 1932 to 1934 he raced an Abbott-Nash at Brooklands.[11] That interest in cars caused him to consider the role motor vehicles would play in war, but his 'advanced opinions' on the subject led him into trouble with Colonel Underwood who was 'thoroughly antipathetic to BALLOON's advanced ideas about military strategy, which he probably considered unbecoming in so junior an officer, and in particular he strongly disapproved of BALLOON's motor racing activities and made every effort to impede them'. His conviction for motoring offences also did him no favours with Underwood, nor his extravagant lifestyle.[12]

On leaving the Army Dicky put his experience to good use by becoming designer and salesman for Messrs Vincent of Reading, a well-known maker of motor horse-boxes.[13] Shortly thereafter, he was employed by the British Red Cross Society as an anti-gas lecturer, having attended an anti-gas course during his Army career in 1933 and been Battalion Anti-Gas Officer, 1933-35. This had made him interested in, and an expert on, the subject.

In May 1937 he was appointed ARP officer for the borough of Mitcham, Surrey; the following May he became the County ARP Instructor for Surrey and Chief Instructor at the ARP school at Artington near Guildford. When war was declared he became Officer-in-Charge of the Surrey County ARP Control Centre. He was well up-to-date on anti-gas measures and had even invented a gas mask for which he held patents in the UK and France.[14]

On 22 December 1936 Dicky had written to Sir Vernon Kell, MI5's first Director, who had known his father, sending him references from Captain A.S. Smedley, Welch Regiment, and adjutant and quartermaster of the Anti-Gas Wing, Small Arms School at Winterbourne Gunner in Wiltshire,[15] who extolled his virtues as an 'excellent lecturer with a sound and thorough knowledge of Anti Gas measures, and has organising ability to initiate and work a scheme suitable for the general public'; Dame Beryl Oliver,[16] of the VAD Department, British Red Cross Society (BRCS), saying that the 'students ... found your tuition most helpful'; Colonel H.E. Weeks, the County Director of the BRCS for Sussex, who said that he was 'a retired Army officer with a good knowledge or organisation, is very capable and has an outstanding personality'; and Lieutenant General Sir George Corey, the County Director of the BRCS for Middlesex, who said that he was highly knowledgeable in his field as well as a good teacher, who 'knows how to approach the general public and to arouse their interest'.

Acting on Kell's instructions, Thomas Argyll 'Tar' Robertson interviewed him at the War Office on 13 April 1939. During the interview Dicky told Robertson that 'for some months past he had been in fairly close touch with a man named [Alexander] POSTNIKOV [sic], who is a director of the British Graphitised Metals Coy. Ltd'. In 1938 the company had been working on the manufacture of a lead-based, anti-friction alloy which had additions of tin, copper, nickel and antimony as hardeners, and impregnated with Acheson's colloidal graphite, the graphite being introduced by a patented process which produced a perfect admixture and homogeneous distribution throughout the metal.[17] It was marketed in various grades for every class of bearing by Johnsteads, Ltd, Whitby Works, Park Royal, London NW10.

He also told Robertson about a consignment of 100,000 Mauser rifles which he and Postikow, a White Russian and arms trafficker,[18] had gone to Paris to check out. 'He discovered that the money for the deal was being put up by the Oil Corporation of America and that the arms were intended for export to India. The curious part about the deal is that no ammunition is required.' Tar advised Dicky to tell 'POSTNIKOV to continue with the deal and asked him to keep us informed of every detail'.[19]

> [Metcalfe] expressed the opinion that as far as he knew POSTNIKOV was absolutely dead straight, that he had taken a considerable amount of trouble in establishing himself in business in this country and also in making a good name for himself in business circles. In his capacity as manager of the British Graphitised Metals Co., he is apparently carrying out a number of Government contracts.
>
> POSTNIKOV is a man, according to [Metcalfe] who is in a very good position to obtain information about the movements of arms on the Continent and for that matter anywhere in the world, as he is a bona fide arms dealer and has a great many contacts all over the world.[20]

A certain Mrs Nita Stoddard, with whom Dicky had had lunch the previous month, was anxious to place an order for gas masks. Her husband was something to do with the Latvian Legation and she lived above a dress shop in Gower Street which she owned.[21] To Dicky it was patently clear that 'she knew a great deal more about gas and gas masks than a woman in her line of business normally would know. He thought it might be worth our while looking into Mrs STODDARD's activities.' Tar commented that

> [Metcalfe] struck me as being quite a decent type of individual, although I am not sure that I should be prepared to trust him far. He seemed to be quite frank in what he told me, and at the same time appeared to be willing to help in any way he could.
>
> I feel that we should check up carefully on the information which he gives us until we become more certain of him.[22]

If MI5 did look into Mrs Stoddard's activities there is nothing recorded, and no file on her. The only evidence available is a list of correspondence sent to her between 24 May and 9 June 1939 from various locations – one, a letter from someone named Mickel in Bergen, and two from Dr Forende Holetter, also in Bergen, as well as numerous letters sent to a Dr Henson c/o Nita Stoddard, from Geneva, Riga, Southampton, London, and Nottingham.[23] The one sent from Southampton was from E. Mary Cubitt of Firgrove House, Moorhill Road, West End. Interestingly, a previous occupant was Air Commodore Arthur Wellesley Bigsworth, the inspiration for Captain W.E. Johns' 'Biggles'. None of these letters are included in any of BALLOON's files.

The only information which has come to light is about Mrs Cubitt. She and her husband had entertained members of the Men's Fellowship group at Firgrove House in 1933, and in the summer hosted a garden party for the Women's Institute in which Mrs Cubitt played the violin.[24] Further evidence discovered by agent M/G reveals that 'there is in London a Russian Jewess who has some kind of dressmaking business which does not pay yet continues to exist. This woman is a friend of Weisblat. Weisblat has asked Mancy to keep contact with her.' However, it is unknown whether this refers to Nita Stoddard. Eduard Casimir Weisblat had reputedly once worked for the OGPU (Soviet intelligence), but was now thought to be a Nazi agent. However, his file and that of Manci Gertler[25] have not revealed any further clues as to who Nita Stoddard might have been, but if this was her she could have been acting as an accommodation address.

Dicky was desperate to rejoin the Army and had unsuccessfully petitioned King George V, so he bombarded the War Office with applications for reinstatement and kept in intermittent contact with Sir Vernon Kell and MI5. In 1938 he had provided Kell with details of an alleged deal in half a million Mauser rifles of German manufacture said to be destined for China. When he wrote to Kell from Paris on 10 April 1939 looking for his advice the quantity of Mauser rifles was now 100,000. 'I do not know if this matter comes within your jurisdiction but I thought perhaps you could advise us. I think the matter rather unusual.'[26] He and a friend (Postnikow) had been asked to supply the rifles but 'On making enquiries we discovered that the conditions were a little odd to say the least of it'. His friend wanted to know whether the rifles' destination was an approved one.

Tar wrote to IPI (Indian Political Intelligence) informing them about the rifles and enquired whether the Indian government had ordered any. The IPI had been established by the India Office in 1909 to monitor attempts to undermine the British government of India by anarchists and revolutionary elements. He also wrote to MI1c about Metcalfe and Postnikow, informing them of MI5's decision to have Metcalfe pass on any information that he might uncover, and would keep IPI informed. He mused, 'A possibility, to my mind, is that they have mixed India up with Burma, and that the arms are really intended for China.' A letter to Tar from 'JMW' (possibly Jock Whyte in B4a) on 16 April stated that the Burma Defence Bureau knew nothing of an order for 100,000 Mauser rifles

> nor is it considered likely that any such an order could emanate from indigenous sources in Burma. On the other hand, a large number of Mauser rifles have crossed the Burma-China border into China, and

more are probably on the way. It would seem probable, therefore, as I mentioned to you at the time, that the enquiry really relates to Arms for China, and that either 'India' is being used as camouflage, or the rifles would be sent to China via Burma.[27]

Kenneth Younger, Assistant Director of MI5's E Division (ADE), confirmed this when he wrote to Major F.A. Sampson of MI1c on 19 May 1939. On 25 May IPI replied to Tar saying that

> it has been suggested by the Intelligence Bureau in India that the term 'India' may refer to the Netherlands East Indies, whose army is equipped with 'Mannlicher' rifles (date of pattern is not known), which are similar to Mauser rifles. This, of course, is only a suggestion, and I myself prefer the theory that the arms are intended for China.[28]

An extract of a letter sent to MI1c on 20 May 1938 stated that he had received the following from Major Hodgeson [sic] of BSA who had been

> approached the other day by a man named [Redacted] who subsequently introduced him to two individuals R.L.C. WADDINGTON, of 28 Essex St, London and a Mr GOULD. At an interview HODGESON had with these three individuals it appears that WADDINGTON had approached B.S.A. on behalf of P.J. PETERS [sic] of the London Armoury Co Ltd,[29] who had been in touch with Kurt H. WEIL.
>
> Apparently this syndicate is anxious to purchase less than 500,000 7.92 Mausers plus ammunition and are offering £10 a rifle. The destination HODGESON understands is to be China and the port from which these are to be exported is Hamburg ....
>
> Neither [Redacted] WADDINGTON [n]or GOULD are known to us.[30]

SIS did not propose to inform the War Office until they knew more about the arms deal, given that the Burma Defence Bureau had already been informed. The author added that, while it appeared the rifles were destined for China, 'there is a vague outside chance that the Japanese are up to some scheme for storing arms, possibly in Siam, for some ulterior motive in British or French possessions'. And while this might have appeared to sound far-fetched, this supposition was based on having already heard 'vague stories of this kind'.[31]

A Special Branch report 'Arms to China' dated 17 June 1938 stated that Metcalfe had been approached by Richard Waddington, a casual acquaintance, of 28 Essex Street, Strand and 'asked to be put in touch with someone from whom he could purchase 100,000 rifles ...'.[32] When Frederick J. Peters wrote to Weil on

13 December 1937 he confirmed that his friend Georg Frank was supplying arms to China.[33] Special Branch had received a letter from Metcalfe at the Naval and Military Club, but who gave his private address as The White House, Bessborough Road, Roehampton Lane, London SW15, who had noticed a paragraph in the Press that the Chinese embassy had issued a statement 'to the effect that a series of bogus enquiries purporting to be issued from that Embassy in respect of the purchasing of arms for China had been circulated'. He informed Special Branch that he had received an enquiry for 100,000 rifles which he had passed on to a well-known armaments firm, although nothing came of it as that number of rifles was not available at that time. He didn't know whether the enquiry was legitimate but 'I was given to understand that although the arms were for China they were to be paid for by German money'. He offered any assistance he could, given that it was being investigated by the English and French police.[34]

***

Kurt Hermann Weil was a Jew born on 26 November 1895 in Leutershausten, Bavaria.[35] During the First World War he served as a pilot in the German Air Force with the rank of lieutenant. The British Air Ministry in March 1934 stated that he was employed by Werber und Handelhaus GmbH of Berlin – 'our agents in Germany'. His MI5 file states that he 'is an expert German aeronautical engineer employed by German aircraft firms and paid entirely by them whilst acting as agent for the supply of German Aircraft material to British firms. He is in close touch with the Air Attaché at the German Embassy who visits him at his house' – 'Oakfield', Wilbury Avenue, Belmont, Surrey; his business address was given as Terminal House, 52 Grosvenor Gardens, London, SW1.'

An extract of Weil's Home Office file sent to Valentine Vivian at SIS states that their information

> clearly shows that he is engaged in collecting intelligence of interest to the German Air Attaché. According to your 'special material' entry 27/2/12/40, PUTLITZ,[36] of the German Embassy, was of the opinion that WEIL's business was of such a kind that the Embassy ought to avoid too close association with it ... the indications are that he is engaged in collecting intelligence for the German Air Attaché in a manner which is not quite proper [and] 'beneath the dignity of the Embassy' and therefore probably amounts to espionage.[37]

A Home Office Warrant was issued on Weil and his wife Charlotte in December 1937. On 31 January 1938 MI5 wrote to the Home Office stating that his was a difficult case as he 'has a plausible excuse for making enquiries and because there is no means of finding out what passes between him and the German Air and Naval Attachés'. On 4 February 1938 Guy Liddell wrote to Vivian expressing his concerns about Weil and requested that his residency permit not be extended as they regarded him as a menace. The Air Ministry was also 'in favour of WEIL being turned out.'[38]

In late February minutes in a Home Office file record that, while Weil had 'done nothing against the law in giving the information mentioned to the German authorities ... Capt Liddell feels that only one construction can be put on his activities and with his technical qualifications and contacts he is certainly a potential danger.' Having spoken with Kell, 'The position is quite simple. No unlawful activity can be proved, but the presence of this man is a source of danger.' Weighed against any advantages that might be gained with trade with Germany and British companies, it was decided not to extend his stay and issue a Deportation Order on 9 March 1938 when he became the subject of a Home Office Aliens' Department review. He left Harwich on 26 March for Germany with his wife following suit on 6 April. However, he tried to return to Croydon airport from Amsterdam on 23 June 1938 claiming to have a meeting with his solicitors, Tobin & Co., but was refused leave to land, in spite of Tobin's intervention on his behalf.

The previous week Major Archie Boyle the ADI (Assistant Director of Intelligence) at the Air Ministry (later, Air Commodore at SOE) had interviewed Lieutenant General Ralph (Rudolf) Wenninger, the German air attaché in London, about this 'somewhat mysterious Jew' and his activities. Wenninger told Boyle that he 'only used WEIL in the most correct ways [by] putting him in touch with firms who wanted agencies in this country, and asking his advice regarding investigations and so on'.[39]

Arms dealer John Edwin Jules Mallet's MI5 file gives Weil's address as Kurfürstendamm 53, Berlin, and lists him as a director of Waffin Munition, Am Karlsbad No.6, Berlin W.5. Weil later went to the United States via Mexico where he became involved with oil magnate William Rhodes Davis of Davis & Co., his oil company based in New York City. Davis had, according to the FBI, a 'bad reputation all over Europe, particularly in the business world', largely due to his business dealings with Germany and his contact with Göring. He died on 2 August 1941, ostensibly of a heart attack, although there is an unsubstantiated claim that he was murdered by William Stephenson, the head of BSC: 'British secret agent, Intrepid, admitted killing Davis some 35 years after the fact .... The reason given by most authors for the murder of Davis was to prevent him from shipping Mexican oil to Germany and Japan.'[40]

Mallet's file also mentions that he was a representative of the Winchester Repeating Arms Co., 10 Ryder Street, Strand; Richard L.C. Waddington, 28 Essex Street, Strand, who was also in close touch with Peters; and Major J.E. Mallet, 7 Park Lane, W1.[41] MI5 issued a Home Office warrant on all three in October 1938.

MI5 reviewed Weil's case 'from the point of view of counter-espionage' and noted in 29 September 1942 that one of his contacts in the UK was 'Max AUFRICHTIG. PF.50019, a banker's agent who was reported to have been allowed to take a certain amount of money out of Germany on condition he worked for the Germans. Case passed to B.4.b.'[42] B4a dealt with suspected cases of espionage by individuals living in the UK; B4b was espionage, industry and commerce under John Craufurd.

Aufrichtig was born in Breslau in 1879 and living at 11 Dalkeith Grove, Stanmore, Middlesex. He had been a banker in Hamburg and was married to Sabine Kalter, a mezzo-soprano opera singer with the Hamburg State Opera. They fled Nazi Germany in 1934 and changed their name to Andrews. He died in 1950.

On 24 May 1939 SIS informed Younger that according to 'an absolutely reliable source POSTNIKOW is unlikely to do anything against British interests'. Their source considered him 'straight' and unlikely to jeopardise his British naturalisation. He had 'got himself and his family out of Russia by joining the Red Trade Delegation to Berlin shortly after the War. While there he quarrelled with the Reds and came to England.' He was

> said to be a clever railway engineer and his main occupation in this country is as a consulting engineer especially over trade with Russia. It is in this capacity that he started and now runs the business of the British Graphitised Metals Co. He is also a director with Serge KARLINSKI[43] of the Industrial Facilities Corporation and an agent for Fairey Aviation Co. In both these latter capacities he has come in touch with the arms trade and has tried to do some reputable business over the sale of arms and aircraft, I gather with no success whatsoever.

Serge Karlinski was a stateless Sephardic Jew and banker's broker associated with the Duchess de Château-Thierry's circle, and living at 24 Brent Street, Hendon. In 1938 he was elected to the London Committee of Deputies of British Jews. The Duchesse's MI5 file adds that he was a naturalised British subject of Russian origin, and manager of P.P. Boeckel of 33 Cornhill, who acted as brokers for the Export Credits Guarantee Department of the Board of Trade. Using this connection, Karlinski had helped to secure the contract between Westinghouse Brake and Saxby Signal Co. of London and the Polish government. 'He is also said to have been successful in arranging loans for Rumania and to have been interested in the supply of arms to China. We have no record of his being directly in touch with the Duchess.'[44] His name would come up in a House of Commons debate on 6 June 1939 when Robert Boothby, MP for East Aberdeen, quoting Major General Sir Alfred Knox, MP for the Wycombe Division of Buckinghamshire, asked

> Is there any truth in the rumour that the Export Credits Department advised the Chinese Advisory Committee to deal entirely with the organisation called Trade Facilities, Limited, of which the chairman is Mr Serge Karlinski: and why were the interests of British traders in China, who have recently been hard hit, disregarded?

Boothby declared, 'I am a director of the Industrial Facilities Corporation, of which Mr Karlinski is chairman.'[45]

The business of the arms deal continued well into November when Gilbert Lennox interviewed Postnikow and Metcalfe at Room 055. Postnikow had recently received a cable from New York with a firm offer of 75,000 Mauser rifles being sold by F. Lovinfosse-Hardy et Fils of Liège, Belgium in four lots:

(a) 100,000 of German manufacture;
(b) 50,000 of Belgian manufacture;
(c) 4,000 of Belgian manufacture, and
(d) 1,000 Vickers type 7.92 or .303 machine guns, presumed to be of Belgian manufacture.

Postnikow wanted to know whether the War Office had any objection to the sale of a minimum of 75,000 Mauser rifles from those of German manufacture mentioned in (a), or to a deal with the Turkish government for 50,000 Mauser rifles of Belgian manufacture, mentioned in (b). He let slip that he had just lost a deal with the Turkish government for 100,000 Mauser rifles, having been advised that the War Office did not approve of the deal as the rifles had been manufactured in Germany. However, the Turkish government had subsequently obtained the rifles from Norman Cooper. Lennox wrote, 'He told me this more in sorrow than in anger and, the moment he had mentioned the name Norman Cooper, I gathered he rather wished he had not.'[46]

SIS informed Captain F.C. Derbyshire at MI5 on 18 December 1939 that the War Office believed the weapons were destined for Turkey but, regardless of their ultimate destination, were not intending to interfere; but, 'They are, however, proposing to consider whether the deal cannot be put into the hands of Norman COOPER [*Redacted*] who is after the same material and is prepared to deposit the profits in a British Bank in London for the duration of the war'.[47]

Postnikow also wanted to know whether the War Office was interested in the 1,000 Vickers machine guns mentioned in (d), in which the Turkish government was also interested. Lennox reported that the cable from America required a very urgent reply and that the decision should be reported to Metcalfe as soon as possible. Postnikow informed Lennox that F. Lovinfosse-Hardy et Fils were a small firm, but they did a lot of business for Fabrique Nationale of Belgium in getting rid of unwanted surpluses.[48]

Tar sought the opinion of Major Tuckey at the department of the Chief of Imperial General Staff (CIGS)[49] about whether the War Office had any objection to 75,000 Mauser rifles being sent to America from Belgium. Tuckey replied that, in principle, the War Office had no objection, but it was 'desirable to prevent the money for this purpose going to Germany and he considered that [Metcalfe] should be warned to this effect'. However, he did not think that the end-user was actually America. Tar sought more details from Metcalfe, and warned him to be careful. Two days later Metcalfe informed him that the arms were destined for China.

During this time China was fighting a civil war between the *Kuomintang* (KMT) Party led by Generalissimo Chiang Kai-shek of the Republic of China (ROC), and the Communist Party of the People's Republic of China (PRC) led by Mao

Tse-Tung which had started in 1927 and lasted until 1949, when the defeated KMT fled to Formosa (now Taiwan). Concurrently, China was also engaged in the Second Sino-Japanese War (1937-45). Exactly which side these arms were destined for was never determined.

In January 1940 Dicky was offered the post of ARP Officer for the borough of Tottenham but declined the offer in favour of joining Postnikow's company, British Graphitised Metals Co., Ltd, who paid him a salary of £500-£600 a year.[50] That spring he made two trips to the Netherlands, again providing MI5 with information about those involved in arms deals and suspected espionage. MI5 arranged to send him back there in May to meet with someone who could provide a lot of information about espionage, but this was pre-empted by the invasion of the Netherlands on 10 May.

Chapter 2

'The man's keen!'

In the opening month of the war Metcalfe had written again to Kell from the Old Court House, Dorking, Surrey, where he was in charge of the ARP Control Centre, requesting his help in securing a job and enclosing various testimonials, hoping that Kell might put in a word for him as he had done when he was looking for an appointment in the ARP. He told Kell that he did not care to be in 'such a sheltered and inactive job' and wished to serve his country and retrieve his reputation. He believed that 'an offensive chemical arm will inevitably be introduced and dealing with the other side I think that given time I could contribute information relating to the movement of arms and leakage of aero information'.[1] He apologised for bothering Kell again, 'but you must agree the man's keen!'[2] So desperate was he that he offered to work voluntarily (expenses paid).

He also wrote two letters to Tar in early 1940, the first of which asked him to whom he should apply as he would like 'to offer my services completely and unconditionally to your department for service in *any* capacity'. While he admitted that his military record was 'none too satisfactory', he hoped that this would be counterbalanced by the glowing testimonials from the local authorities, and that being a 'nonentity', as he put it, 'might have its advantages'. Certain enquiries he'd made were soon to pay dividends and he would soon 'have a *real story* for you', which was quite exiting! [*sic*].

His second letter mentioned an Army friend, C. Wright, a former lieutenant in the 104th Battalion, MG (Machine Gun) Corps, who had left the Army at the end of October 1920 and claimed to have invented 'some marvellous type of shell'.[3] Wright was now in Holland boasting about his invention and how he was well-known to the War Office, as well as trying to sell his patent and ammunition. Some of Metcalfe's friends were considering dealing with him but he was 'not at all happy about him' and he sought Tar's unofficial opinion as to whether he should deal with him. Tar replied that there were no vacancies at the present time; nor was he in a position to comment on whether he should deal with Wright, but suggested that 'you should be guided by circumstances'.

The first intimation that MI5 was leaving the door open a crack to employ him was at the conclusion of Tar's letter when he said that he was always interested in any information that he could supply. At the end of January 1940, over lunch with Major Hodgson of BSA, Tar learned that Metcalfe was hoping to rejoin the Army in the near future. The implication being that this was actually in the Ministry of

Supply where he hoped to be able to provide Postnikow with information which would be of use to him in his business activities. Hodgson thought that MI5 should keep an eye on him and see what job he would be getting. Tar noted that Postnikow was currently supplying foreign governments with arms, although did not know his source, but was mainly concerned with dealing with countries which had been given loans for the purchase of arms by His Majesty's Government.

Tar thought it worthwhile finding out whether in fact Metcalfe has been called up and what type of job, if any, had been earmarked for him,[4] so he contacted MI5's C2, under Captain A. Johnston, responsible for the examination of credentials of military personnel, asking that he be informed of anything about Metcalfe from the Ministry of Supply. C Division was headed by Colonel H.I. 'Harry' Allen, who was also in charge of D Division – security and travel control. C1b responded that the Ministry of Supply had reported no trace of Metcalfe being employed by them, but since the establishment Branch only had knowledge of certain classes of employee, their statement did not necessarily mean that he wasn't being employed by them at some outstation.[5]

Tar informed Metcalfe that the information he'd supplied had been passed to 'our friend', and he would be in touch with him about it. Metcalfe informed him that the enquiry he'd mentioned 'has progressed further to-day and came from a man called Brooks':

> Furthermore, to-day a Major Mallet has been in touch with us for 75,000 rifles, and 30 million [rounds] of ammunition. He is coming to the office at 5 p.m. tomorrow Jan 18th. He states that he has the full permission of the War Office to transact this deal even though the arms may be of German or at least Goering origin.

Mallet's name was unknown to him but he would be present at the interview. He'd also heard that the civil war in China was coming to an end and that Mitsubishi were cashing in on this by offering arms and aircraft. His friend Reynell (possibly fighter pilot Flight Lieutenant Richard Carew Reynell, later killed on 7 September 1940, the first day of the Blitz) was 'active in this respect'. He thought that Mallet 'may prove of interest', and gave Tar a telephone number where he could be contacted, but if the information was of no interest he shouldn't bother to reply.[6] Tar passed on this information to MI1c.

Back in July 1938 Dick White had reported that

> one Major J.E. MALLET, a director of Tourist Transocean Economy Cheques Ltd of 7 rue d'Artois, Paris 8e, is taking an active interest in the arms traffic. He is in communication with Kurt WEIL[7] [*Redacted*] and J. VELTJENS of Waffin Munition, Am Karlsbad No.6, Berlin W.35, apparently on the subject of the deal in 300,000 Mausers concerning which we sent you a copy of a Special Branch report dated 18.6.38, under our 76/China/B3 of 6.7.38.[8]

Mallet worked for W.W. Greener Ltd of Birmingham, a sporting gun manufacturer founded in 1829 and government contractor to the War Office.

Josef 'Seppl' Veltjens had been a German fighter ace in the First World War, credited with thirty-five kills. Later, he worked as an international arms dealer and acted as a personal emissary from Göring to Mussolini. In the 1920s he became involved in shady arms deals, delivering to China and Turkey. In 1929 he joined the NSDAP but resigned in 1931 after an argument with Hitler. In the 1930s he was involved in arms smuggling to Finland, the Soviet Union and Spain, where he supplied arms to the Nationalists in 1937 during the Spanish Civil War.[9]

At the beginning of the Second World War he was recalled to rejoin the Luftwaffe. He was killed on 6 October 1943 when his Junkers Ju.52 crashed in the Apennines near Gervellino on a mission to finalise the distribution of the Italian national gold reserves to prevent their capture by the Allies. A post-war report dated 25 June 1946 in the National Archives in Washington prepared from information in the secret files of the *Devisenstellen* (exchange control office) details his career as an arms dealer, in which it describes how Germany allowed Finland to purchase German arms in October 1940.[10]

An intercepted telephone conversation between Mallet and Bernstein of S.A. Industrielle, Armament Manufacturers of Brussels on 4 April 1940 refers to 'Moskers' (Mauser rifles) and their being cheaper in London than Brussels.[11] Bernstein mentions that when he came to London he wanted to see Robert Boothby, the MP for Peterhead. Further information regarding Mallet's arms dealing activities can be found in his MI5 file.[12] An entry for October 1938 states that 'There are indications that these arms are being exported to China, certain South American states (not specified) and Spain, and there are strong indications that Palestine is to be included as well'.[13]

Chapter 3

Going Dutch

Information was beginning to emerge about arms deals in Holland, so Metcalfe obtained a visa from the Finnish Legation to go to Belgium and Holland; however, the Passport Office required a letter from the War Office first. But when he enquired whether he should obtain this from Major Tuckey or someone else, neither Derbyshire nor Tuckey knew anything about it. It was finally sorted out by Lennox.[1] Metcalfe told him that Lovinfosse & Hardy of Liège had 15,000 Schmeissers and 1,300 heavy type Vickers machine guns, so Lennox contacted Outram at the War Office about it.[2] As far as the War Office was concerned, Outram could see no objection to Metcalfe's departure to Belgium being facilitated.[3] The Passport Office was informed that the War Office had expressed no objection to an Exit Permit being granted and Metcalfe was advised to call there the following morning.

Metcalfe intended to leave for Brussels on the first plane the following day and could be contacted at the Metropole Hotel in Brussels and the Krasnapolski Hotel [*sic* – Krasnapolsky] in Amsterdam. While in Brussels he would be dealing with Colonel Heise of the Finnish Legation. He asked Tar, 'Were you really serious about offering the War Office the Schmeissers and Vickers? I naturally concluded that you knew all about them.' He intended to be away for a week and hoped that the trip to Amsterdam would be successful, but in case anything should go wrong in Brussels Tar should let him know if he wanted them. Postnikow had also told him that he knew of more Schmeissers which were available.[4]

Upon his return Lennox interviewed him on 20 March about his eleven-day trip. The arms deal for Finland had collapsed as the arms involved in the transaction were still in Germany. While staying at the Krasnapolsky Hotel he reported that his room had been entered and his luggage and papers searched, but nothing had been taken; however, the chambermaid was German.

His Dutch acquaintance was a 'temperamental, artistic sort of person … temperamentally very unsuitable as an espionage agent'. However, amongst the information he learned from him was that information and specifications relating to British aircraft, and the Air Ministry's policy, had been getting across to Germany before the war, and continued to do so, which he described as 'remarkably serious', but when Lennox pressed him for the Dutchman's identity he demurred, saying that if MI5 were to contact him he might become spooked and slip up. Instead, he suggested that he should employ him on MI5's behalf, but Lennox didn't consider that as 'a particularly satisfactory arrangement'.

In fact, the Germans *were* receiving information about aircraft from another source –Ludovico von Karstoff @ Krämer von Auenrode, the Abwehr's *Leiter* of KO Lisbon – described as 'a colourful Viennese intelligence officer ... [who] kept a pet monkey named Simon'[5] was supplying the Germans with monthly production summaries from the Society of British Aircraft Constructors, and from other contacts in Sweden, one of whom, codenamed JOSEFINE, was thought to be Count Johan Gabriel Oxenstierna, the Swedish naval attaché in London.[6] British intelligence had identified JOSEFINE as Oxenstierna through ULTRA intercepts, and German diplomat Fritz Kolbe @ George Wood whose correspondence was being read by a secretary working for the Germans. In September 1943 Britain demanded Oxenstierna's recall to Sweden, but it would take until the spring of 1944 before this occurred.[7]

The CIA would later describe Kolbe as 'the most important spy of the war', with Allen Dulles writing, 'George Wood (our code name for him) was not only our best source on Germany but undoubtedly one of the best secret agents any intelligence service has ever had.'[8]

However, Nigel West, reviewing Delattre's biography of Kolbe,[9] refutes Dulles's claim of the value of Kolbe's information, which had been exaggerated, and merely confirmed intelligence already gathered by MI5, or even unwittingly jeopardized operations such as ULTRA and TRIPLEX,[10] of which Dulles would have been largely ignorant. West concludes that Kolbe was 'an exceptional character in every way, but also a menace bearing unwanted gifts to an eager suitor ... it is doubtful that Kolbe could ever be considered the most important spy of the Second World War.'[11] Claude Dansey of SIS declared that 'there is nothing in them [Kolbe's cables] which could affect the course of the war'. Much to Dulles's chagrin, his OSS colleagues in Washington considered the 'George Wood' material as 'museum pieces', and he blamed his OSS superiors for not making the best use of Kolbe's intelligence.[12]

Metcalfe told Lennox that he was not looking for any financial reward and that Tar knew the circumstances under which he had left the Army. What motivated him was his desire to regain his commission and his original rank. He had learned that arms traffic was very active in Holland and that the Dutch were probably forming a group to deal in German small arms.[13] Lennox noted:

> He added that any amount of small arms could be obtained from Germany just now, but no heavy guns. He told me that he expected this group would shortly begin shipping arms in large quantities to some neutral country, possibly Brazil, this country merely acting as what he called a 'pavilion'. I gathered that he meant cover for the real purchasers. [Metcalfe] expects that the market will shortly be flooded with Mauser Rifles, and he said that there are 511,000 Mauser Rifles at present available in Holland. This attempted sale of arms on a vast scale by Germany, is, of course, with the object of obtaining foreign currency.[14]

Two persons engaged in arms trafficking – Schulz and Messerschmidt [sic] – were said by Metcalfe to have connections in Portugal and/or the USA, and he offered to find out more about them.[15]

Lennox told Tar that he didn't think that Metcalfe was trying to double cross them as he had nothing to gain from it, but it concerned him that they didn't know his Dutch contact's identity, nor was he happy about Metcalfe acting as a go-between. However, he was confident that sooner or later he would learn his identity, but didn't want to rush things. What made him suspicious was the Dutchman's request for information about German codes.

When Metcalfe met with Lennox again in Room 055 he was told that MI5 would be interested in whatever information he had, in particular about the Air Ministry leak. He agreed to be paid cash on delivery, and he would pay 300 guilders to the Dutchman when he returned to Holland shortly. Lennox told him that they would give him 'every facility, but nothing more'; if he produced reliable information he would be reimbursed his 300 guilders. After that MI5 would consider other requests. He then made a request on behalf of his partner, Postnikow, who was Herr Erren's agent, for his 'hydrogen engine', the files and legal documents of which were in Postnikow's possession.[16]

Rudolf Arnold Erren was a German inventor and engineer, born on 11 September 1907 in Rokitsch, Germany, who converted trucks, buses, submarines and internal combustion engines to run on hydrogen.

> Before the Spanish Civil War, Postnikow was negotiating with the Spanish Government, which showed great interest in the hydrogen engine, because of its suitability for coastal submarines. Postnikow has now heard that the Franco Government is also interested in the hydrogen engine, and in view of the new Anglo-Spanish Trade Treaty [1938] he is anxious to enter into negotiations as soon as possible. [Metcalfe] explained to me that a very big and expensive plant would be required for the hydrogen engine, and that government financing would probably be necessary. So far so good, but Herr Erren is unfortunately in a concentration camp in England!
>
> Postnikow wants to know if it is possible for him to visit Erren, or alternatively write to him and get a power of attorney, so as to enable him to open negotiations with the Spanish Government. He is very anxious to know what the position is, and would be extremely obliged if we would let him know, either by letter to him or to [Metcalfe]. As I think you are aware, the [Metcalfe] and Postnikow firm is British Graphitised Metals, Shell Mex House, W.C.2.[17]

Erren had been interned under the Prerogative on 10 October 1939 at Olympia in London, but later released. On 21 June 1940 he sailed to Canada on the SS *Duchess of York* with 3,000 German PoWs; on 24 July 1945 he returned on the SS *Ile de France* for continued internment and was repatriated on 28 October 1945; in 1946 he applied for naturalisation.[18] Tar sent a copy of Lennox's report to Vivian at SIS pointing out the deal they had made with Metcalfe.[19]

When Metcalfe went to see Lennox on 6 April he explained that his intended return to Holland had been delayed because he had been seeing the Ministry of Economic Warfare about a chemical deal his firm was negotiating in Holland. Therefore, he would combine this with seeing his Dutch contact, so MI5 promised to arrange his Exit Permit for the following week.

The Turkish government was negotiating a deal for the purchase of Mauser rifles, some of Czech manufacture, others German, which Metcalfe's firm, and another dealer, Otto Anderson of Arthur R. Brown, Dashwood House, Old Broad Street in the City of London, were negotiating. Turkey was not fussy about the origin of the arms, so Metcalfe suggested that it might be advisable to waive certain regulations of the Trading with the Enemy Act (1939). Boher Jessurum would be handling the business in Amsterdam regarding 400,000 German-made units, and China was enquiring about 100,000 units.[20] Specifications of the Mauser rifles, bayonets and ammunition were attached to Lennox's reports.

When Metcalfe wrote to Tar on 11 April he stated that he had

> talked up a case that I am going over to see our agent in Rotterdam about B.S.A. motorcycles his name is Schrameier Verbrugge and he sells B.S.A. motorcycles through us.[21] Actually, I have no business to do in Holland this time and I am simply going on your peoples [sic] behalf. I shall take about £40 extra with me in cash for my contact over there. He purports to have valuable information. Mr Postnikow has also submitted two suggestions which I brought back last time [...] the Ministry of Economic Warfare. They have expressed great interest in both propositions and have intimated to us unofficially that they approve and have asked us to submit a full report of ways and means when I return. This we have agreed to do so that I will try and fix this while I am over there as well. It is not exactly a pleasant time to visit Holland but I consider it well worth it.[22]

Part of the arms deal to Turkey was successful as Postnikow received an order to supply them with 50,000 Mauser rifles, as well as 7.2mm Mauser ammunition and grenades, both destined for Norway or Sweden, to which the War Office expressed no objection.

In Metcalfe's letters to Tar on 23 and 26 April he reluctantly revealed that his Dutch informant's identity was R.L. Boissevain of Van der Elst & Matthes, Heerengracht 286, Amsterdam, who was anxious to come over to Britain and work for British intelligence. He had told Boissevain that he worked for British intelligence to gain his confidence, which Boissevain accepted. Tar noted that 'Both Major Lennox and I agreed that the information which [Metcalfe] had brought back was in all probability a plant of which [Metcalfe] is unsuspectingly the victim'. They believed that he was 'sincere and honest in what he is doing and believes in the information which he is given by his informant'.

Metcalfe had informed Tar that he had obtained information from Boissevain. Dr Gruner and Dr Klose[23] had arrived in Amsterdam from Berlin and Klose was soon going to Brussels to meet an Englishman with some important information. He told Tar that he might possibly be able to obtain Klose's address in Brussels and pass it on to MI5 immediately. Tar added that '[Metcalfe's] sole motive is giving us information of this description is in order that he shall be able to regain his commission in the Army'.[24]

Robert Lucas 'Bob' Boissevain, born on 27 April 1895 and married to Helena Suzanna Sonia (Sonja) van Tienhoven, joined his father, Dr Charles Ernest Henri Boissevain, in the chemical industry working for Van der Elst & Matthes which delivered chemical fertilizers for agriculture produced by German companies such as I.G. Farben (later to produce Zyklon B, the gas used in concentration camps).

> By 1935, the three Dutch companies [I.G. Farben Holland-DSM (Dutch State Mines), Hoogovens, and Shell] succeeded in ousting Van der Elst & Matthes from its leading position in the fertilizer business in Holland and it eventually went bankrupt in 1936. I.G. Farben may have intended to place itself in the position of Van der Elst & Matthes, but it failed, at least until the 1940 occupation.[25]

The company bankruptcy forced Boissevain to sell his house at Emmaplein 2, Amsterdam and relocate the family to Zandvoort, but soon after the German invasion of Holland on 10 May 1940 the SS evicted them from their house. The family moved four times in six months, ending up in a house at Spruitenbosstraat 11, Haarlem. On 3 August 1940 MI5 informed Felix Cowgill, head of Section V at SIS, that Boissevain's name was being put on the CSW Black List (Central Security War Black List).

Boissevain was anxious to receive a British decoration after the war and to meet with MI5 and the Ministry of Economic Warfare, so Metcalfe proposed bringing him to England 'on the pretext of doing business with us as he has often done in the past. I propose ... that he comes over with a view to purchasing certain goods, gas masks etc.' as he was more likely to obtain a visa if he was coming over to purchase. But Tar informed him that while MI5 was not prepared to defray Boissevain's expenses they would be prepared to meet with him if Metcalfe could bring him over 'for business purposes'. He agreed to approach the MEW to see if they would agree to Boissevain coming over to England – 'He apparently has a scheme which he is anxious to put up to us in connection with the collection of information.'[26] Tar asked SIS to provide any information they might have on him, but whatever papers SIS sent over they are not available.

When Metcalfe returned from his visit to Holland (13-18 April 1940) he provided MI5 with a report (see next chapter), a copy of which was sent to Vivian at SIS. Tar's accompanying note stated that '[Metcalfe] considers BOISSEVAIN to be reliable but I am rather inclined to think that he is leading [Metcalfe] up the garden path'. He wrote to Metcalfe on 8 May expressing interest in meeting Boissevain if he were to visit England and offered his assistance in Boissevain's application for a visa if there were any problems.

W.S. Mars of D4a1 wrote to B3b stating that 'The P. & P.O. now wish to know what attitude they are to adopt in future, so perhaps you will let me know if you wish me to take any further action'. However, Michael Ryde's (D4a1) reply on 24 April stated that they were interested in information Metcalfe might obtain but were now not prepared to support his application for an Exit Permit to Holland, only the previous one.[27] Tar added that 'Everything connected with his reports appears to be incomplete.' They were looking into Metcalfe's personal request and would keep him posted.

During the war the Boissevains were responsible for hiding four Dutch Jewish families from the Nazis, including the Goldbergs – Leo (Lowske) Goldberg; his wife, Lyubova Elperin Goldberg, and their daughter, Anya Goldberg, later Anna Ormont; and Dr Jacob Vecht ('Mr Knoppers'), a Jewish dentist. The Goldbergs survived the war, but Dr Vecht committed suicide, having learned that his wife, Sophia *née* Levie, and daughter had died in Auschwitz on 12 October 1942. He should not be confused with another Jacob Vecht, married to Schoontje Polak, who died in Auschwitz on 28 February 1943.[28]

Since Bob had been educated at an English public school and had served in the navy during the First World War, he had become a 'skilled Marconi telegraph operator' and at some point became involved in Resistance work.[29] But in 1943 he was betrayed and sent to the 'Oranjehotel' camp at Scheveningen, then in June 1944 to a concentration camp at Vught. From there he was transferred to the Orianenburg camp, until the end of the year when he was moved to Langenstein-Zweiberg, Silesia, a sub-camp of Buchenwald. As his son Charles recounted: 'He died April 12, 1945, the day that the camp was liberated. He was completely exhausted by torture and hunger, and deadly ill with high fever, dysentery and typhus.'[30] He is commemorated on a plaque at Yad Vashem in Jerusalem, and his entire family is included in the Yad Vashem List of the Righteous for The Netherlands.[31]

Chapter 4

BALLOON's Report on Holland

Metcalfe's report on his second visit to Holland[1] attracted a comment from Tar that he was only a go-between and that Postnikow, 'a White Russian with some peculiar antecedents', was actually running the show. He also thought that the excuse given for not obtaining the name of the Air Ministry official was a lame one.

Metcalfe had flown to Holland on 13 April and stayed at the Krasnapolsky Hotel in Amsterdam. Postnikow paid all his expenses and provided £40 for his contact's information. Unfortunately, he failed to find out who was responsible for the leakage 'from a very high source', but did obtain other information which he hoped would be of value. He was satisfied that he hadn't been followed; nor did the German chambermaid go through his things, apart from letters he left laying around. However, he believed that it was official policy that his telephone calls had been tapped since he was speaking English.

He reported that Norman Cooper had been trying to take over certain German companies, such as the New Atheneum Corporation of 91, Moorgate, 'which is really Otto WOOLF [sic] of Cologne.[2] I was informed that a member of the Turkish Embassy in Brussels tipped him off to leave this alon[e] as you knew about it.' Tar commented that 'This may be interesting, but it certainly is not very important.' He also thought that the Nazi plan to invent a banking institution in Holland or Brussels, from which they would control an actual bank in Tangier, sounded 'like ordinary newspaper talk'. The Germans had paid '"the Native Ruler" (Mohammed V) a large sum of money for the bank to obtain control of the radio of the port and permission to make extensive extension of the port under cover of which guns etc. will be smuggled in.'

Metcalfe also said that German troops being sent into Norway and Denmark, who were nearly all Bavarians and Austrians, had already been reported in the newspapers, as had North German (Prussian) troops who had been sent to the Brenner Pass for the Nazi attack against Russia. He was unimpressed by the fact that Nazi armoured troops and pilots were dressed in 'a sort of "Triplex" type of steel called Molybdenum', which again, was already known.

He mentioned 'Martin Michmoller' [sic] (brother of Pastor) who was operating in Greece, Belgrade, Brussels, and came to Amsterdam frequently where he spent a lot of time in the German Legation and had a false passport.[3] As to the Gestapo being very active on trains to the Belgian frontier this was to be expected. Tar commented: 'I presume he means trains in Germany; but if he means on trains between Holland and Belgium, it is rather more interesting and quite likely.' Metcalfe's contact could also get details of an air torpedo if MI5 was interested.

Metcalfe reported that the Secretary of the British Legation in The Hague had recently married and it had been suggested to him, based only on hearsay, that his wife '(formerly German?) might be only helping her husband but that she certainly has many German friends with whom she still has contact.' Tar presumed that this was Lord Chichester whose wife, he was told, was 'a very charming person'.[4] Also German consulate officials in Amsterdam had 'made a great point of the Russian weaknesses discovered as a result of Russia's repeated requests for this and that during the war in Finland.' As Tar noted, 'So have British officials.'

German officials had claimed that at the Brenner Pass meeting between Hitler and Mussolini on 18 March 1940 Hitler had handed Mussolini copies of the actual original notes of admitted Allied weak points said to have emanated from the discussions of the Anglo-French Supreme War Council in Paris. At that time Mussolini said that while Hitler was working with Russia he would not help him as Italy and Hungary were ready to fight Russia. It was Hitler's intention to occupy Murmansk, which it disputed with Russia. He also intended to occupy Scandinavia, and when he did he hoped that because the Finns hated the Russians they would side with him. That left Russia very anxious about German moves in the Baltic. Mussolini assured Hitler of his naval superiority in the Mediterranean and that he had some unspecified 'surprises' for the English. Tar commented that 'This is all very interesting, but is probably sheer guess work. I certainly do not see how [Metcalfe's] informant could have got this information as I understand that no on[e] else was present at the Brenner Meet[ing other than] the two D[ictato]rs ... .'

The Germans had obtained sixty U-boats from the USSR which were being reconditioned near Danzig, where chief German naval engineers were supervising the fitting of new engines etc. New aircraft factories had been set up near Munich and Metcalfe hoped to be able to supply a map. The aforementioned Drs Gruner and Klose from Berlin were operating in Holland and Brussels. That weekend Klose had met his English contact, who has had his visit held over for two days 'as [he] is expected to bring over something valuable'.

The report stated that there had been fewer messages over the past two months as the Germans were using an ultra-shortwave radio based on an island near Emden, and they received news from London or Southampton after 9.00pm and again between 2.00am and 4.00am. The last word of the code used indicated the time and which station would be sending next. Gruner and Klose were reported to have said that there were only three or four people in the whole Chancellery who control German espionage. They remarked that 'only one system worked in the last war and that we now use for everyone'.

German morale was low as state employees were being taxed to pay for the Winter Relief Fund; Metcalfe thought it provided a good opportunity to act now, 'before the German propaganda machine has an opportunity to smoothe [*sic*] it over'. His Dutch contact in Holland was convinced that if he were given money now he could get much information from disgruntled employees.

Michael Holzmann, described as an 'international rogue', had been expelled from Holland and was believed to be in England. During the Spanish Civil War he had worked for both sides. There was a big scandal in Holland as he had private dossiers on many prominent Dutch officials which the Department of Justice seized when he was expelled.

Metcalfe concluded that

> as I have made certain observations while abroad and have suggested plan whereby I believe that much valuable information can be obtained regularly, and as I also have a comprehensive report for the Ministry of Economic Warfare that I am given an early opportunity of expressing my suggestions.

His Dutch contact was 'a man of breeding and culture and has the entré [sic] to German official circles and friends on Goering's staff' who he regarded as reliable but whom he had once believed to be a member of the Dutch Secret Service.[5] And while he appreciated that these titbits of information were incomplete, with the exception of the aircraft leakage, he told Tar that his contact had been given no work plan and passed on whatever he managed to obtain. Several times his contact had asked him for a list of information required, but as a layman he had only been able to make a few suggestions.

> In view of his intimate connection with a member of the Göring staff and an ex-Austrian secret police agent, together with his brother's position and that of his brother-in-law (Holbeck) I am still convinced that he is a valuable contact and has, I believe, been approached by both Dutch and German agents in the past. Postnikow saw W.A. Burton of Economic Warfare on Wednesday and they are considering the suggestions put forward by him ... I am only too willing to assist your department in any capacity although naturally I should prefer to do so as a proper soldier.[6]

Chapter 5

The Air Ministry Leaks

MI5 had hoped that Boissevain might be able to provide the name of the Air Ministry official who had perpetrated the alleged leak, but their investigation was thwarted by the German invasion of the Netherlands on 10 May 1940. However, the list of suspects could be narrowed down since 'the person concerned was bound to have the following attributes':

1. He must be a man of considerable technical knowledge, who probably is aware of the latest types of aircraft, even before they are put into production, as reports would seem to indicate that these became known to the Germans very quickly.
2. He must be high up in the Air Ministry, so high that he probably attends meetings of the Air Council.
3. It was indicated to Postnikow that the name would be a tremendous shock to the British Government, should it ever leak out, and that therefore the official must be someone who in the ordinary way is above suspicion.

It had been suggested during Metcalfe's and Postnikow's interview on 20 July 1940 that Postnikow had once actually heard the name of the official, and that if he were allowed to look through the *Air Force List* he might remember the name. However, later on he claimed that he had *never* heard the name. Lennox noted that, since Postnikow had gathered some of this information before the war, whoever was in the Air Ministry at that time must still be there now. Postnikow was allowed to browse through a copy of the *Air Force List* for August 1939, but while he had no one particularly in mind, he narrowed it down to four possible suspects in order of probability:

- Air Chief Marshal Sir Cyril Newall
- Sir Arthur Street, the Permanent Under-Secretary of State for Air
- Air Marshal Sir Wilfred Freeman
- E.J.H. Lemon, Director General of Production.[1]

However, all were eliminated as,

> Lemon is no longer on the Air Council. It must be clearly understood, of course, that Postnikow is not accusing any of these eminent

and distinguished men of being enemy agents! He was merely trying to find someone to fit the bill. He also said ... that a name he had heard several times on the Continent was Galpin. He had nothing against Galpin but thought it peculiar that his name should have been mentioned so often. I find from the Air Force List that C.J. Galpin, D.S.O., was, before the War, Assistant Secretary in the A.R.P. Department of the Air Ministry. He is now one of the assistant secretaries of the P.U.S. for Air, but has been seconded to the Home Office. It is always possible that Postnikow got the name Galpin wrong and there is certainly another name I can think of which does not sound unlike Galpin![2]

Lennox commented that 'There is no definite proof that Boissevain will divulge the information, even if he is approached, but according to [Metcalfe] he would on conditions, and his price would probably be to get him out of Holland. I suppose it is possible that someone from S.I.S. might contact him, although I can see difficulties.' He attached two letters and a note given to him by Metcalfe about Boissevain, with his contact information.[3]

Postnikow thought that someone in Holland called Warneck, thought to be engaged in the arms trade, might be able to supply the name. He had been in trouble with the Dutch police, causing him to flee to Belgium, or possibly to England.[4] On 15 May Metcalfe informed Tar that he had no news from Boissevain but might still be able to help if they could get in touch with him: 'He would I think be able to get news of impending air attacks on this country or at least of troop (parachutists) concentrations. If I can help in any way let me know. Perhaps I could go over as an American.'[5] There the matter appears to rest as MI5 does not seem to have taken it up.

Metcalfe reproached Tar in a letter on the 18th for not bringing Boissevain over saying that 'I did invite your people to get him over a long time ago and it was only when this was turned down that I arranged to get him over at our own expense'. He said he could try getting in touch with him but it would take a long time. Ironically, had MI5 decided to bring him over it would have saved Boissevain's life.

On 28 August 1941 Tar contacted Squadron Leader Henry Arnold of Air Intelligence about information Metcalfe had picked up from Wing Commander Spencer,[6] whom he had met quite casually the previous week and on two or three other occasions, but did not consider him as a close friend. He was anxious that under no circumstances must his informant's identity be revealed, and expressed that Tar be responsible for 'the handling of the security side of this matter. Although I realise that the leakage is a serious one, the interests involved, as far as my agent is concerned, are very great.'

The plan was for Bill Younger to meet Metcalfe at the Dorchester where he would introduce Spencer to Younger and John Bingham, who would try to get him to 'commit an indiscretion', thus alleviating the need to provide Metcalfe as a witness at any court martial.[7] Arnold investigated the leak, then handed it over to the Air Ministry. However, Tar reported on 7 September that Spencer hadn't turned up for the meeting he'd arranged with him. He wondered whether it was really necessary to proceed with the investigation as he felt strongly that it might prejudice Metcalfe's position. If Air Intelligence wanted to catch Spencer 'they should spend some time and take some trouble over the problem themselves, and should not expect us to endanger the usefulness of our very valuable informant.'[8]

The following day he reported that 'Wing Commander Spencer is to be given a severe choking off for being too talkative and will in all probability be seen by the A.C.A.S.I. [Assistant Chief of the Air Staff (Intelligence) – Air Vice-Marshal Charles E.H. Medhurst]'. Arnold had given strict instructions that, on no account, was the source to be revealed.[9] That afternoon when Spencer dined with Metcalfe he committed further indiscretions. Tar spoke to Arnold and agreed that he should take Metcalfe to lunch with him at his club the following day so that they could discuss the best way to approach the problem.

Luke spoke to Metcalfe about his concern about being compromised and on 11 September he, Arnold and Metcalfe lunched at Arnold's club. They decided that Spencer's case should be left to Arnold's discretion – 'He fully appreciates the necessity of keeping Metcalfe out of it and will probably make arrangements to ensure that Wing Commander Spencer's indiscretions will be discovered locally.'[10]

In February 1942 BALLOON would provide 'more nonsense', in this case concerning an Armenian tail gunner, and also Group Captain Gerard Combe. Before Flight Lieutenant Charles Cholmondeley passed this information to the Air Ministry Luke wanted to have a chat with him about it.[11] Tar confirmed to Air Commodore Douglas Leslie 'Gerry' Blackford, appointed Director of Intelligence (Security) for the RAF in 1941, the above information.

Combe, who had just been appointed Vice President (Air) of the Ordnance Board on 24 January 1942 was, according to Tar, 'a great personal friend of the agent'. Cholmondeley's query and BALLOON's report are not included in the files, so the exact nature of the 'nonsense' about heavy calibre cannon is not known. Tar pointed out to Blackford:

> As you know I am most anxious that any action which is taken of a disciplinary nature should not in any way jeopardise my agent and if you are contemplating taking action on this information I should be glad if you would let me know. I fully realise that it hampers any security measures which you may wish to take but at the same time I am sure you will appreciate the position into which I am put with regard to my agent.[12]

In 1943 Combe was appointed Chief Superintendent, Chemical Defence Experimental Station at Porton Down. In 1946 he received the Legion of Merit from the US President, Harry S. Truman. He ended his career in the RAF as an Air Vice-Marshal and AOC No.41 (Maintenance) Group, Maintenance Command. In 1943 he was appointed air attaché in Washington. He retired from the RAF due to ill health.

Chapter 6

'A man of intelligence and resource'

Metcalfe's 'official' recruitment by MI5 came most likely on 4 March 1941, although the date of his long petition to the Under-Secretary for War in February 1945 suggests that he had been working for them even earlier:

> In February 1941 Lieut Colonel Lennox, who knew of my efforts to regain my commission, asked me if I would work for Lieut Colonel Robertson of MI5 on work of a highly secret nature. I at once agreed and was so employed up to the end of April 1944 ... MI5 have informed me that it would be improper for me to include in this petition particulars of this work, which was of a most secret nature, but that they will themselves submit to VCIGS personally details of my work and why they support this petition ...
>
> In May 1940 ... MI5 asked me if I thought that I could procure for the Ministry of Supply certain 40mm Bofors guns and small arms believed to be in France. I agreed to try and flew over to Paris on 1st June 1940, where I reported to the late Lord Suffolk at the Ministère de l'Armement. Although I found the alleged owner of these weapons, a Spaniard, nothing could be done as he declared that the arms were then situated in a Baltic port.[1]

Brigadier Sir David Petrie, the wartime Director General of MI5, confirmed that Metcalfe's association with MI5 began 'some time before the war' when they required 'the services of a man of intelligence and resource for secret work', as they were building up a network of '"German" agents ... working under our control'. He wrote to Lieutenant General Sir Archibald Nye, the Vice Chief of the Imperial General Staff, on 24 March 1945 explaining the details of Metcalfe's work as a double agent for MI5 owing to his work as a registered arms dealer: 'It was thought that [Metcalfe's] past history was such that, with suitable exaggeration, it could be made plausible to the German Intelligence service that he was prepared to be a traitor to this country.' He had 'acted under our control as a high grade German agent in this country' from early 1941 until April 1944. Petrie said that Metcalfe's work had been entirely satisfactory 'and assisted the control by us of information reaching the enemy from this country'; he was 'an important link in the organisation', allowing them to substantially control 'the whole of the German espionage network in this country'.[2]

Nevertheless, a note on 18 April 1940 from Luke to 'Jasper' Harker and Guy Liddell, the Deputy Director General, and head of B Division respectively, reveals that MI5 had had certain reservations about employing him, even though the periodic information with which he had provided them was useful. Luke explained that Metcalfe was anxious to get back into the Army and recently they had found it 'desirable that we should find a sub-agent in this country for Tricycle who was one of our agents, and it was decided that [Metcalfe] would be an extremely suitable person to undertake this work'. That being said,

> We have every reason to believe that he is a loyal subject, but his history and background suggest that he is in certain ways somewhat unreliable and of course in appointing a man of this kind to perform duties of this nature there is an unavoidable risk, particularly in view of the fact that he is a licensed arms dealer and is serving a company with international connections.
>
> In view of the importance of the work which we hope he will undertake it is most desirable that we should have a check on his correspondence at any rate for a short time, although it is not suggested that his telephone calls should be intercepted at this stage, and I should be most grateful if you would give your approval to our application for a H.O.W.[3]

On 31 May 1940 Metcalfe reported to MI5 that he had located a quantity of 150,000 Mauser rifles on a ship believed to be in Dublin Bay. There were also other parcels of arms which he hoped to locate which could be bought for Britain. Acting on this information, he and Dr Otto Andersen of Messrs Arthur R. Brown in the City of London flew to Paris on 2 June 1940 in an attempt to locate and purchase them. There he was introduced to Dr D.H. Benjamins, a Dutch national, formerly the director and manager of the Nedeil Handelsbank in Amsterdam, who had also acted as a broker between the French authorities and contractors for the construction of the Maginot Line, as well as assisting in the financing of arms deals. He was therefore familiar with most of the German-controlled arms syndicates operating in Holland and Belgium before the war.

Benjamins knew that the arms cache, part of it belonging to Lovingfosse Hardy et André of Herstal, was located in Liège and Antwerp; a second supply was owned by a syndicate, the principal of which was ballistics expert Professor Fernand Pâques, 47, rue Carnot, whose firm, DAPAC, had invented a high-explosive bomb, details of which had been given to Lieutenant Colonel F.A. Blake, the British military attaché in Brussels. A third supply belonged to Colonel José Calvino Ozores of 61, rue Emile Victor III, Paris, and 59, Boulevard Carnot, Vichy, although the arms themselves were located in Tallinn, Estonia. All this information Metcalfe passed on to the Earl of Suffolk at the Ministère de l'Armement on 3 June.[4]

Charles Henry George Howard, 20th Earl of Suffolk and 13th Earl of Berkshire, had been posted to Paris in 1940 as a liaison officer with the Department of Scientific and Industrial Research, established in 1915. Major Ardale Vautier Golding was in France as a liaison officer with the French Ministry of Defence. Golding and Suffolk left Paris with their secretaries on 10 June 1940 after the fall of France, together with the German-Jewish physicist Hans Heinrich von Halban and Lew Kowarski, carrying with them a dozen canisters of the only supply of heavy water smuggled out of Norway, and escaped via Clermont-Ferrand and Bordeaux. After arriving in Falmouth on 21 June, Suffolk joined the Ministry of Supply as a research officer learning how to defuse bombs. He was killed while defusing a German bomb on the Erith marshes on 12 May 1941, earning him a posthumous George Cross.[5] In 1941 Golding became the assistant military attaché in Washington, DC.

Owing to the German invasion of France on 10 May 1940, it was not until 13 June that Metcalfe was able to return to England. He described his flight from Paris on 10 June 1940 as eventful and hair-raising – the pilot got lost and was instructed to return to Paris but they were shot down in flames over the Cherbourg peninsula by a British AA battery at Montreuil-l'Argillé, Normandy:

> We took off for Paris at about 3.45 p.m. and after flying for about half an hour at an altitude of about 1,000-ft. we were fired upon by small arms fire from the ground. The pilot circled round and almost immediately a battery of Bofors anti-aircraft guns opened fire on us and shot us down in flames. The pilot managed to get the wheels down and effected some sort of landing in a clover field on a hillside. The small arms fire continued from a company of French Colonial troops and the wireless operator was hit in the leg. He eventually persuaded these troops to stop firing on us and that we were not German parachutists, and after a few minutes the British officer in charge of the Bofors guns came up and informed us that we were at Montreuil-l'Argillé – his name was Second-Lieut J.B. Legge (No.14429) Fourth Light A.A. Battery.[6]

With Legge's help he and Monsieur Riza, the Turkish counsellor at the embassy in London, escaped in a Morris truck which they drove to Paris, only to find it had been evacuated and their embassies closed. After sleeping in the forest of Fontainebleau they proceeded to Tours, whereupon Riza reported to his ambassador and Metcalfe to Golding. The following day he accompanied Golding to the headquarters of Air Vice-Marshal Playfair who sent them on to Air Marshal Barrett who 'arranged for me to have a car to take me to Chateaudun from which place I went in a van by night to Houssay and was flown back to London early on Thursday morning in a Bombay aircraft which was evacuating secret documents from France under the charge of Flying Officer John A. de Laszlo. We arrived at Hendon about two o'clock'.[7]

On 29 August 1940 Tar wrote to Lennox regarding Metcalfe's commission, enclosing a note signed by Petrie, asking if he could 'possibly shepherd this through and see what can be done for him', saying that he had done 'some good work for us in various directions and I should like to have it placed on record that he has been of considerable use to this Department'. He added that Metcalfe was trying to regain his commission and get into either the Royal Armoured Corps or a cavalry regiment. He hoped that Lennox could get his commission restored in appreciation for the services he had already provided to MI5.[8]

***

Dušan 'Duško' Miladorov Popov was born on 10 July 1912 in Titel, Austria-Hungary (now Serbia), and had travelled as a representative of the Savska Bank, Belgrade, and an 'export and import Commission Agent' [sic]. In 1937 he was arrested in Germany, put into a concentration camp and told to work for the Germans. He claimed he could obtain information from business friends in England, such as Ivan 'Vane' Ivanović who ran Yugoslav Lloyd Shipping Company, through the Yugoslavian diplomatic bag. When he had walked into the British Legation in Belgrade in July 1940 he was already working for the Abwehr. He was recruited as double agent SKOOT (later TRICYCLE), a pun on the name 'pop-off', by Captain Clement Hope, the passport control officer, the cover for anyone working for SIS, the Secret Intelligence Service. His elder brother, Ivan ('Ivo'), was codenamed DREADNOUGHT.

After Popov's recruitment he arrived at Whitchurch, near Bristol on 20 December 1940 and was whisked off to London by 'Jock' Horsfall, the MI5 A3 Division transport officer, accompanied by a Mr Andrew of B24, the section of MI5 based at the Royal Victoria Patriotic School (RVPS), later known as the London Reception Centre (LRC) on Wandsworth Common which interviewed aliens to determine whether they were genuine, or enemy agents. An SIS document in his file dated 18 December 1940 chronicles the sequence of events detailing his recruitment to British Intelligence.[9]

When BALLOON met with Luke at Imperial House on 25 March 1941 he asked him 'whether he should pass on to us certain information which he had discovered during a visit with a friend to certain aerodromes. This information could not be obtained by the average citizen, but of course if BALLOON was really a German spy he would undoubtedly have passed it on'. Luke decided that a ruling was needed on this 'as to whether this priveliged [sic] information should be submitted to the services for approval'. All his messages sent to a cover address would be signed 'Ralph'. He wanted to know whether he should mention that he had obtained the Ministry of Supply circular currently in his possession. He expressed his concern that they not meet at Imperial House in case he was being watched. In future they would meet at Luke's club or his flat, but the decision was up to Tar.[10]

Luke informed BALLOON that TRICYCLE would be returning from Lisbon soon, as did 'Gwennie' (Mrs Charles Wilson), one of TRICYCLE's girlfriends, who had received a cable from him saying he would be returning inside a month. He was also told that they were vaguely interested in Irsey de Irsa [sic], his friends, and what his movements were.¹¹ Luke followed this up on 4 April in a note to Tar recommending that as 'he is in the armaments racket and is an ex-Army officer with something of a past ... as an elementary precaution I think we ought to have a note of his correspondence'. Therefore, a Home Office warrant (HOW) was placed on BALLOON's correspondence.¹²

Special Branch recorded that George Irsay de Irsa was a Pole who may at one time have been Hungarian. They alleged that he was on the German General Staff at the time of the Treaty of Brest-Litovsk on 3 March 1918. Described as 'boastful and unreliable', he '[h]as apparently not been thought to be dangerous'. He claimed to be acquainted with unnamed high Nazi officials and was suspected by the Polish authorities of being a German agent working from Danzig.¹³ He is shown as holding patents for inventing a process and apparatus for the drying of wood, and drying bearings.¹⁴

***

On 17 April 1941 BALLOON wrote to Lennox regarding notes Luke had asked him to prepare 'in the part of a would-be German agent trying to become established with them' and enclosing his observations. Major Frank Foley of SIS had rung up Gardiner, BALLOON's assistant, who had lived in Berlin for sixteen years to ask him whether BALLOON knew anything about Schirnick who he presumed was at Ham (Camp 020). Luke intended to get a look-up on him.¹⁵ Another report followed on 24 May, also addressed to Mathews (Lennox):

> I R.A.F.
> At Northolt Aerodrome (Fighter Command) along the railway line and on the edge of the landing ground are a series of metal mushroom-shaped hoods as per sketch below:
> I hear that similar apparatus can be seen at Slough Trading Estate. The hoods are spaced at regular intervals and great secrecy as to their use is observed. I believe them to be a smoke producing plant to screen the area similar to those used on Clydeside.
> I hear that the magazine feed for the 20 mm cannon in the 'Beaufighter' are disliked as at 20,000 ft the gunner has the greatest difficulty in lifting the magazines to fit them on to the gun. All the newest cannon are being fitted with a belt feed to overcome this difficulty.
> Quite a number of Hurricane Fighters have been fitted with four 20mm Hispano cannon, two in each wing, instead of 8 machine guns. These are very formidable and popular with the pilots.
> The German aircraft shot down in Kensington was inspected by an expert from MAP who considered that your valves were badly carboned up and showed that the engine had not received a

top overhaul for an ~~very~~ unduly long period. The camshaft casing showed signs of fracture and the joint had been made good with red lead.

II Royal Navy
Your 'E' boats are giving quite a lot of trouble and the armament being fitted by ships for defence against these craft are .8" Orlikon [*sic* - Oerlikon] guns (you may remember I spoke of these last week). I know these guns well as I had them in 1928[?] as an anti-tank gun in the army. I do not think much of them and if your MTBs can attack from a fair range they should prove ineffective.
23/4/41[16]

Chapter 7

A Network Evolves

The day after Popov's arrival Tar, John Marriott, John Bingham, and Andrew (known as Mr Norman) interviewed him in room 430 of the Savoy Hotel. During that first debriefing he gave them an account of his life. Marriott stated that he 'left an exceedingly favourable first impression upon all of us. His manner was absolutely frank and we all considered without question that he was telling the truth. He particularly impressed upon us that *he desired no money from us* and only stipulated that he should be allowed to go home as early as conveniently possible in January so that he might attend to his own business.'

In subsequent days he was interviewed by members of the Twenty Committee (also known as the Double-Cross Committee) – Tar, Masterman, Marriott and Montagu, Naval Intelligence Division (NID). Attached to the report on the meeting on 21 December was SKOOT's mission, a list of his German secret service contacts, and his first meeting with Marriott when Andrew had collected him from Bristol.[1] On the 23rd Marriott reported that he would be interviewed by Oreste Pinto at the RVPS 'who will obtain from him his whole story in French in which language SKOOT is fluent'.

On Christmas Eve William 'Bill' Younger (aka 'Mr Younge') explained to Popov that a casual friend of his, 'Mr Norman' (Andrew), had told him that Popov was on his own, and invited him to spend Christmas and Boxing Day with him. He told him that he was still a student at Christ Church, Oxford (having been taught by Masterman) and was due to return there, having been rejected from the Army on health grounds, which was only a white lie – he had suffered polio as a child, resulting in restricted growth and a withered arm.[2]

Younger was a poet and stepson of author Dennis Wheatley, originally recruited to MI5 by Maxwell Knight to penetrate Communist meetings; he would later fall in love with Friedl Gaertner. According to Joan Miller, another of Knight's agents talent-spotted by Younger, he was 'very anxious to marry her up until the point when his mother, Joan Wheatley, took a hand in the business. Bill invited his mother to lunch to consult her about an engagement ring for Friedl, and some hours later, with the crucial meal behind him, he found himself buying a string of cultured pearls instead. That was the end of the romance.'[3] In the 'fifties he wrote several thrillers under the name 'William Mole'.

Bernard O'Connor mistakenly claims it was Tar who entertained Popov at Quaglino's, then at Younger's club, the Lansdowne, Berkeley Square, where they

A NETWORK EVOLVES

played billiards, but it was actually Younger. They were joined by some of his friends, one of whom worked in MI5's Registry at Blenheim Palace. From there they moved on to the United Universities Club where they drank sherry with Masterman. Dinner was at the Savoy where Popov 'took part in the usual Christmas bonhomous rioting, well lubricated by champagne' and danced the night away. On Boxing Day he took Popov to lunch with friends of his (a Mr and Mrs Valli) in Leighton Buzzard. It was only after they set out that he remembered that Popov should have had a permit. He was told later that Leighton Buzzard was a protected place but was not aware of that before.[4]

***

There is conflicting information about when Popov was first introduced to 'C', Sir Stewart Menzies, the Chief of SIS, as well as GELATINE. Several authors claim that his first meeting with 'C' was likely at a New Year's Eve party in December 1940 at Dassett, the country home of Menzies' mother. Also present were Menzies' brother, Major Ian Graham Menzies of the Scots Guards and his Austrian wife Lisel [sic], also referred to as Alice née Stöttinger,[5] and Lisel's sister, Friedl Gaertner, a cabaret singer. However, Knight, writing to Harker in August 1945, states that 'it was through C. that we were first introduced to her in 1938'; Joan Miller simply says that it was 'At one of the Menzies parties' as does O'Connor, who gives her birth name as Friedericka Stottinger [sic – Stöttinger].[6]

Friedl was born on 17 January 1911 at Raitham [sic – Roitham], Austria, and had arrived in England on 12 March 1938 following the *Anschluss* in Austria. A telegram in her file from João Almeida dated 15 October 1941 gives her name as 'Friedl Stockinger Gaertner' [sic] living at 18 King's Court, King's Road, Chelsea, London SW3.[7] She had previously visited England in 1937 as well as making frequent visits to Palestine where she had gone to live with her former Jewish husband from whom she was now divorced.

Popov (TRICYCLE) was totally entranced by her. Menzies had invited her so that she could 'provide Popov with the entrée into British society that was expected by his German masters'. However, the alleged New Year's Eve encounter with TRICYCLE contradicts the official account in GELATINE's MI5 file which states that they didn't meet until 28 February 1941, as on 26 February Luke, Tar, Knight and Masterman met with her to discuss a plan to put her in touch with TRICYCLE.[8] The account of TRICYCLE's first visit to England (20 December 1940 – 2 January 1941) makes no mention of their first meeting on 31 December, although the account of his second visit to England (4 February – 15 March 1941) mentions '28.2.1941'. A further meeting with GELATINE, who was subsequently introduced to TRICYCLE', suggests that they *had* met before, either on New Year's Eve or 26/27 February. Russell Miller also acknowledges this in his book, as does Larry Loftis, but that the meeting with Menzies *was* on New Year's Eve.[9]

Initially, Menzies had tried to recruit her to work for SIS and send her to Germany, but when she refused he put her in touch with Knight via Guy Liddell.

Knight suggested to Tar that she be recruited as a double agent since she 'was German and in touch with the German Secret Service representative in this country prior to the outbreak of war, although she had never got the length of doing any work for them'. He considered that the type of information she could provide to the Germans should be more political than military. Her contacts, through her brother-in-law, would give her the opportunity to pick up a great deal of extremely valuable information of this kind, and become the Germans' link with people in high society in England. Luke agreed. TRICYCLE should inform the Germans that 'although she was willing to do everything she could for the Fatherland, it would be impossible for her to obtain the fullest amount of information unless she received from them some contribution towards her inevitable heavy expenditure' as she was doing the work out of loyalty for her country.

Knight interviewed her on 27 May 1938 and reported the following Monday:

> Although previous information about this girl had rather prejudiced me against her I must confess that she struck me after an hour's talk as an extremely level-headed and intelligent person. Her one aim and object in life is to secure a permit to work in this country and to remain here, and in order to achieve this end she is willing to do anything in order to ingratiate herself with the authorities. There is only one thing she refuses to do and that is to go back and live in either Germany or Austria.

She was unknown to the German authorities as being opposed to the Nazi regime. The only negative point against her was that her ex-husband was a Jew. But since she was prepared to tell them that her general opinion of the Jews was the same as theirs 'the fact that she divorced a Jew who is now living in Palestine may not prove a serious obstacle'. She would require some instruction on the NSDAP in Britain.

Knight assigned her to spy on the Anglo-German Fellowship (AGF) as an honorary member, and attend meetings of the Deutsche Arbeitsfront (DAF) at Cleveland Terrace 'where she did excellent work in connection with German organisations up to the outbreak of war' as a part-time informer.[10] She was given the codename GELATINE, because someone in MI5 thought she was a 'jolly little thing', and joined Popov's network of agents.[11] At the same time, she worked as a secretary for Knight's friend, Dennis Wheatley, 'a fact which must interest the Germans in view of the important and confidential work which this gentleman is undertaking at the present time'.

Wheatley was a prolific author best-known for his novels about the occult. During the Second World War he was a member of the London Controlling Section (LCS) established in September 1941 to co-ordinate strategic deception and cover plans under the command of Colonel John Bevan. This begs the questions: (a) Was Friedl ever privy to his work for the LCS? (b) Was she only working for him in his capacity as a novelist or also with the LCS? And (c) What, if any, of their deception plans was she instructed to pass on to the Germans as part of a disinformation campaign? No answers to these questions can be found in her files so must remain purely speculative.

Knight's report to Liddell on 21 September 1939 about a follow-up interview he'd had with her the previous day stated that he was satisfied that her anti-Nazi views were perfectly genuine

> and it is worth noting that she is completely out of sympathy with her sister and her sister's relations-in-law on nearly all matters. [Frau Gaertner] is, if anything, definitely Left Wing in her politics, but I have no reason to think that she has Left Wing associations in this country which might prove to be embarrassing to us ....
> (In future I intend to refer to [Frau Gaertner] as M/G.)[12]

However, as noted in Chapter 1, he had already been referring to her as such in 1938.

TRICYCLE was instructed that when he returned to Lisbon he was to tell the Germans that he considered GELATINE might be of considerable use to their organisation in Britain. How he should introduce her to them would be left up to him as he 'would be in a position to judge the effect on them of his revelation. But he should not press the matter in any way, simply say that this was a young woman whom he had met during his stay in this country and with whom he had formed an attachment'. Tar informed Knight that when TRICYCLE returned 'We shall then know presumably whether [Friedl Gaertner] has met with the reception we hoped it would and that they will take her on.'[13] But when he met the Germans in Lisbon they told him they were disappointed with the information he had brought them, saying that it was too general, and asked if, after he had returned to England, he would be prepared to visit America to appoint an agent who could pass information to them in secret writing. After that he was to proceed to Egypt and remain there as their agent.

TRICYCLE was amenable to doing this, and was given a questionnaire which he was told to memorise; when he returned to England he was to obtain answers to approximately fifty questions mainly concerning the RAF and air force production, which were 'of great interest to the Service Intelligence Directors', who provided him with a good deal of information which he took back to Portugal on 15 January, much of which was written in secret ink by BALLOON and GELATINE.

When he returned to the UK on 4 February he brought the original questionnaire in German as well as some secret ink 'of a somewhat primitive kind for his own usage', as well as for GIRAFFE (George Graf),[14] and given three cover addresses in Lisbon to which he should send his communications:

> Maria Gonçalves de Azevdo
> Lisbon
> Calcada do Desterro, 5.11coj (5, 2nd floor, c)

DOUBLE AGENT BALLOON

Paolo Simões
Lisbon
Large Santo Antominho, 1st Loja.

Paulo Pinto da Lima
Lisbon
Praca Duque de Terceira 25.

The Germans expected him to appoint someone as a suitable agent in the UK who would pass on to them further information from time to time. The original idea was that he should pretend that he had appointed someone in the Yugoslav legation, although in fact the work would be carried on by one of MI5's nominees. However, it was decided that, given Yugoslavia's position vis-à-vis Germany, it would be better for him to tell the Germans he had appointed a British subject (BALLOON) instead. He would tell the Germans that his Yugoslavian friend had in any case intended to obtain most of his information from BALLOON, but owing to the present international situation, was not prepared to get involved and had placed TRICYCLE in direct contact with him. As for GELATINE, MI5 hoped to re-introduce her to the Germans through him. The objects of his visit to the UK on behalf of the Germans were as follows:

(1) To take back as many answers as possible in detail to the questionnaire.
(2) To send back by secret ink any information which he might obtain during his stay, if he considered it should be sent on at once.
(3) To carry a package of secret ink for Giraffe which he would post in this country on arrival.
(4) Before leaving this country to find someone, preferably his friend in the Yugoslav Legation, to take over his job and write in secret ink information in answer to these questions which he himself was to answer.
(5) To send a postcard in ordinary writing to one of the cover addresses in Lisbon giving a cover address to which letters could be sent in this country. (Unfortunately it has subsequently been discovered that this message was written on a picture postcard and it seems likely that it was destroyed by the Censors as the sending of picture postcards to Portugal is prohibited.) ... .[15]

Metcalfe officially became double agent BALLOON when Tar Robertson decided that he would be the most suitable person for TRICYCLE to leave behind, 'particularly as his background was particularly suited to the task'. He, Lennox, and John Masterman met with BALLOON at Room 055 on 4 March where they outlined their scheme. While they couldn't promise that his commission would be restored, they 'undertook to have him released from his application under the

National Service Act, and steps have already been taken to ensure that he will not be called up for military service'.[16] 'We explained to him that much would depend on the success which attended TRICYCLE's interview with the German Secret Service in Lisbon, but we had every reason to hope that they would be glad to avail themselves of BALLOON's services and to pay handsomely for them.' Any money Metcalfe received from the Germans would belong to MI5, but he would be given a proportion of it. They would control any messages he sent, and any information he received would be passed to the Service Intelligence Departments. BALLOON was 'willing and anxious to undertake these duties and if necessary to visit Portugal and see the Germans'. Tar then took him to meet TRICYCLE. TRICYCLE set up his network, as Luke recorded on 24 March 1941:

> TRICYCLE, who is one of our double agents, was instructed by the Germans to leave behind him a suitable agent who would send messages to an address in Portugal in secret ink. At first it was his intention to pretend that this agent, who would of course be appointed by ourselves, was one of the members of the Yugoslav Legation, but we decided that it would be better in view of Yugoslavia's international complications if an Englishman were appointed for the task.

BALLOON and TRICYCLE would meet several times after that. Luke explained that

> TRICYCLE should tell the Germans that he had met BALLOON through a member of the Yugoslav Legation who was originally supposed to send the messages. TRICYCLE would explain that his Yugoslav friend had in any case intended to obtain most of his information from BALLOON and that owing to the present international situation he was not prepared to appear in the matter himself and had therefore placed TRICYCLE in direct contact with him.

Together with Marriott and Tar, he met with BALLOON on 9 March at Imperial House, when they decided he should write certain notes in secret ink for TRICYCLE to take back with him to Portugal, which BALLOON did the following day. 'In Portugal TRICYCLE will have told the Germans that BALLOON really provided him with practically all the information which he is giving them in answer to their questionnaire.'

> BALLOON is not officially aware that Lieut Commander Montague h[as] shwon [sic] TRICYCLE a chart which displays the gaps in the mined area off the East coast of Britain, but he knows all about TRICYCLE's movements in this country and has been given a copy of his itinery [sic] which is attached hereto. It has been arranged

that if BALLOON should be telephoned by someone in this country in connection with his work for the Germans, he should try and arrange an appointment with him two hours ahead. He will of course immediately get in touch with us the moment he receives any such communication. The Ministry of Supply circular is being handed to him. ['Given to him 25/3/41'][17]

TRICYCLE's schedule records that he was busy with BALLOON on the afternoon of 8 March, the following day when they lunched at the Savoy, and again on the 10th when they had drinks. Guy Liddell recorded in his diary for 15 March 1941:

> SKOOT left for Lisbon this morning taking with him notes on his questionnaire and notes about the Ministry of Supply circulator for which he was asked and certain particulars of mine fields put forward by the Naval Intelligence Division. All these notes were written in secret ink on innocuous correspondence from Friedle Gaertner (his girlfriend), BALLOON and his business cover.[18]

On 1 May 1941 TRICYCLE reported that what the Germans had been told about BALLOON's background was essentially true, that he was resentful about what had happened to him, which didn't seem to bother the Abwehr providing TRICYCLE's organisation functioned: 'That's why I have to stay in Lisbon for 2-3 weeks to see how it works, as they said: "If you are there it works and when you are not there it doesn't work".' The Abwehr agreed to send BALLOON some money and would make arrangements for further payments. TRICYCLE told them that BALLOON would not be sending any information until he got paid: 'So when BALLOON receives money he should send quite a lot the first time and later on a little information week by week. He had better sign himself Ivan II.'[19]

MI5 had decided to pay BALLOON a salary of £5 per week, in addition to 5 per cent of whatever money the Germans paid him, for which he was perfectly satisfied, as it was more generous than he had anticipated. But if he were to receive a large sum of money, they would have to restrict his commission to £500 per annum, although he thought this unlikely. MI5 had already received £300 from TRICYCLE, for which his commission would be £15. BALLOON's salary would be back-dated to when he started work for MI5, namely 4 March. He was given £60, composed of his salary to date (4 March – 9 May) – £45, plus £15 commission.[20]

BALLOON sent three letters in secret ink to three separate addresses in Lisbon: from 'H.J. Spenser' to João Maia; 'E.J. Edwards' to Paulo Pinto de Lima; and 'W.P. Newman' to Arthur Soares (see Chapter 9). Luke sent instructions to Colonel H.M. Allan at the GPO as to how they should be marked by the Censor and air-mailed to Lisbon post-haste. On 14 May 1941 he reported that:

> When I saw TRICYCLE yesterday I discussed with him further the question as to how BALLOON should be paid in the future.

We decided that if Plan Midas [see next chapter] did not go over he should try and get the Germans to pay the money to an agent in Dublin. He could explain that BALLOON would visit Dublin periodically, not necessarily at regular intervals and would collect the money from their agent while he was there. If the Germans do not like this idea they could perhaps arrange to have the money paid into a bank account in Dublin in BALLOON's name, or at worst arrange for the money to be paid into his account on this side direct.

The trouble is that the matter can hardly be left in the air as TRICYCLE has been left by the Germans with the task of finding some channel through which BALLOON can be paid.

I have also told TRICYCLE that I wish him to inform the Germans that he has handed over to BALLOON the re-agent of the secret ink that they can write to him in secret ink sending him questionnaires and ask whatever information they particularly want. It is much more satisfactory that there should be correspondence both ways.[21]

***

Memorandum for Metcalfe

The memorandum which Luke had drawn up on 2 August explained TRICYCLE's organisation in London and set out the terms of reference by which BALLOON became one of his sub-agents.[22] TRICYCLE passed this on to the Germans, and a copy was shown to BALLOON on the 14th.

The Germans gave Popov the codename Ivan I[23] and Metcalfe Ivan II. MI5 did not tell Metcalfe the whole truth about his being an ex-British Army officer who had lost his commission by passing 'bounced' cheques; instead they told him, 'In point of fact your past history as given to the Germans has been made to look pretty black.' For the Germans' benefit they were told that he was an 'excellent spy' who worked for British Graphitised Metals Co. and was interested in armaments; that he was discontented with the current regime in Britain, and felt 'outlawed' because of his past and would do anything for money 'with which to rehabitate yourself' [sic]. His main problem was that he had a habit of overspending. He also knew 'R' (Ralph), who was probably intended to be Ivanović, the name by which the Germans knew the imaginary Yugoslav diplomat who was going to work for them from the beginning. Metcalfe was told:

> You may remember that Popov was sent to this country with the idea that he could obtain information from this person. You have only known Popov since his second trip to London. Formerly you did all the work for Ralph who passed on the result to Popov. It should be explained here that during his first visit in December 1940, Popov

'obtained' certain information which he took back with him to Lisbon. You were responsible for this although it was given to Popov by Ralph. So that you may be fully aware of the exact nature of the information which you passed on, I attach copies of the notes which Popov took back with him, last January.

During his second visit to this country Popov was informed by Ralph that it would be easier for him to work in direct contact with you. Since then for all the work he has done and for practically all the information which he has obtained, the Germans have you to thank. Being English you are able to go around without very much danger. It is with you that Popov always travelled when he went to inspect aerodromes etc. but you have often travelled alone without him. It may also please you to know that Popov has told the Germans that your brain and personal courage are worthy of admiration.

It seems likely that you will be paid by the Germans $500 a month but this will be made in fairly frequent payments as you spend money easily and often lose in gambling. You have been borrowing money from Ralph for sometime [*sic*] and indeed that is what enabled him in the first place to recruit you. You have also asked Popov to lend you money on more than one occasion. With regard to Ralph he is an entirely legendary figure and is supposed to occupy some position in the Yugoslav Legation. The Germans know nothing about him and they have dropped the subject so far as he is concerned. If you should ever be in touch with the Germans yourself, however, they will no doubt press you for more informatio[n] and you will have to refuse to give it.

Since you do all the work Ralph now does practically nothing except to give you political information from time to time. He is very much afraid of compromising himself with his own people and will therefore be unsuitable as a direct agent for the Germans. Popov only retained him in his organisation because he knows about you and really brought you into the services of the Germans.

The following are important observations in case you should make a trip to Lisbon.

(a) Popov explained to the Germans that you have volunteered to go to Lisbon, but that it was most difficult for you to obtain an Exit Permit. In order to have this it is necessary for you to have a real reason to make the trip. In order to help you towards this end the Germans are going to em[plo]y one of their agents in the Arms business and will start [fr]om today to correspond with you making you a big offer for sporting guns. In this way they hope to provide within two or three months a reason for travelling from London to Lisbon.

(b) As you know our present inclination is to avoid sending you there but if we should decide to ask you to do so and you are willing to go you will have to be extremely careful. It seems that your best plan would be to occupy yourself with genuine business. Whilst we have every confidence in you and feel that if you went there you would be more than equal to the occasion, it is only fair to point out that if anything should happen which would disclose to Karstoff [TRICYCLE's copy says 'the Germans'] your true position and that of Popov, the repercussion on his family in Yugoslavia might be tragic.

When you are writing or cabling your representative I should be grateful if you would ask him to thank TRICYCLE on Major Robertson's behalf for the letter which he wrote to him.

Although TRICYCLE's mistake about the name of the 'coldfooted Jew' in this country who was anxious to change pounds into dollars was serious, I do not think that any useful purpose would be served by taxing him unduly on the subject. He has done very well to push through Plan Midas and we would prefer that he should be complimented rather than blamed. You could perhaps arrange for him to be informed that we shall take every precaution to ensure that the Germans do nto [sic] discover that he has been working for us in view of his anxiety regarding the repurcussions [sic] on his family which such a discovery might entail.

In the meantime at any rate we are not at all anxious that BALLOON should go to Portugal.

(c) All the work with secret ink has been done in your flat and for the most part Popov has travelled in your motor car.[24]

TRICYCLE wrote from the Estoril Palace Hotel (undated), 'In any case it would probably be best that Ivan II not go to Lisbon.'[25]

***

After some difficulty with his visa, TRICYCLE left for Lisbon on 23 April. When he finally met Karsthoff on the afternoon of the 27th they discussed the letter which he was to take back to GIRAFFE, and details of financial arrangements for paying BALLOON and GELATINE. He was allowed to make his own plans for these two agents, but the Germans showed very little curiosity about his affairs in England or how he managed to obtain permission to enter the country; it was understood that he was capable of managing everything through his acquaintance Bozo Banac, which they regarded as sufficient.[26]

When he first mentioned BALLOON they told him that he was free to employ anyone he pleased, provided he told them who it was, but when he mentioned

GELATINE neither Karsthoff nor Warnecke responded. Later Berlin sent a telegram saying that she would be useful as she had already worked for von Ahlefeld.[27] Gwyer reported that:

> TRICYCLE did not appear to think that Dr WARNECKE was necessarily KARSTHOFF's superior, though if they were on an equality, it seems curious that he should not have bothered to inform KARSTHOFF when to expect TRICYCLE back in Lisbon. He certainly does not seem to have done so, to judge from TRICYCLE's difficulty in getting hold of KARSTHOFF on his return; but this may have been due to the uncertainty caused by TRICYCLE's perennial visa trouble.
>
> There is also the question of Dr WARNECKE's two 'specialists', whom TRICYCLE never saw. What did they specialise in, and why was it necessary for them to come at all, if only to advise Dr WARNECKE in the background? The most plausible explanation seems to be that they had nothing to do with TRICYCLE, and were there to advise (in whatever capacity) the wholly separate organisation run by LENZ in Madrid. That it was separate is indicated by the fact that no attempt was made to contact or entertain TRICYCLE in Madrid until JEBSEN's arrival. On the other hand, after a friend of his had overheard two Germans (the specialists?) discussing TRICYCLE in a hotel, it was with LENZ and not with Dr WARNECKE that TRICYCLE made trouble.[28]

TRICYCLE described Gustav Wilhelm Lenz @ Wilhelm Leissner @ 'Papa', *Leiter* Abwehr Madrid as 'LENZ alias "Fruhling"' based at the German Embassy, Madrid, and 'Said ... to be head of German SS in Madrid'. According to a CIA report on Oberstleutnant Franz Seubert, Lenz's cover name was SOMMER, but his real name was Leiser.[29] Luke added that if Plan MIDAS were adopted TRICYCLE should mention that it would provide a means of paying GELATINE, thus strengthening its attraction from the German point of view. They agreed that she should be run as an entirely separate agent from BALLOON, the only connection being TRICYCLE. He added:

> From the purely domestic point of view, I emphasized that any information which GELATINE has to send over to the Germans should pass through this office for approval and that the letters should be written in the presence either of one of the B.2a officers or at any rate under their auspices. Whilst no mention of the subject was made by Major Knight it is fairly clear that as long as she is used as a double agent it is desirable that GELATINE should become a B.2a agent and responsibility for the payment of remuneration may have to be transferred to B.2a.[30]

A NETWORK EVOLVES

On 1 May 1941 when TRICYCLE had returned to England he reported:

> Regarding Friedl, I just followed through the plan as arranged. I told Karstow [sic][31] first and he just said: 'Thank you, thank you.' I then told the same story to Warnecke who said the same thing but made notes. Just before I left they had several cables, one Fritzi Gardner geborene [born] Sottinger [sic] could be very useful to come into contact with. Just mention the name von Ahlefeld and ... I said I would think about it but it is too dangerous for me. If I do it I am supposed to give her some of these addresses and some of the ink and in future they will explain to her, but she is not going to be paid as she is not doing it for money but for patriotic reasons. She has already done some work for them for von Ahlefeld.
>
> When I gave them the report about Friedl I told them both that I did not want to have anything to do with it as I am often in the same society as she is and she would not like to know that I know and vice versa. I can say that I did not want to do it and maybe they will send someone else to her. Friedl will sign Fritzi.[32]

Chapter 8

Plan MIDAS

TRICYCLE had conceived a scheme codenamed Plan MIDAS whereby the Abwehr would provide funds for his notional network of agents in Britain, but in reality the money would be channeled directly to British intelligence. Eric Glass, Popov's nominee, was 'a flamboyant figure, half-Austrian and half-British' theatrical agent who had arrived in Britain in 1932 and founded a literary agency in 1934.[1] His cover story was that he had met Glass through a young actress when he was last in the UK. He had not paid much attention to him but Glass

> being a Jew, was smalmy [*sic*] and tried to make up to Tricycle, asking him to have drinks etc. Tricycle again saw him at various times this time and gradually this proposition developed. Probably some chance remark by either one of them started the whole thing … . He is quite a successful theatrical and film agent and well enough known for Tricycle to have made some general enquiries about him. In 1938 [Glass] applied for British naturalisation but has not got it yet. He is married to an English Jewess …
>
> When the drive to lock up all aliens started, [Glass] like a good many others went automatically inside although there was nothing against him, and stayed inside for nearly 6 months, finally in the Isle of Man. Since then he bears the British Government a grudge. Apart from that he is not at all sure that England will win this war. Nor does he fancy the idea of being in this country if the German invasion succeeds, but there is probably nothing he can do about it. The least he can do, however, is to try and get some money to America, and although he has told Tricycle that he is acting for somebody, Tricycle has a shrewd suspicion that at least part of the money is [*Redacted*]
>
> The only thing [Glass] would not do is to trust Tricycle to such an extent that he would leave the money in his care in America. He would nominate somebody, probably a Jew, to whom it should be paid. For some reason or other, he has not given Tricycle the name of this man yet, perhaps he has to arrange things first. Therefore, as soon as he hears from Tricycle that the proposition is accepted and Tricycle is in New York [Glass] will cable him the name of the man

to whom the money should be paid. Then, as soon as he hears from his friend that everything is all right he will pay the money in here.

There is a certain amount of mutual trust required, On the other hand, Tricycle is or should be in a position to have the whip-hand over [Glass] to assure that [Glass] pays the money in this country. And this I think he would have as soon as [Glass] has sent the cable giving his friend's name to whom the Dollars should be paid, as Tricycle could expose the whole scheme to the British Government if [Glass] did not pay up.

To complete the picture [Glass] has a weak heart.[2]

Lennox provided further information about Glass and explained that 'These are not the facts about [Glass] but it is merely a suggestion for Tricycle's story'. TRICYCLE asserted that Glass 'had made a tidy sum in London and was anxious to export his cash to America'. Major Albrecht von Auenrode @ Ludovico von Karstoff, a Viennese aristocrat and *Leiter* of the Lisbon Abwehrstelle was 'particularly impressed'.[3]

When Glass became naturalised in 1946 his wife's name was given as Blanche, but in 1983 he had married Australian Janet Ruth Crowley who succeeded him in running the agency when he died in 1995, until her death in September 2018. Her obituary in *The Stage* described Eric as 'legendary' and mentioned that he had represented actors such as Jim Dale, Ron Moody and Edward Woodward,[4] as well as being Sean O'Casey's European literary agent from 1929 to 1932.[5]

As Lennox recounted to Marriott on 4 June, Glass 'was in a complete flat spin and scared nearly out of his life'. Lennox reassured him that he didn't have to do what MI5 had asked, without revealing too many details of what that was, but before leaving their meeting Glass told him that he was 'willing to do anything'. Lennox commented that 'he had been given an opportunity, but on the whole I felt he was wise to refuse. All he had to do now for his own safety and liberty was to keep his mouth shut.' Lennox proposed that they would use Glass but without him knowing:

> After all, Tricycle has seen him, can describe him if necessary and what more do we want? In due course, if the plan works we can adopt either one of two methods. I guarantee that if [GLASS] gets a message or a cable he will burn the telephone wire in his excitement to let me know immediately. Probably better would be that we put a 'How' [Home Office Warrant] on any messages to him from Portugal or America. Then he need not know that he is being used until we want him. If and when we do want him I guarantee that he will walk into the mouth of hell if need be. Sorry to appear somewhat ruthless but we are at war and I see no reason why the fears of a little Jew should in any way deflect us from our path.
>
> I would suggest that you make it utterly clear to Tricycle that if [Glass] is used for our purposes he can be trusted not to tell

anyone. This trust is based on the one thing that in this case really counts – sheer fright. I am convinced that you can set Tricycle's mind absolutely at rest in this matter and I think you should do so in no uncertain terms. After all, he is risking his neck and deserves the reassurance.

Personally I am rather glad that [Glass] tried to back out. It really makes it more simple for us.

Please note that [Glass's] present address is [*Redacted*] this is both his office and his house. He is shortly moving his office to Piccadilly House. The offices in this building have no numbers and simply [*Redacted*] Piccadilly House, Piccadilly Circus, S.W.1 will find him. Both addresses may be useful. [Glass] is actually sleeping at the White House, but for reasons which I have already explained I think this address should not be given. His name appears in the telephone directory with the address of [*Redacted*].[6]

Marriott, TRICYCLE, Glass, and Luke met on 5 June 1941 to discuss details of the rate of exchange. The cover story was that the whole plan was designed to catch out certain illegal currency operators, but Glass had not been told about espionage. It was noted that 'TRICYCLE disliked and distrusted [Glass] whose appearance and general demeanour are scarecely [*sic*] prepossessing. Under these circumstances the meeting could hardly be expected to be very successful.' They worked out the following arrangements for the deal:

(1) That TRICYCLE should try and exchange a maximum of £20,000 at a minimum exchange of $2.25 to the pound sterling.
(2) He should receive himself ten percent of total amount of dollars received. This will have the effect of encouraging him him [*sic*] to exchange as many pounds as possible up to the limit of £20,000.
(3) The basic exchange rate for the deal between [Glass] and TRICYCLE would be $2.50. Any excess on this quotation being divided between the two partners equally (e.g. the amount to be exchanged being £12,000 @ $3 to the pound, will give a sum of $36,000 of which TRICYCLE will retain 10% = $3,600. If he had only been able to bargain for the dollars at $2.50 the amount received would have been $30,000, so in addition he will receive ½ of the difference viz. $3,000, making his total remuneration $6,000.
(4) As soon as he has negotiated the deal he will cable to [GLASS] as follows, either from Portugal or from the U.S.A.:

> 'X had a <u>son</u> yesterday weighing Y kilos please inform Z.'
> daughter

(a) N.B. 'X (woman's name) signifies 1,000 ~~dollars~~ pounds if the name begins with the letter 'A', 2,000 if 'B', 9,000 ~~dollars~~ pounds if 'I', 10,000 ~~dollars~~ pounds if 'S', etc.etc.etc.

As a double check the infant will be a son up to and including 10,000 ~~dollars~~ pounds and a daughter between 10 and 20,000 ~~dollars~~ pounds.

(b) 'Y' (weight of infant) will indicate the rate of exchange the table being as follows:-
3.25 kilos = an exchange of 2.25 dollars to the pound.
3.30 kilos = "   "   " 2.30   "   "   "   "
4   kilos = "   "   " 3   "   "   "   "
                                                etc. etc.

Thus the actual exchange rate has been stepped up one point in order to ensure that the child will carry suitable weight.

(c) 'Z' (man or woman's name) = equals name of the agent to wh[om] the sterling is to be paid by [Gl]ass.

Just before the meeting ended Glass spoke with Marriott alone in another room. He was 'behaving like a frightened rat and was not prepared to go ahead with the plan willingly.' MI5 would use his name without his knowledge, but 'In the meantime however we are investigating the possibility of finding a more suitable Midas.'[7]

The following day Luke and Liddell saw William Stephenson who was in London and decided that Glass should ask TRICYCLE to pay the dollars into his own account at the banking company of Ladenberg Thalmann of New York.[8] Luke saw Sir Edward Reid, who confirmed that 'this arrangement is quite suitable.'[9] Reid was formerly a partner in Baring Brothers, the City bank, and now working in an auxiliary section of B1b which dealt with finance and currency enquiries.[10] He was also a first cousin of Guy Liddell by marriage – Liddell was separated from his wife, Calypso Baring.

On 7 June 1941 Cowgill wrote to Tar about the comments which Reid had made on Plan MIDAS:

> Firstly, the intermediary brokerage or commission should be 10% or 25 cents per £. Any wide variation from this figure would be suspicious. This would mean that the Germans would furnish in America $2.75 for each £ made available to them in this country.
>
> Secondly, the Germans are unlikely to accept the plan if they have to have direct dealings with the Jew in question. There must be an intermediary between TRICYCLE and the pseudo-provider. *This opinion is based on long experience of German methods of exchange dealing.*
>
> Thirdly, it is important that the Treasury and Bank of England should be taken into confidence to some extent. I can arrange this for you if you like.[11] [To which Tar added 'Yes']

As arranged, TRICYCLE would send a cable to the UK on 31 July, as well as a second one to Berlin confirming the despatch of the first telegram and asking that Harry (TATE) should confirm by cable immediately he had received the money, so that dollars could be paid to IWAN (TRICYCLE) before he left for America. TRICYCLE postponed his departure on the Clipper until around 10 August.[12]

On 6 July Cowgill informed Tar that

> Plan Midas is under discussion this weekend with a financial expert whom KARSTOFF [sic] has brought from Berlin [Töppen – see below] for the purpose. TRICYCLE asks, therefore, that 'DICKIE' (presumably BALLOON) shall not press for funds, and particularly that no money should be sent to TRICYCLE in Lisbon. I gather from what you said at last Thursday's meeting, though I have not yet seen the relative papers, that BALLOON has already pressed very hard for funds, but subject to anything that you may have to say, I do not think it is worth while [sic] informing TRICYCLE of this fact, particularly as we wish to make communication between him and our organisation in Lisbon as infrequent as possible.[13]

On 15 July he reported to Tar that

> We have heard that BEYER (presumably Walter BEYER of whom we have no other record), who came from Berlin to examine Plan MIDAS, has accepted it subject to some slight modifications.
>
> They are:
>
> (i) The name of the man who will contact S. will not be given in the cable to England;
> (ii) Instead KARSTOFF will write to his agent in this country telling him to call on S. using a name to be agreed on (e.g. Harry).
> (iii) TRICYCLE will cable S. telling him to expect 'Harry'.
>   All this will happen between the 20th and 24th July. (I presume S = X).
>   We shall probably be getting a fuller report in which case I will write to you again.[14]

Beyer was actually Oberstleutnant Martin Töppen, the Abwehr's financial supervisor/chief accountant.[15] Guy Liddell noted in his diary for 16 July 1941:

> The Twenty Committee has got a plan known as MIDAS. The idea is to get the Germans to send over a large sum of money which will be held here by some selected individual who will make the necessary payments to agents in the United Kingdom. TRICYCLE

has succeeded in getting the Germans to bite but they propose to send over their own representative who will effect the disbursements. He will get the money from our agent who will be reimbursed by the opening of a credit which TRICYCLE will take with him to America.[16]

That afternoon Luke, Tar and Marriott met to discuss 'the latest development in connection with this scheme' with Lennox also present for part of the meeting. Luke reported:

> It was decided that [Glass] would now have to be told that we had told TRICYCLE to use his name in connection with this money transaction and Major Lennox did not consider that this would present any great difficulty. He suggested that we should offer [Glass] British nationality if he played his part and brought the affair to a successful conclusion but Major Robertson did not consider that it would be prudent for us to make an undertaking of this kind, and it was therefore left to Major Lennox to use his own discretion in approaching [Glass].
>
> It is evident from S.I.S. letter to us dated 15.7.1941 attached hereto, that TRICYCLE will send the cable giving in code the amount of pounds to be exchanged and the rate of asking [Glass] to inform the third party of the happy event he will say that the third party is to be told when he calls on him – the cable will, therefore, read something like this:
>
> 'Anastasia had a daughter yesterday weighing 3½ kilos. Both well please inform Harry when he calls upon you.'
>
> There is not much we can do until the cable arrives but it will probably be desirable for us to place microphones in [Glass's] offices and also to find a way of getting a photograph of KARSTHOFF's agent.[17]

At the B2a management meeting on 24 July it was agreed that there would be nothing to gain by sending BALLOON to Lisbon. As Luke pointed out:

> If he went there he would probably have to give them valuable information for which we should obtain nothing in return, and they might ask him to obtain other information in this country which it would be difficult for him to avoid. On the other hand, if the Germans suggested that he should come to Portugal and pressed him to do so, the matter could be discussed again. Meantime BALLOON should hint that the present means of communication with the Germans is not particularly satisfactory or safe, in the hope that they may suggest that he should obtain a wireless transmitter.[18]

As a follow-up Tar requested that Liddell hand a copy of Luke's note on Plan MIDAS to Stephenson so that he could be briefed on TRICYCLE's connection with the plan. He asked that Stephenson supply them with a name and address to which the money in dollars could be paid, which Glass would transmit to TRICYCLE when he arrived in New York 'by means of an open cable'. Luke's note of the 24th explained Glass's involvement in MIDAS and how the scheme was intended to work, but

> There has, however, been a slight variation in this original scheme, because the people with whom TRICYCLE has been negotiating the deal in Portugal, i.e. the German Secret Service, have insisted that their representative in this country should get into direct communication with [Glass] and in the coded cable that TRICYCLE will send over to [Glass] he will simply mention that this person will be calling on him.
>
> There are two alternatives which might be adopted as regards the payment in dollars:
>
> (1) [Glass] could be satisfied on receiving the cable that the dollars have actually been paid to TRICYCLE, and could trust him to pay them over to his nominee in New York, whose name he would provide at a later date.
> (2) He could insist that before handing over the pounds he would have to be sure that the dollars had been paid into the account or personally handed to his nominee in New York.
>
> The latter course might be more realistic, but at this stage would be rather more troublesome, but whichever course is adopted, it is essential that a suitable nominee, who is not known to be connected with the British Secret Service should be found in New York with as little delay as possible, and I think it should be possible for such a name to be produced on this side without previous reference to anyone in New York. We could then cable [John] Maude or the S.I.S. representative telling them to warn the nominee that he must expect the payment of this sum in the near future.
>
> It is desirable, I think, that [Glass] should be able if necessary to produce the name at his first interview with the German Secret Service representative who is to call upon him.[19]

But on 1 August TRICYCLE sent the following cable:

> MR ERIK SAND PICCADILLY HOUSE PICCADILLY CIRCUS LONDON W1 TILLY HAD YESTERDAY A DAUGHTER WEIGHING 3 KILOS PLEASE INFORM HARRY WHEN YOU MEET HIM MARIA GONCALVES[20]

PLAN MIDAS

The following day Dick White wrote to Cowgill asking how TRICYCLE had managed to make such a hash of everything. Not only had he mistakenly addressed the cable to 'Erik Sand', 'which might have been catastrophic', but he had also mistakenly given the baby's weight as 3 kilos:

> [This would] indicate that he had negotiated the deal at a rate of exchange of 2 dollars to the £ which is 25 cents below the minimum which we authorised. As he personally would stand to gain nothing out of this transaction and would therefore not be in a position to give any cut of pay to Karsthoff I can only assume that in quoting the weight of the infant he has forgotten to add on 1 kilo to the actual rate of exchange.
>
> In addition to these two major errors there is the fact that it was made quite clear to TRICYCLE that when he sent the cable the dollars would already be in his possession and your representative has informed you that this is not the case. On receiving TRICYCLE's cable [Glass] SAND would assume that the dollars had actually been paid over to TRICYCLE. The other alteration in the plan – viz that Karstoff's representative on this side would call on [Glass] and obtain the money – was made I gather with the approval of Captain Jarvis [SIS Head of Station, Lisbon] so there is no need to say any more about it. It is quite evident then that if 'Harry' [TATE] had not himself been the agent controlled by us the whole Plan Midas would have had to go by the board and TRICYCLE would have to extricate himself from his difficulties as best he could.
>
> It is providencial [*sic*] that TATE has now received instructions to collect the money from SANDS [*sic*] and there is now no reason why we should not complete the plan in spite of all the errors, ~~inhibitions~~ and doubts which surrounded it. In fact TATE is this evening sending a message to say that he has been in touch with SAND and has already obtained part of the money, the balance to follow on Tuesday. It is for you to decide whether Captain Jarvis should be informed of the developments, but you may think it best to leave over all question of an inquest until TRICYCLE reaches America.
>
> The next move in the game after TATE has received the balance of his payment is for Karsthoff to hand over to TRICYCLE the dollar equivalent of £20000. This I think will almost certainly be at the rate of $3 to the £, i.e. $60000, but if TRICYCLE has negotiated the deal at a rate b[etter than] the minimum authorised, the account will only be $40000. If this is the sum paid to him by the Germans it should all be handed over to us in New York by him. If the sum is $60000, TRICYCLE is entitled to retain 10% of this amount i.e. $6000. The basic dollar rate which we fixed was $2.50 and any advantage TRICYCLE was able to obtain on this quotation was to be divided

> equal parts between him and ourselves i.e. GLASS [...] SAND. As the rate of exchange is $3 to the £, TRICYCLE has been able to obtain 10000 more than the basic figure, so he himself is entitled to retain in addition to the 6000 dollars, 5000 dollars, giving him a total remuneration of 11000 dollars. When Captain Liddell saw Mr Stephenson last week it was arranged that the latter would open an account in the name of Eric [Redacted] at Ladenberg Thalmann bank in New York (I think this was the name of the bank) and asked Stephenson to let us have a note of it before he left, but obviously he did not have time to do so. It is desirable that Mr. Stephenson should now be asked to change the name of the account from [Redacted] to SAND. It should be clear then that TRICYCLE is expected to pay over to our representative in New York the sum of $49000 which should be placed to the credit of SAND.

The payment was to be made in cash or banker's draft which TRICYCLE would then pay into his own account in New York. When he arrived he would then withdraw the amount due to MI5 and hand it over to their representative. White saw

> no reason why this part of the plan should not be altered if the Germans have actually paid the cash to TRICYCLE except that it is difficult for him to get in touch with Jarvis in order to hand over the money. TRICYCLE should be given clear instructions by Jarvis however that he must not carry the money with him in the Clipper in the form of notes to the considerable risk of loss. He should be told that he is to credit his own account in New York with the total sum and then hand the major portion of it, which is our share, over to our representative in New York.[21]

He presumed that Jarvis would be informed and the arrangements made with Stephenson in New York would be confirmed. Jarvis should also be advised of 'the alteration of the name and of the exact amount which we consider TRICYCLE is to hand over to him'.

While Marriott was informing Lennox of this development, a greatly agitated MIDAS had telephoned to say that the cable (above) had been delivered to Piccadilly House, Regent Street but addressed to Erik Sand. Another firm in the same building had brought it to him wondering whether it was meant for him. Glass had replied that he knew nothing about it. Therefore, after being taken all over the building in search of the true recipient, the telegram was returned to Cable & Wireless. Luke made arrangements through Alan Grogan for the original telegram to be extracted from Cable & Wireless and delivered to MI5. Grogan explained:

> With Luke I then went to Special Branch to explain the position to Supt. Foster and to ask him to take the following action which had

been discussed with Major Lennox, namely that Special Branch should arrange for the porter or lift man at the building to reply to anybody asking for Eric SAND by saying that he had just gone out and would not be back till the afternoon. The idea was that as soon as this had been done, Major Lennox would instruct MIDAS in his part and that thereafter the staff of the building would have instructions to send up to MIDAS anybody asking for SAND.

I then visited Piccadilly House with Sergeant Feltwell and we at once discovered that there was no porter, that the lifts were automatic and that any staff in the building were girls believed to be employed by the Eire Government who have large offices there. It was decided that it would be too dangerous either to take anybody in the building into our confidence or to put up on the board at the entrance of the building the name of Eric SAND and it was also decided that it would be preferable not to employ MIDAS himself in this operation at all. After discussion with Major Cowgill and A.D.B.1 [Dick White] it was decided that it would also be too dangerous for the building to be watched for anybody apparently studying the list of firms at the entrance to the building with a view to having any such person followed away. MIDAS will therefore be instructed by Major Lennox to deny all knowledge of SAND if anybody asks him who he is.

The following cable will be sent to-morrow as from SAND to TRICYCLE in Lisbon.

'Thanks for cable which I have only just received. It was wrongly addressed. Please tell Harry I have had to give up my office and am looking for other accommodation but telephone Regent 1774 will always find me.'

Regent 1774 is I.H. [Imperial House] and if Mrs Barton receives a call for SAND she will say that he generally comes in for messages at about e.g. 4 o'clock and suggest that the caller rings him then. At the second call the telephone will be answered by a substitute for the original MIDAS who will suggest a meeting place somewhere outside. We ought to be ready with another office in the name of Eric SAND where subsequent meetings can take place.

The ideas under-lying the above cable are as follows:

1. The cable addressed to SAND was incorrectly addressed to Piccadilly House instead of e.g. Regent House and that it was therefore delayed in delivery.
2. If anybody makes any enquiry at Piccadilly House and he gets, as he will, the answer that Eric SAND is unknown, an explanation will be provided by our cable.[22]

Cowgill confirmed that Menzies had approved the supply of £20,000 for Plan MIDAS if required. He also informed Marriott that a Yugoslavian named Matic, Chef de Cabinet to General Dušan Simović, Prime Minister of Yugoslavia, would shortly be departing Lisbon carrying in the diplomatic bag the latest type of transmitter intended for BALLOON to pass on to 'some other person unspecified'. They would only know for whom it was intended once they had received their own diplomatic bag containing instructions for its disposal, but Cowgill was unable to tell Marriott what Matic's position was and 'whether he knew what he was doing, or whether he was an innocent courier'.[23]

Marriott informed D4b (Port Intelligence) that anyone arriving at Whitchurch (Bristol) airport with a transmitter should be detained, but to take no further action until they had spoken on the telephone. The following day he told Cowgill that he and Masterman disagreed with the calculations in Dick White's letter to him, and Luke did not agree with the letter:

> [I]n our view TRICYCLE's basic 10% ought to be calculated on the amount of dollars produced by a rate of $2.50, i.e. in this case $50000. According to our view therefore TRICYCLE's commission is $5000 being 10% on the amount produced by $20000 which is $50000 @ $2.50 plus $5000 being half the amount by which the actual dollars obtained exceed the basic amount. TRICYCLE should therefore account for $50000.[24]

It was with a certain irony that in an undated letter from TRICYCLE in Estoril to Tar, referring to the telegram sent to E. Sand two days previously (1 August, which would make his letter 3 August), he said: 'I hope that you have been able to arrange everything so that the pitiable SAND does not make a mess of the affair and I wish you good hunting.' Liddell noted on 3 August:

> There has been great anxiety over Plan MIDAS. TRICYCLE made a number of mistakes and began by sending his telegram from Eric Sand instead of Eric Glass. This led to endless complications but the situation cleared up when we found that instead of somebody from their side arriving to collect the money, TATE received instructions to do the job. It then became clear that what we thought to be an independent plan by the Germans to build up TATE and make him a centre for running agents was in the minds of the Germans Plan MIDAS. The two plans married and all is now well. TATE is in the position of paymaster and we should before long have £20,000 to our credit in New York.[25]

Also that day Luke reported that TATE had received the following message:

> Urgent as the giver of money is about to leave. A smaller amount is not possible – please administrate it. Go at once to the theatre agent

Eric Sand, Tea House, Piccadilly House, Piccadilly Circus, name plate is on entrance of teahouse. Introduce yourself as 'Harry' and say 'how do you do Mr Sand – I am Harry and appreciate very much to meet you.' You will receive £20,000. Please give acknowledgement of money to us at once, as we have to reimburse at once a similar sum to a friend of Sand. It is better to hide the amount in parts.

But Luke added that there was no need for him to go to Piccadilly House as

GLASS @ SAND is our nominee in Plan Midas which has been put over in Lisbon by TRICYCLE. In point of fact there is no such person as SAND and the Germans have mentioned his name because TRICYCLE erroneously informed them that this was the name of the Jewish Theatrical agent with whom he had arranged to put through the illegal currency deal.[26]

Marriott noted the following day: 'When TRICYCLE left England in June he took with him the name of Eric GLASS of Piccadilly House, Piccadilly Circus, London with instructions to inform the German I.S. in Lisbon that GLASS would play the part of MIDAS.'[27] But when he spoke with Töppen @ Beyer who had flown in from Berlin especially to meet him in Lisbon he mistakenly referred to GLASS as Erik Sand. That left MI5 to assume that 'there is a possibility of their attempting to communicate with this non-existent person'.[28]

Reid informed Masterman that someone like SAND [sic] would not want to collect a large quantity of small notes in small denominations as it would arouse suspicion. However, it would be unnecessary to record all the serial numbers as he was supposed to collect them gradually and they would therefore not run in a long series. Furthermore, it was unlikely that TATE or anyone else would receive many of them from him, but 'if at any time he does have to make a payment, Sir Edward will secure numbers of notes which were in fact in circulation, or could have been, in July 1941'.[29]

TRICYCLE was scheduled to leave Lisbon for America on 10 August, but delayed his departure because he had not been paid. MI5 noted that he would not receive his dollars 'until HARRY [TATE] has received payment from Midas and has reported back to that effect by cable'. He and Karsthoff were also anxious that there had been no news from Berlin. The same day, Karsthoff instructed him to send BALLOON the name of the unknown person to whom the transmitter was to be delivered, which would be included in the suitcase containing the set.

Discussions had taken place all day regarding how MI5 should handle MIDAS. However, Marriott decided not to record their decisions as that evening they had heard from TATE. '[T]he other side' had instructed him to 'proceed to Eric SAND, at Piccadilly House, as soon as possible in order to collect £20,000'. Under the circumstances, MI5 decided that 'MIDAS should be considered to have received and accepted the telegram notwithstanding the numerous mistakes in it, and that the operation should be reported to the Germans as having gone through in as normal a fashion as possible'.[30]

The Yugoslav courier smuggling the set into Britain had left Lisbon on 4 August 'using the good officers [*sic*] of a non-existent friend in the Yugoslav Legation in London' (Ralph?), but he'd arrived without the set as he'd been unable to obtain diplomatic immunity for it at the last minute.

> TRICYCLE therefore, handed the case back to KARSTHOFF who congratulated him on not having forced the issue and thereby giving the game away. (Incidentally, we are informed that the set is of the same type as that which will be given to TRICYCLE when he gets to the U.S.A.
>
> Instead of the set, BALLOON will shortly receive instructions for sending messages by microphotography one page being reduced to approximately 1/10 mm. These instructions are already in the possession of our representative in Lisbon, but he is quite rightly withholding them until the next Yugoslav courier comes to this country in order that KARSTHOFF's illusion may be complete.[31]

As TRICYCLE explained:

> 1. Very often during recent months, the Germans do not write any more to their first class agents in secret ink. They employ full stop marks. These are diminutive photographs of letters reduced to about this size. It is possible to read the whole letter with a microscope. I received 6 for my trip to America. I will show them to J. I am doing what I can to arrange for the future correspondence with Ivan II with these full stops. The full stops are stuck on to the interior of the envelope. I have marked on this envelope the places where the full stops have been stuck in my presence for one of their agents. Unfortunately I do not know for whom or where, but they do not always stick them onto the same places. My six full stops have been stuck on an old telegram and in the letters which I shall receive at New York they will be inside the envelope.
> 2. I have seen two letters coming from England written in secret ink, they have been signed one, XZ and the other IDEM. The ink seems to be the same as mine.[32]

Luke was trying to find out from Grogan about two letters which had arrived from England signed in this way.

TRICYCLE left Lisbon on the Clipper on 11 August and arrived safely in New York where he contacted the SIS representative. The FBI was also co-operating with his handling. BALLOON supplied answers to a questionnaire and secret letter

PLAN MIDAS

concerning various aviation-related subjects he'd received from TRICYCLE on 2 August. But as Liddell's entry in his diary for 25 August states:

> Plan MIDAS does not appear to be working quite as we arranged. The traffic indicates that the money is to be used for building up an organisation under TATE rather than for payment of other agents already established. This is deduced from the fact that DRAGONFLY used to receive his money from other sources. TRICYCLE has arrived safely and our £20,000 has been safely banked in New York.[33]

On 22 August TRICYCLE sent a note to BALLOON explaining that how future instructions may not always be written in secret ink. Instead, they would be in 'special "points" [microdots] which will be stuck in the inside of the envelope as this illustration shows you'.

> Those 'Points' are practically invisible, about the size of a full stop and is brownish in colour. [sic] They are very small photographs, each representing one page of typewritten instructions. You will need a small microscope which can magnify about 2-300 times. For that reason dont [sic] throw away the envelopes before you have inspected them.
> Be good and work hard. Yours IVAN[34]

Chapter 9

BALLOON's Reports

On 5 May 1941 BALLOON had supplied a report illustrated with a thumb-nail sketch showing defences on the southeast coast, whereby tubular steel scaffolding was being used on the beaches He described it as:

> anchored deeply in the beach and is cross braced and strutted. At high tide the scaffolding which is about 10' high is practically covered. From the construction it would appear that the harder one pushes against 'A' the further 'B' is driven into the ground. I presume that if a tank obstacle from the seawards [sic]. Actually two sea mines were washed against a section some little time ago and breached it badly. This might be used effectively when attacking it. The beaches (Deal area) are mined extensively with small round flat shaped mines many of which are not even detonated yet! In any case an English Divisional Commander Maj. General C.C. Maldon [sic] killed himself when walking on one recently.[1] These mines seem to shift considerably when laid in sand. A great deal of cable laying is also going on inland from the beaches.

Security had been lax. A security policeman disguised as a German infantry soldier was able to wander about unhindered for four-and-a-half hours, and also enter an HQ where he was known personally, before a despatch rider had apprehended him, having seen him on the road. BALLOON had also discovered an RAF direction-finding station hidden in a field about two miles from Ashford through the village of Kennington.[2] He revealed that MI9 was located on the common outside Richmond Park in an old house which 'should be easy to break in and rob', but that after September 1940 they had moved to Beaconsfield (Wilton Park).

***

On 16 May 1941 Dick Brooman-White of B21 (also known as B1g), MI5's Spanish counter-espionage section, proposed that BALLOON be put in touch with the Spanish military attaché, Colonel Alfonso Barra, who might be able provide information on arms deals, which might also shed some light on his activities and those of other diplomatic personnel, or possibly enable BALLOON to be sent out to Spain under Barra's aegis.

Barra had been DMI in Madrid before coming to the UK and, while not a Fascist, he 'has a respect for the German army, which is fairly common in Spanish military circles'. First of all, BALLOON should try to 'get wind of some bona fide transactions in arms to justify his approach'; then he should get in touch with Barra using his own Spanish contacts: Palomero, Jaime, Martinez, etc. If that didn't work, he could approach Polish intelligence which had good contacts with Barra, as he had also been military attaché in Warsaw, and could facilitate an introduction.

Brooman-White asked the Poles if they could assist MI5 in planting on Barra a man interested in arms trafficking. They suggested a young lieutenant who was dating Barra's secretary and could be approached while skating in Kensington. He could talk to the secretary and ask if she could wangle an introduction to Barra. Alternatively, the officer who had guided Barra while he was in Warsaw could entertain him one evening, and they could meet BALLOON in a bar or restaurant. Whichever option was used would risk exposing BALLOON's identity to the Poles, but not that he was a double agent.

The Poles thought that the first suggestion was more indirect. SIS assured Brooman-White that the Poles involved were members of their intelligence service, not their counter-espionage branch, and were entirely reliable.[3] Luke agreed with their suggestion and would discuss it further with Brooman-White, saying that he should bring BALLOON with him as 'I believe he has a means of getting to know the Spanish Military Attaché'.

Tar and Brooman-White agreed that they would not provide any assistance to him in getting an introduction to Barra since, being an arms dealer, he was already in a good position to obtain that himself. Nor would B21 (White's section) give him any direction on what they were interested in 'but if BALLOON comes across anything suspicious he will of course report it to us through Mr Luke'. And if the Spanish asked him to go to Spain he would be encouraged to do so 'but he will use this as a cover for getting to Spain and will at the same time be able to communicate to the Germans that he is going on legitimate business'.[4]

Luke duly provided Cowgill with a short history of BALLOON. He explained that Lennox, who was in charge of Room 055, should approach BALLOON and propose that he act as a double agent for them and carry on TRICYCLE's work as he seemed to be the ideal candidate.

When he went over to Lisbon in March TRICYCLE took with him a lot of information which BALLOON had written on the back of the pages of ordinary letters. He explained to the Germans that BALLOON was thoroughly disgruntled, having been thrown out of the Army, and was prepared to work against his own country provided he received adequate payment. The Germans fell for the ruse and gave TRICYCLE £300 as an initial payment for him. BALLOON then wrote several letters to the following contacts supplied by TRICYCLE – Paulo Pinto de Lima, as well as:

Artur Soares,
Lisboa,
Rua João Menezes 18-5.

João Maia,
Lisboa,
Rua Passos Mannel 56-1º

How future payments would be made would be settled before TRICYCLE departed for Portugal. Luke noted, 'I think BALLOON has now been well established with the other side.'[5]

Luke and Brooman-White (introduced as Herne) met with BALLOON on the evening of 21 May 1941 to discuss the possibility of his getting in touch with the Spanish military attaché. They impressed upon him that under no circumstances should he prejudice his position as a double agent 'but that if he could get to know the workings of the Spanish outfit and particularly the Military Attaché, it might be well worthwhile'.

> No indication was given to BALLOON of any suspicions we may entertain about any of them as it was felt that this would be dangerous knowledge for him to possess, and would perhaps prejudice his judgement. If he is not able to make any progress with the Military Attaché, Mr Brooman-White will try and arrange for an introduction through another channel. It was agreed that all BALLOON's reports on this and any other matter would be passed through myself or Major Robertson and there would be no direct contact between him and Mr Brooman-White.[6]

***

For the Germans' benefit BALLOON produced a memo on 22 May 1941 stating that during Operation CATAPULT, the British assault on the French naval base at Mers El Kébir in French Algeria on 3 July 1940, the French battleship *Richelieu*, attacked on 8 July by Fairey Swordfish from HMS *Hermes*, was not put out of commission and was still seaworthy. And when the *Bismark* was attacked on 27 May 1941 the new 14-inch guns of *George V* and *Prince of Wales* failed to live up to expectations, but the 16-inch guns of the *Rodney* had done the damage.

He said that Vosper Ltd of Portsmouth had won the Admiralty contract to build seventy MTBs, but the British Power Boat Co. of Hythe, Southampton, would continue to build rescue launches and small craft for the RAF. It is unclear what he meant by 'The Admiralty is considering the use of metal containers (1,200 tons each) found behind or strapped to powerful ships in convoy', but he claimed to have details of them. He added that the Royal Navy had ordered 1,400 8" Oerlikon guns [*sic*] from the factory in Switzerland but their production had been delayed by the Germans' sabotage of the factory. Consequently, the guns could not be brought out of the country.

HMS *Excellent,* the Navy's gunnery school at Whale Island near Portsmouth had every type of AA gun from .5-inch up to 6-inch – 'and it might be a good thing to go and brown them up'. A 'British Panzer arm' – the Guards Armoured Division – was created on 17 June 1941 and was training at Sandhurst and Bovington. Part of this formation was the Irish Guards stationed at Woking. He was told by an officer of the VIIIth Hussars [*sic*] that they would be going to the Middle East in a few weeks' time. (In July 1941 the 8th King's Royal Irish Hussars, equipped with Stuart tanks, formed part of 4 Armoured Brigade for Operation CRUSADER which took part in the three-day battle of Sidi Rezegh airfield on 23 November 1941.)

Other information concerned fortifications in east Kent, particularly 'strongpoints' at Deal, Dover and Ashford, but that defence against airborne troops landing well inland was still inadequate, 'especially if they have anti-tank rifles or light A/T guns as the British seem to think that light tanks will do the job. The press are crying out for tank defence at aerodromes.' There was also a reference to a hidden camp near Horsham (between Dorking and Horsham), 'guarded and wired', where experiments with special 'fire shell guns' fitted to tanks, were being carried out.

Both the RAF and Fleet Air Arm were considering using seaplane fighters either with a retractable float or two fixed floats, which could be hidden under the lee of cliffs, coves and bays, away from Stuka attacks, or if aerodromes had been damaged. He suggested that extra petrol or cannon could be fitted in the floats. Experts, he said, were criticising the American Allison engines, which were 'so long that the crankshaft whips and causes lack of power'.

There was a 'great steel wall-like structure' at Shrewton, Wiltshire which had been used at Manby (No.1 Air Armament School), to enable aircraft to land downwind. He also reported on the bombing of the BSA factory at Small Heath, a suburb of Birmingham, on 26 August 1940, which produced small arms and bicycles, and the Parnell factory at Yate, Bristol, which produced gun turrets, on 27 February 1941, killing fifty-three people, and in March 1941.[7]

***

On 12 June Susan Barton of B1a, the cover name for Austrian-born Gisela Ashley, reported that BALLOON had asked her whether she knew the name of the Spanish military attaché, without revealing why he wanted it. He told her that the blueprint of a Czech gun had arrived in America 'and that now the Treasury had woken up to the fact that this cheap gun would probably be sold in America'. She didn't know the name but after their conversation he'd somehow discovered that it was Colonel Alfonso Barra. What is surprising is why neither Tar nor Brooman-White had told him the name.

DOUBLE AGENT BALLOON

On 16 June BALLOON wrote to Barra, referring to a conversation they'd had during their meeting on 12 June 1941, arranged through the Spanish consul (Miguel de Lojincho) at the Spanish Embassy, 24 Belgrave Square. His original enquiry, dated 16 May 1941, bears the name R.S. Davidson.[8] His pretext for meeting was that he wished to purchase arms from Spain, and attached his company's formal enquiry for small arms for re-sale to China. He reported to MI5 on 16 June that 'This is in some measure true as I have had enquiries for military weapons and I had heard that Spain was willing to sell. Indeed there was a rumour that some of the captured Dunkirk material had found its way into that country.' Barra smiled knowingly when BALLOON mentioned this to him. He behaved very courteously to him and listened while BALLOON explained what he wanted: '[H]e asked me who the arms were for. I told him that I had enquiries from Turkey, China, and some of the Allied governments. He … replied to the effect that it would be easier if they were for China and would I be so kind as to put this in a letter together with a list of what I was after', preferrably before Thursday 19th so that it could be sent in the diplomatic bag. There were some Russian rifles captured from the Reds, and arms had been supplied to Finland. BALLOON told him that he really preferred German-made arms if possible.

Barra struck BALLOON as well-bred and courteous, and reminded him of a schoolmaster: 'He gives the impression of being a man of character and shrewdness, indeed the word "deep" or "still waters run deep" was what I actually said to myself as I left.' He told Barra that if any arms were available he would be able to get an Exit Permit through the Ministry of Supply who had always been 'helpful to the arms trade as a whole.'[9] His letter to Barra included a list of the arms he was seeking – various Mauser rifles, sub-machine guns, machine guns, cartridges, anti-aircraft guns, anti-tank guns, mortars, hand grenades and pistols. Barra told him that 'the Oerlikon factory in Switzerland with which the Admiralty placed an order for 1,400 20mm guns was under complete Nazi control'.

On 19 June Luke forwarded a copy of BALLOON's report, complete with details of his enquiry for armaments, to Brooman-White 'from which you will see that he has set the ball rolling'. He had asked BALLOON to pay a visit to Claridges where Barra regularly dined and was trying to chat up 'a rather unreceptive young woman', in the hope that a more sociable atmosphere might produce results.[10]

***

BALLOON also supplied three reports to MI5 in June 1941 for the Germans' benefit. The first covered RAF-related topics, such as the Liberator bomber, and how they would be using a new automatic bomb-sight (most likely the Norden); the number of Me 109s shot down, attributed to the success of the 20mm Hispano-Suiza cannon; German Soluthorn 12.5mm machine guns found jammed on crashed aircraft; how the British had captured some of the German 15mm Mauser high velocity guns, which BALLOON claimed were better than the British 15mm Besa guns; and how the RAF was now using 20mm shells in their cannon. He added that a Typhoon squadron would be stood up that week picked from specially selected pilots. (In fact, the first Typhoon squadron (56 squadron) did not come into service until September 1941.) There had also been a shortage of Miles Master I and II advanced trainers, and problems with the cooling system on the Mark I. The RAF and RN had adopted the Lanchester sub-machine gun, while the Army was using the Thompson, Smith & Wesson, and Sten guns.

During a defence exercise in Worcester security had been lax: an Army subaltern had been able to walk into an old factory with a home-made pass and distribute paper bombs (cards with writing on them). Also someone disguised as a paper boy got into the police CID branch and placed a 'bomb' in the control room. Aircrew from a crashed German bomber had had to walk eight miles before they could surrender to the village constable. And the Beaufighter was being equipped with 40mm cannon for ground strafing.[11]

The second report covered military activities in the Ashford, Kent area where he saw transport bearing the sign of a black cat on a red and black background. 'This is the Divisional crest of the 44th Div.', whereas it was the sign of 56th (London) Division.[12] Two battle HQs were situated between Ashford and High Halden – one at Wye, the other at Witherstane; Corps HQ was at Southborough. There were cables being laid in the Dymchurch area. Some of the tubular-steel coastal defences had large gaps blown in them. Morale was low among the troops who were complaining about a lack of transport, and 'the two 48-hours schemes which they are having each week'.

An RAOC officer, formerly with 45 AA battery at Dover[13] to whom he gave a lift, told him that he thought the Vickers 3-nch Predictor was very good but complained that the American Sperry model I was unreliable. (However, there was no 3-inch predictor: the Army was using the Vickers No. 1 Predictor with its 3.7-inch AA guns, having previously used it with 3-inch AA guns.) He also said that the gun-laying radar Mark 1 (GL Mk 1) developed in 1935 was working very well. This artificer told him that optical instruments in the North African desert had been causing problems as the Canada balsam used to cement lenses and prisms melted and became dislodged. A secret cloth used to distinguish British from disguised German troops had been found in the possession of two civilians who had been arrested.

He recalled a very experienced pilot who had been stationed in Gibraltar telling him that the aerodrome there was 'very tricky and is practically in Spanish Territory. Planes are frequently fired on by small arms AA from the Spanish Pill Boxes.' The pilot suggested placing a line of buoys in the sea to guide pilots on their approach so that they didn't overshoot the aerodrome. BALLOON commented cynically, 'The matter has been referred to London so probably nothing will happen for a month or two.' The same pilot had also complained that the bombs supplied for attacking ships were incorrect and that they had often been forced to attack at low level with instantaneous fuses, 'which is of course very dangerous'.

Some of the recent raids on Germany were on undefended towns and villages, heralding more ruthless bombing in the future. And contrary to popular belief, the

AA defences of Malta were 'terrific and they have huge supplies of ammunition'. He reported that an officer of the Seaforth Highlanders arrived in Britain with eighteen soldiers, having come from Paris via Gibraltar. They had been imprisoned in Spain several times but managed to escape. And a suitable bombing target might be the building in Hayward's Heath, Sussex where the Air Ministry stored inflammable material such as paint, dope, and cellulose finishes.[14]

The third report, dated 3 July 1941, concerned military manoeuvres on 2 July between Newmarket and Royston, consisting of 'lorries, Bren-gun carriers and light mobile AA guns (40mm Bofors) and anti-tank guns carried in trucks, with guns actually facing forward!' Vehicles were marked with the numbers 73, 74 and 77 and a crest bearing a mailed gauntlet (6th Armoured Division). Also in East Anglia, a simulated attack carried out on Norwich by 'Fifth Columnists' disguised as undertakers complete with hearses, had surprised the defenders. BALLOON observed that

> The change of command in the Middle-East is not very popular as Wavell[15] is publically considered our best general and it is thought that he should have been left where he was or else made CIGS [Chief of Imperial General Staff] if indeed any change was necessary. It is commonly believed that he advised against the Greek and Crete campaigns but was overruled by politicians.

He reported seeing Hurricanes, Tomahawks, Lockheeds 'and what appeared to be a Glenn Martin bomber in the distance' at RAF Duxford and that the airfield was well defended by light AA guns (Bofors 40mm). Fighters were distributed in concealed temporary hangars on subsidiary landing grounds near the Cambridge Road. He commented: 'Tomahawks are popular with pilots as they climb very well and are very manoeuvrable – all out speed is rather low 324 m.p.h.'[16]

The Luftwaffe night raid on Lowestoft the previous weekend had been successful, with a gasholder and the pier badly damaged, but a visitor there during the raid was unimpressed by the volume of AA fire put up. Careless talk in the downstairs bar of the Ritz Hotel had caused many COs to put it out of bounds for young officers; likewise, the pavilion at Bournemouth.

The Turkish embassy was negotiating with the Admiralty for the purchase of a large number of 500hp Napier Marine engines with McAdams gear boxes for use in MTBs to be constructed in Turkey. And an unnamed 'influential Rumanian' had provided news that Rumanians were 'most unwilling to fight Russia and that the Germans have to watch them constantly'.[17]

***

On 20 June Susan Barton reported that BALLOON had told her about 'Hector MacNeil' [*sic*][18] and his invention of fire-proof clothing. Sir Hector Murray MacNeal, known as the 'black knight', was a Scottish ship owner and director of

BALLOON'S REPORTS

MacNeal & Company of 120 Pall Mall, London SW1, who during the war worked for Lord Beaverbrook at the Ministry of Aircraft Production (MAP). He was short of money and had been hawking his invention around the City of London, in spite of it being placed on the Secret List. One person he'd approached was Lord Sempill who put him in touch with a Dr Kronisch.[19] According to BALLOON Dr Kronisch

> is a refugee and a crook and Possnikow said that he knew Dr. Kronisch in Poland but that he then had a different name. Dr Kronisch is supposed to be anxious to get to America as soon as possible and take him with anything [sic] in the way of assets that he can lay his hands on and Balloon considers that Dr Kronisch is perfectly capable of evading or juggling with the foreign currency restrictions.
>
> Furthermore, Dr Kronisch is apparently in touch with a man called Leigh Gray (I think his name is Robert Leigh Gray, but I'm afraid I don't know how he spells it.) Leigh Gray used to be one of our Consuls in Germany and is supposed to have said that he can get anybody an American visa (presumably for a small payment) as he is in touch with the Americans.
>
> Balloon also tells me that Possnikoff [sic] is endeavouring to find the money for MacNeil's invention and "put the business on a sound footing" and that he thinks it will go through now.[20]

An intercepted letter from Kronisch to Metcalfe on 13 June 1941 read:

> My dear Dickie,
> Before rushing off to High Wycombe yesterday, I handed over your letter and enclosure to our Chemists who discussed the matter with their solicitors, who have advised them that the proposal as put forward by Mr. Postnikow should not be considered. The Solicitors point out – and I quite agree with them – that the effect of the proposal would be to hand over control of our Company and therefore the policy would rest entirely in the hands of the new parties coming in.
>
> They also pointed out that although the 'Owners' are receiving a loan of £5000, this has to be repaid 3 years after the termination of War, out of £30,000, which has to be handed to them by the Purchasers from monies accumulated out of the profit of the 'Owners' own formula and in addition the £10,000 now to be advanced by the financiers has also to be repaid.
>
> I am sorry now that I showed the document to our Chemists as evidently their Solicitors have passed some rather 'unfavourable' comments about the proposal in general.
>
> From a personal point of view nothing would have given me greater pleasure than working with you and your associates, but in

all fairness it would be impossible to work out a deal on the terms indicated.[21]

Tar requested that F4 – the section of F Division (Subversive Activities) run by Roger Fulford – check up on Leigh Gray. Luke added that he would prefer to obtain the intelligence on Kronisch then have a similar look-up done on 'Leigh Gray' [*sic*] [Robert Lee Grey]. A further note from Luke to Cowgill on 28 June 1941 refers to Grey as being American vice-consul in Zurich.[22]

Dr Kronisch

Based on information provided by BALLOON, a Special Branch report dated 18 June 1941 revealed much about Kronisch's suspect dealings:

> Dr KRONISCH, believed to be a Polish Jew ... is negotiating large scale loans on rather peculiar terms. KRONISCH represents himself to be acting on behalf of a bank holding Czechoslovakian monies. The loans are made without interest and all agreements are verbal. The borrowers give a verbal assurance that the loan will be repaid abroad, at the exchange rate ruling at the date of repayment. If the borrowers are unable to repay in foreign currency, then 20% in sterling will be charged, of which 6% will be interest and 8% commission.
>
> KRONISCH is stated today to be visiting two firms with a view to arranging a £50,000 loan with each. These firms are: Finchley Engineering Works, director Gordon L. PADLEY, and Strachan Gurney & Co., Finsbury Place, director Mr PALMER.
>
> Further caller stated, an acquaintance of his, Sir Hector MacNEAL, of St James Street, W.1, [*sic*] who is in financial difficulties, recently attempted to form a compan[y] with a view to marketing or supplying to the Government a special fire resisting substance for treating the clothin[g] of pilots etc. The invention has been examined by Air Ministry and placed on the secret list. However, it had been learnt by Mr [Metcalfe] that KRONISCH had approached Sir Hector MacNEAL with an offer of £10,000 to take over the whole business. Caller also stated that he knew that KRONISCH, Sir Hector MacNEAL, one Robert L. GRAY, British, (late Consul-General in Germany) and a man named MYER were all endeavouring to get visas to travel to the United States of America. In the application for MYER's visa this person was represented as an 'inventor' and presumably the inventor of the process for treating clothing referred to above, whereas, MacNEAL had informed the authorities that the inventors were the brothers named PETZEL.[23]

BALLOON'S REPORTS

Caller considered that KRONISCH's one idea was to draw his commission and get to the U.S.A. with as many cashable assets as possible – including the secret process referred to.

Mr [Metcalfe] could not give KRONISCH's address and stated that as far as he knew the latter had no office in London. He offered to procure KRONISCH's address, howeve[r] and to render any assistance possible to Police in the event of future enquiry.

Another point which added to his suspicions regarding KRONISCH's intentions was that his [Metcalfe's] principal, Mr POSNIKOFF [sic], had, on seeing KRONISCH, stated that he had met the latter before somewhere, he thought in Moscow, when KRONISCH had gone under another name – what name, he could not remember.[24]

Luke wrote to Cowgill at SIS stating that he was aware of SIS's record of Kronisch: 'BALLOON ... has told us that KRONISCH is trying to get an American visa and is being helped by one Lee GREY who was the American vice Consul in Zurich and is now in this country.'[25] But Cowgill replied that 'The only record we have of KRONISCH is contained in letter no. CX/ [Redacted] of 14.12.39 which is probably in your file.' A further Special Branch report dated 1 July 1941 provides more details on Kronisch:

'Dr. KRONISCH' has been identified as Eugen [Olgen] KRONISCH, German Jew, born 17.10.07 at Berlin [died 10 September 1980, Fredericksburg, Virgina], described as of no occupation, and living in a furnished flat at 1, Arlington Court, Twickenham. This man is registered with Police under serial No. EZ. 328489 and holds Registration Certificate No.725057 and German passport No. K.271/38, issued at Berlin on 28.3.38. His wife, Edith [Daniel], is still living in Berlin [1910-2003; married in Berlin, 1934].

KRONISCH first came to the United Kingdom on 16.1.1939, being landed at Croydon for one month on a 'no employment' condition. He has been allowed to remain here since – vide Home Office correspondence K.15474, but still on the 'no employment' condition. He was exempted from internment as a refugee from Nazi oppression by H.O.[?] Tribunal on 2.12.39, but was interned on 19.7.40. He was subsequently released from Kempton Park Internment Camp on 25.7.40.

... Special Branch report dated 20.1.40 revealed that KRONISCH had been a doctor of medicine in Berlin, but being a Jew, had been forced to give up his profession in 1933 and was held in a concentration camp until he signed a document renouncing his medical status. He then lived on the procee[ds] of some property and his earnings in commercial life until [he] was able to leave

Germany. With the assistance of a friend in a foreign embassy in Berlin, he managed to smuggle £300 out of Germany and at the time of enquiry (January 1940) professed to have been living on this money since his arriva[l] in this country. KRONISCH came to England mainly on the invitation of Lord SEMPILL, who wrote to the Chair of the Aliens Tribunal, Kingston-on-Thames, on 30.11.39, stating that he had asked KRONISCH to come to this country in connection with negotiations for manufacturing a German hardboard here. KRONISCH was stated by SEMPILL to have represented the interests of Ryken & Co., bankers of Amsterdam. It was further reported that KRONISCH, together with two other German refugees, Erich Nikita Wilhelm BRUST, an engineer, and Kark Georg Remy EYSSEN [sic], a chemist, was in possession of a secret German process for the production of artificial rubber, insulating materials and lacquers, and had sold for £750 [?] a three month's option on the process to Messrs. Catomance Ltd., 94 Bridge Road East, Welwyn Garden City, [H]erts.[26] An agreement between Catomance Ltd. and KRONISCH, dated 3.8.39, stated that if the option was taken up by Catomance Ltd. KRONISCH would act as consultant to the firm, without salary, but would receive 30[%] of the net profits. The major idea behind the scheme was the manufacture of clo[th] which was fire, water and acid proof, and the taking up of the option by Catomance Ltd. depended upon the exemption fro[m] internment of KRONISCH's collaborators – BRUST and EYSSEN. Both these aliens were exempted from internment. BRUST on 7.12.39 by No.7 Tribunal and EYSSEN on 30.10.39 by No.4 Tribunal. BRUST and EYSSEN are dealt with further, below.

At that time KRONISCH had a current account with a balance of £50 at Barclay's Bank, Fleet Street branch, and the option of £50 per month as his share of the sale of the option on his process to Messrs. Catomance Ltd. the furnished flat he occupied (as now) at 1, Arlington Court, Twickenham, was rented at 35/- per month.[27]

On 13 December 1941 John Noble in B4b wrote to John Craufurd in B4b, about the Kronisch case:

We have been dealing with Eugen KRONISCH since July 1941. Having had a report from Special Branch, we proposed to suggest his re-internment. As there was evidence that S.I.S. were at one time interested, we enquired from them before putting forward the suggestion.

S.I.S. replied that they were not interested and added 'I presume you have seen Luke's letter B2a/BAL/WEL of 28.6.41 to me, regarding KRONISCH.'

We had in fact not seen the letter and there was no evidence in the file to show that there was any information other than what was contained in our file.[28]

Luke's letter is cited above but the letter from SIS is not in the files. Later, on 17 December 1941, he provided Noble with a few more details about Kronisch based on notes provided by BALLOON on 14 December 1941:

> I confirm my telephone call re KRONISCH and attach a copy of our letter to S.I.S. dated 28.6.1941, which was written, of course, before you became interested in the case. I saw my agent yesterday and he gave me some information about KRONISCH which adds very little to the information which is already in your possession.
>
> KRONISCH, according to this source, is a Polish refugee who at one time used a different name, either in Poland or in Germany. He is about 42 years of age, short and plump, with the appearance of a white slug, and possessing a Polish passport. He is in close touch with Polish and Czech refugees, whose finances he handles, and in my agent's view is trying to defeat the currency regulations and get away to the United States with money thus entrusted to him. He is a friend of Lord Sempill and of a man called Robert LEIGH GRAY, who last June professed to be able to obtain American visas quite easily. He also knows Sir Hector MacNeil [sic], in whose fire-proofing system for clothing he showed great interest. At present he is classed as a C category alien, but in the source's opinion should be classed A. Recently he was interrogated by Scotland Yard.[29]

He neglected to mention that the Special Branch report of 1 July 1941 (above) stated that Kronisch was also a friend of a man named Meyer who BALLOON had never met – 'In view of the fact that no outside enquiries have been made, it has not been possible to identify MYER [sic] (mentioned in my previous report) as one of KRONISCH's associates attempting to travel to the U.S.A.'[30] Kronisch had tried to introduce Postnikow to various businesses but BALLOON had advised him to have nothing to do with the 'able rogue'. Postnikow believed that he had met Kronisch in Germany or Poland before the war.

Robert Lee Gray

The same 1 July Special Branch report provides details of Gray:

> Robert L. GRAY is probably identical with Robert Lee GRAY, United States citizen, now resident at Pilston Manor, Bridport, Dorset, and registered with Dorset Police. This man was born on

28.6.1886 at Virginia, U.S.A., held American passport No. 481076 issued at Washington on 13.12.37 and was previously registered with Metropolitan Police under serial No. EZ.84643. His last known London address was 31 Coleherne Road, S.W.10.[31]

Robert Lee GRAY first came under notice of Special Branch on 9.11.35 when Captain L.R. ROWE (retired British Army) of 37 Hornton Court, Kensington, W.8, called at this office to give information that there were certain suspicious aliens at 12 Vicarage Gate, W.8. GRAY was referred to by caller as Consul GREY and was alleged to associate with a man named BURNETT or BERNAISE, a German woman named Frau KOCHMAN and one Baron IRSAY – all said to be strongly [an]ti-Nazi.

On 27.11.35 an anonymous letter was received by Police alleging that suspicious aliens lived at 12 Vicarage Gate – apparently referring to the same group of persons.

On 4.12.35, M.I.5 letter PFR.2235/DS.7a (of that date) was received, requesting information regarding 'Consul GREY' and others. Special Branch report dated 18.12.35 shows that Consul GREY was in fact Robert Lee GRAY who described himself as being a member of the U.S.A. Oil Commission and a representative of the Sultan Abdul Hamid Estate Company, Virginia, U.S.A. It was reported that he married Maud Christian TRIPP, American, at Marylebone, London on 28.3.25. His wife however died on 15.12.1928. Records also show that GRAY was fined 20/- at Bow Street Police Court on 30.10.1928 for being drunk and disorderly. At the time of enquiry he was residing at 31 Coleherne Road, S.W.10, together with George IRSAY de IRSA, and was stated to make frequent visits to the Continent usually by air.

Brust and Eyssen

Erich Nikita Wilhelm BRUST was born on 21.8.1895 in [Mag]deburg, Germany and arrived in this country from Paris on 3.12.35. He is registered with Police under serial No. Q.54246 holds Registration Certificate No.585090 and German passport No.23816 issued in Paris on 8.7.33. He was granted permission to remain in this country, vide Home Office correspondence B.13630 and allowed to act as manager and technical adviser to Messrs Gold Seal Electrolyte Ltd, 634 Crown Buildings, S.W.1. BRUST was interned until further notice on 16.7.40, his last address having been 205 Endsleigh Court, Upper Woburn Place, W.C.1 (the same as that of FRIEDMANN). His wife, Helene, is registered with Police under serial No. HZ.61748.

BALLOON'S REPORTS

Kark Georg Remy EYSSEN was born at Frankfurt-am-Maine on 4.3.1899 and arrived in the United Kingdom on 31.8.34. [*sic*] He is registered with Police under serial No.EZ.241344 and holds German passport No.10104 issued at Hamburg on 1.8.32. This man was interned on 19.7.40, his last address having been 20 Hothan Road, Putney, S.W15 [*sic* – Hotham] ...

George Karl Remy EYSSEN. P.F.49682.
At present interned. There are conflicting reports from the camps about his reliability. Is a chemist of some ability; claims to be a refugee, but was a member of FREIKORPS EPP, a Munich anti-red organization in 1923 and was in touch with Nazi H.Q. in 1933 about membership; was also in touch with SCHALLIES. His father is said to control a large factory at Frankfurt engaged on war contracts.[32]

GELATINE described Gunther Schallies as a 'typical Nazi Prussian' whom she had 'cultivated' in 1938 at the Deutsche Arbeitsfront (DAF). He was deported from Britain in April 1939, three days after Dr R.G. Rösel, the London correspondent of the *National-Zeitung*, along with Richard Frauendorf, Captain Adolf Jaeger, Ernst Lahrmann and Friederich Scharpf. She reported that he fully expected to be sent to Budapest, but by 5 June 1939 he was still in Germany.[33]

***

BALLOON supplied another report on 10 July 1941 in which he stated that 'Much of the War Office has been moved to Cheltenham'.[34] Nine regiments of the Royal Corps of Signals were to be disbanded, most likely due to the lack of equipment 'or they may be required in civil capacities'. Given that they were fully trained, it was a waste of money. A brigadier (CIA)[35] and several officers were flying from London via Aberdeen to Orkney for consultations the following Thursday (17th).

As a follow-up to the mention of MacNeal, he reported that, in addition to the RAF, the tank designs branch at Egham, Surrey was very interested in the fire-proof treatment of clothing. They considered it 'especially suitable for troops using the flame throwing apparatus'. There was also mention of the 16-ton Valentine tank and how the engine compartment was fire-proof. He predicted that prior to 1 August there would be an invasion of the northern French, Belgian, or Dutch coast by a force of two mechanised divisions which would stay for two-to-three weeks. For the Germans' benefit he noted, 'The idea appears to be to personify your dislike of a "war on two fronts" to to [*sic*] upset communications, and to gauge th[e] reaction of the population to such a manoeuvre.'

A senior naval officer had told him that the Germans would lose the war if they hadn't beaten the Russians by 1 August. Also, a QVR officer[36], part of 27 Armoured Brigade in the Northampton district, expected to be sent overseas in September. A civil servant employed in the Ministry of Aircraft Production, who had just returned from America with fifteen people in a Consolidated Liberator, reported that the Ferry Service was working very well. He said that the Home Guard now have a weapon called the 'Northover mortar', which is breach loading and used for firing 'Molotov cocktails' and high-explosive '68 grenades'.[37]

The Russian ambassador, Ivan Maisky[38] had recently stated that he believed his country was capable of fighting for a year even under present conditions, but land operations would be brought to a virtual standstill when the snow arrived early in October. Stalin had assured General Sikorsky that he wanted no Polish territory, only to occupy part of the country to act as a buffer state between Russia and Germany. He intended to release all political prisoners from Siberia to act as saboteurs, agents, etc.

BALLOON referred to the British Secret Service representative in charge of commercial counter-espionage, etc. in America as 'a very able man' [name redacted],[39] who before the war had operated in Berlin. He thought that Sir Frank Nelson of 41 Davies Street was the British equivalent.[40] He'd heard from a regional commissioner that during heavy air raids on Southampton the fire services 'went to ground' and major fire appliances had to be sent from London. The mayor, who was never around after 5.00pm, was sacked and the Chief Constable, also in charge of the Fire Services, was given leave pending probable retirement.[41]

Colonel F. Thornton of MI11, the War Office section responsible for the Field Security Police, enquired where BALLOON had acquired his information about the camp near Horsham, referred to in his 7 June report, as he said that it was 'quite true and is very hush-hush. It is still very much in the experimental stage'.[42] When he met with Cholmondeley on 14 July he expressed his horror at the accuracy of the information, and wished to be allowed to 'take some action in order to deal with leakages'. But if he were to do so 'BALLOON would have to give rather more chapter and verse'. Cholmondeley thought that Thornton would raise it at the next meeting of the Twenty Committee, and told him that 'we would never allow any agent or officer of this section to appear as a witness', a fact Thornton fully appreciated. He asked Cholmondeley to investigate it and 'possible sources of leakage'. Luke replied that BALLOON had obtained it from a woman in the MTC who had driven a Ministry of Supply official to the factory. The driver had asked the military policemen on duty what they were building in the factory and was told 'the information which I have passed to you'.

Luke requested that Thornton keep BALLOON's 'name and the circumstances under which the indiscretion took place as far as possible to yourself', while expressing that some disciplinary action was necessary. He suggested that they send either someone in plainclothes or an ATS driver and 'try the same trick' in order to make a case for disciplinary action.[43]

Tar assigned Luke to deal with the problem. When Luke saw BALLOON on 15 July he was told that the information about the nine signal regiments came from a very old personal friend of his, now a gunnery captain, who had recently attended the Oxford Military Training College and was due to be posted to York. Following that, he would go to Orkney, and then probably the Middle East. Luke recounted: 'In the circumstances I did not press for his name as obviously it would be a mistake to divulge this to Colonel Thornton. The fact that the informant is such a close friend of our agent reduces the gravity of his indiscretion so considerably that the matter hardly seems to be worth pursuing.' He told BALLOON that for security reasons he must always divulge the source of his information to him, but that he (Luke) would 'take every care to ensure that his own identity never comes to light'. At the same time, he would not ask him to name an informant 'unless it is essential from the national standpoint that we should have the information'.[44]

But Thornton *had* raised 'the horrifying accuracy of BALLOON's information' at the Twenty Committee meeting on 17 July and requested that this should be used for taking security action. The committee agreed that, when requested, BALLOON should disclose his source's name and how he had come by the information; each case would then be judged on its merits as to what security action, if any, should be taken.[45]

Chapter 10

Plan STENCH

Guy Liddell reported in his diary for 4 October 1941 on a plan codenamed STENCH conceived by MI5:

> Plan STENCH is in operation. Porton Down is being asked to make a special gas mask which will contain certain ingredients which will puzzle the German scientists. They will think that because we are introducing these ingredients we have some very special gas about which they do not know. The mask will also have earpieces in order to give the impression that we have some new gas which affects the ears. There have already been rumours about such a gas. It has not yet been decided how this gas mask is to reach the Germans.[1]

On 10 November Luke reported:

> I saw BALLOON yesterday and discussed with him Plan Stench. He was quite enthusiastic about the idea but did not consider that Lord Rothschild's gas mask looked sufficiently complicated for use by shock troops. He asked if I would show the experts his own gas mask which he designed himself and which he thinks would be more suitable provided that it is treated so that it embodies the special features which have been applied to the mask submitted by Lord Rothschild. Incidentally, I have not told BALLOON the nature of the special treatment.[2]

The same day he saw Rothschild who was going to send BALLOON's mask to Porton for their input. Rothschild wrote to L.T.D. Williams at the Ministry of Supply on 10 November asking that the gas mask be shown to Pratt, and also Major Sadd, and posed four questions (below).[3] He emphasised that a timely answer was of the essence and hoped that Sadd would be able to look at it and return it by the end of the week. John A. Sadd was a leading authority on the production of respirators and continued to work as a senior civilian scientist at Porton until the 1950s.[4] Two days later Williams returned the gas mask, saying that it had been examined by James Davidson-Pratt and Sadd,[5] and provided the following answers to Rothschild's questions:

1. Would this respirator have certain advantages compared with the other one for Assault Troops?
   Answer – No.
2. Does this respirator incorporate any features that are so hopeless from the production point of view that it would be realised that the respirator must be a plant or a very experimental model?
   Answer. It is doubtful; probably not.
3. Has it got any totally useless functions which again might suggest it was a plant?
   Answer – No.
4. Could the peculiar container on the other model be substituted for the 'Carrier' container which is on the other one?
   Answer – not immediately but one could be made; this, however, would bear traces of improvisation.

   Major Sadd points out that this respirator was a modification by a private firm to the official civilian duty respirator and that it was turned down on account of the weakness of the bakelite valve holder, and because the projection of the container from the face was too great.

   With regard to your fourth point, there appear to be two possibilities; that the Carrier people be asked to provide container tops with the screwed spigot and to use these tops to close the containers of the official type filled in the same way as the ones you have already received; or alternatively to obtain from the Carrier people canisters containing their filter but without the charcoal and with the tops loose. These containers could then be filled at Porton with the special mixture and the tops seamed on there.[6]

On 17 December Luke reported that after Rothschild had sent BALLOON's gas mask to Porton Down, Wiltshire, it had been decided to use Rothschild's original mask, and BALLOON now had it; however, he had not heard anything about it from the Germans.

No further information appears to be available as to whether this plan was ever implemented or connected in any way to the articles published in the *Jerusalem Post* and *The Times* on 13 September 2016 – 'Britain's secret World War II plan: Stink bomb Hitler'. The plan was for SOE to use a liquid based on a bacterial compound called skatole which reeked of faeces.[7] The Americans also developed their own version to be used against the Japanese which reeked of vomit, goat and smelly feet, but it was never used as they dropped the atomic bombs on Hiroshima and Nagasaki on 6 and 9 August 1945 respectively.[8]

Chapter 11

The 'mythical Christmas card'

At the end of December 1941 BALLOON received a 'mythical Christmas card' and envelope thought to have been posted by air mail in Estoril on the 17th which appeared to contain 'duff' – a fact confirmed by H.L. Smith of their scientific section, A6. 'Duff' was the MI5 codename for a microdot, because their distribution was random, rather like the raisins in a 'plum duff' pudding. Smith observed that there was evidence of one missing spot, possibly two, which fits with TRICYCLE's earlier description of the microdots: 'The fact that the spot photograph is marked II tends to support my assumption that there was another spot. Note also questionnaire starts No.8.' (The first seven questions are missing!)[1]

Wilson showed BALLOON the questionnaire contained in the 'duff' so that he could provide answers to questions about where the Ministry of Food and Food Control Board stored supplies of food; the quantities of main foodstuffs (grain, meat – including tinned meats, butter, lard, margarine, seeds, whale oil, principal imported animal feed, type and quantities of food supplied by the USA under the Lend-Lease bill so far; which harbours were out of commission due to heavy bombing, and which ones were being used in the interim; quantities and location of mineral oil stocks being stored; and whether toilet and washing soap can be freely purchased (they were rationed).

The card was signed by Manoel Almeida and Francisco Azavada. Tar asked Colonel Allan of the GPO about 'when the letter would have been received by the addressee, (a) if it had not been intercepted, and (b) if the fact that it came by air mail and not by sea mail is due to some accident in the Portugese Post Office'[sic]. Wilson was informed that it could have been an accident of sorting or that there had been space in a partially full air-mail bag. BALLOON had admitted in his last cover letter to receiving the card 'and probably in his next secret letter he will explain that neither of the Christmas cards containing "Duff" were received only until just after his last letter was written'.[2]

Early in the New Year BALLOON received another series of letters containing microdots. Luke noted that Censorship had missed the first two but they were intercepted just before delivery; the third was intercepted before it went to Censorship. Wilson's report of 5 January 1942 outlined the recent messages BALLOON had received:

THE 'MYTHICAL CHRISTMAS CARD'

(a) re the Short Sunderland factory.
Received December 31st, the cover being a Christmas card sent air mail postmarked December 17th.

(b) Night fighter devices etc. received by us December 30th through Colonel Allan. It would presumably have been received by BALLOON himself on say 31st December. Post mark undecipherable. No indications of postage by air mail but the amount of postage is the same as that of the letter (c).

(c) Enquiries regarding army units etc.
Received by us January 3rd through Colonel Allan. Presumably would have been received by BALLOON January 5th. No air mail indication, but obviously came by air mail as post marks are 29th and 30th December. The cover letter in this case is dated 21st December, and the writer hopes that BALLOON will have received his letter of 22nd [sic] December, as well as the transfer of money.

He suggested that BALLOON's next outgoing letter should be dated 6 January, noting that his letter of 29 December said, 'Very many thanks for your letter and Christmas card', but at that date he had neither received a letter nor Christmas card and it was 'mere fiction'.[3]

On 7 January J. Whiffen, a second-class clerk in the GPO Investigation Branch, Special Section, wrote to Tar about the letter and returned the envelope with an additional photostat copy, confirming that it had arrived in Britain via Clipper air mail, the postage was correct, and the postmark indicated that it had been treated as air mail matter. He added, 'In normal course i.e. without interception, the item would probably have been delivered at the place of address on the [7th?] January 1942 after subjection to Censorship.'[4]

But a recent memo from BALLOON to MI5 included the sentence 'From what I have seen of aerodrome defence in this country I believe that when you invade you will *not* find it difficult to occupy many aerodromes.' Luke observed that 'This information was approved by the Service authorities after they had removed the word 'not', and the approved material was handed to BALLOON for him to copy'. However, when BALLOON noticed that the word 'not' did not appear, he added it. It was not until Masterman read the traffic sheets that he spotted the mistake. Fortunately, they were able to stop it, and it was rewritten.[5]

Luke raised the matter at the Management Committee on 14 January where it was decided that Masterman should see BALLOON and explain the seriousness of his error. At the Royal Aero Club late that afternoon BALLOON apologised for having inserted the word without drawing Luke's attention to it. Luke felt sure that 'There is not the slightest suggestion that he made this addition wilfully, and it is quite easy to understand how it happened'. It was decided that in future an officer would oversee the writing of his letters in secret ink just in case some query of this kind was raised again. However, Luke cautioned that it would not be possible to check the text of BALLOON's secret letter without developing it, which would therefore make it impossible to send. When, on 10 January, BALLOON had written another letter, Luke reported:

> I went over all his recent questionnaires with him and he asked if he could have copies of the questions over the weekend so that he could memorise them. As he has to obtain the replies I have given him copies which will be returned to me on Monday. He is of course very pleased at interest the Germans are showing in him but feels the questions they have asked on this occasion will be very hard to answer, particularly those which concern the food stores and food stocks.[6]

Chapter 12

'Gardiner is all right'

In December 1941 Luke began making enquiries about Gardiner, BALLOON's assistant, who was staying with him as a paying guest and had recently joined the Inter-Services Research Bureau, the covername for SOE. On 17 December Luke's report to Alex Kellar in F2b, the section investigating Comintern and Communist refugees, stated that Gardiner was

> exceptionally reliable, he is a good type of man, fond of his wife and family and two children, and completely loyal to this country. His wife is a Russian, has slightly Bolshevik leanings, but according to my informant need give us no cause for alarm. I know that he has applied for an Aliens War Service Permit to attend a Government Training Centre and should not think that you would be running any undue risk if you were to give him an open permit to work anywhere.[1]

He suggested to Tar that BALLOON's latest note about Gardiner made good reading and that he might like to show it to Senter, 'but I am sure you will agree that it is most undesirable that it should be left in John's possession' and perhaps he should treat it as today's 'after lunch tit-bit'.[2]

BALLOON had provided MI5 with some important background on Gardiner who for many years had been the Export Sales Manager of the A.E.G. in Berlin (Allgemeine Elektrizitäts-Gesellschaft AG – General Electricity Company) and was also employed by the same company as himself. In what was probably more information that he should have known, he confirmed that Gardiner had now joined the 'Secret Operations Branch' [sic] at 64 Baker Street, W1, whose head was Sir Frank Nelson and disguised as the '"Inter-Services Research Dept", [sic] whereas in reality it studies methods of skilled sabotage and the use of secret weapons and devices'. He added that Gardiner worked under Professor Newett [sic],[3] and with a man in the RAF called Bird.[4]

> They travel about the country by car a great deal and apparently the work is very interesting. The Department is very secret and they are paid in cash like the M.I.5 people monthly tax free. GARDINER gets £900 p.a. free of tax, and has been made a Major G.S.O.2.[5] As GARDINER's family is in the country – his wife, a Russian ... once married to Dick Ellis.[6]

When Gardiner first joined SOE Lieutenant Colonel Tommy Davies and their Security Officer (presumably Senter) had given him a lecture on security, threatening to lock up anyone who talked about their work, as a result of which BALLOON remarked, 'he is extremely security minded and I can get little or nothing out of him, although he is a great personal friend of mine and trusts me implicitly'. He commented on the irony of this 'considering the indiscreet approach to GARDINER made by Davis [sic], who interviewed him in our outer (partitioned) office with POSTNIKOW and myself in the office, to say nothing of an odd client or two.'[7]

Luke pointed out to Lieutenant Commander John Senter, Head of Security (A/DP) at SOE, that 'it seemed rather unwise for a high official of his organisation to interview a prospective employee of his organisation at the employee's office', and could easily have been overheard by 'a German spy and a Russian arms dealer'.[8]

Senter wanted to mention it to Air Commodore Archie Boyle, Director, Security, SIS Liaison at SOE, but Luke preferred that the fewer people who knew about it the better. He impressed upon Senter that BALLOON's position was extremely delicate and that under no circumstances should Gardiner learn that BALLOON was employed by MI5. BALLOON had been unable to prise out of Gardiner any information about his work and 'the man had now gone into his shell and was acting very discreetly'.

BALLOON observed that Gardiner tended to be 'a bit indiscreet on the telephone' even though he understood that all incoming and outgoing calls to and from Baker Street were monitored. He noted that 'When they go out into the country they are driven by M.T.C. girl drivers – a point which I have not overlooked.'[9]

What is known about Robert Drummond Gardiner from his sparse SOE file is that he was 'put through the cards' (i.e. vetted) on 5 December 1940[10] having enlisted on 25 May 1940 as a sapper in the Royal Engineers (RE); from 9 October 1940 to 1 March 1941 he was an officer cadet and later commissioned as a lieutenant.[11] He was married to Dorothy Kathleen with whom they had one daughter, aged two, living with his parents at 2 Royal Villas, Lansdown, Bath. In peacetime he had worked in various railway capacities from 1928 to 1940. 'Major R. Gardiner, REME [Royal Electrical & Mechanical Engineers], took over the Production Department in the summer of 1943, on the departure of Major Moreland Fox to the USA.' He 'had a fairly short SOE Career joining SOE in Feb 41 and leaving on 17 Sept 41. He was employed as a railways expert and assistant to RICHARD to HQ' [sic] Between August 1944 and February 1945 he was in charge of railway operations in the Ancona area of Italy and was gazetted for an MBE, having previously been Mentioned in Despatches.[12]

Professor Dudley Maurice Newitt, SOE's Director of Scientific Research (DSR) based at Station IX, The Frythe, Welwyn, Hertfordshire, was described as 'outgoing, clubbable and his good sense and natural kindliness "tinged with a delicious sense of irony" made him a notable leader' as well as 'a typical absent-minded Professor'.[13]

On seeing Tar's report, Senter declared that 'Gardiner is all right'; however, someone named Lund had accused him of being indiscreet and unsuitable for

'S.O.2.', but in Senter's opinion, he too 'was … not altogether above suspicion'. Lund had once told Senter that Gardiner had worked for SIS in Germany before the war, 'that he had become brule [brulé – 'burnt'] in Germany' and had had to give up his work. It was possible that MI5 could try to find out discreetly from BALLOON whether Gardiner was ever employed by SIS, or knew Lund, given that he and Gardiner were friendly, and perhaps he had met Lund occasionally.[14] According to BALLOON, Gardiner was never employed by SIS although the Germans believed him to be an intelligence officer and requested that he leave the country.[15]

Chapter 13

The Scandinavian Connection

Mystery and confusion surrounds Lund's identity as there appear to be two people named Lund, both of whom worked for SOE, and the information in MI5 and SOE files is conflicting.

The Lund to whom Tar appears to refer in his report to Luke must have been Knut Lund as an extract of a Home Office file in BALLOON's file[1] states that he was a Norwegian consulting engineer born in Oslo on 1 February 1898,[2] and 'a Norwegian engineer of many years' experience in China ... [who] was in fact the China hand for the firm Perin & Marshall, an American steel engineering firm'[3] who had also represented H.A. Brassert & Co. Ltd. In collaboration with Perin & Marshall, he was 'involved in and built steel production factories in Japan, China and India before World War II'.[4] In early 1939 he came to England and was allowed by the Home Office to stay until 30 April 1940 to establish himself as a consulting engineer.[5] During the latter part of August and early September 1939 he was in Istanbul representing Brassert's on a contract to construct steel works in Turkey.

Kaj Ronald Lund/K. (Kaj) R. Lund was a nurseryman from Jutland, born in Brønderslev, Denmark on 20 February 1921[6] and recruited into SOE by Paymaster Lieutenant Commander Ralph Cooper Hollingworth RNVR, head of the Danish Section (SD). He was commissioned into The Buffs (Royal East Kent) Regiment as a lieutenant, later captain, and employed by SOE from 9 April 1943 to 1 January 1944, although his file also says he joined SOE on 21 April 1941. On 17 February 1941 he was unknown to MI5 'and that as he was working for M.E.W., it is up to them to satisfy you both on the question of his bona fides and on the necessity of his naturalization.'[7]

On 6 January 1942 Luke wrote to Tar about Lund: 'BALLOON considers that LUND is a rather stupid person who is very jealous of GARDINER. Apparently he is known to his friends as "Hush-hush" and although moderately pleasant is not thought to be very intelligent.' His SOE instructors at STS 2 Bellasis created mixed impressions describing him variously as 'Intelligent and takes an interes[t] in his work. He should develop well'; 'not very intelligent'; 'a steady, likeable chap but is liable to become confused when given an order'; 'good at Signals'; or 'a little childish at times.'[8]

When Tar wrote to Senter at SOE on 1 February 1942 he managed to confuse things by referring to Knut Lund as a captain when in fact he was a war substantive lieutenant in 1942:

> With regard to Captain Knute LUND [*sic*] we have really nothing against him. I believe that in 1935 he was a representative of Messrs. Braithwaite & Co., engineers in China, Manchukuo and Japan, and that he was also employed by H.A. Brassert and I.G.I. I am enclosing for your information an extract from the Home Office file relating to LUND.[9]

No personal file exists for Knut Lund, and his information does not concur with what is in Kaj Ronald Lund's SOE file. Confusingly, both appear to have been associated with Brassert's. In K.R. Lund's file a note from Colonel F.T. Davies to Air Commodore Archie Boyle at SOE, dated 6 May 1943, also confuses the issue even more when he states

> I agree entirely that Lund should be allowed to accept Brassert's invitation to rejoin the firm. I have a feeling that A.D. may have some feelings on this matter but my own impression is that he would be far better working for Brassert's than being discontented as he is with S.O.E.
>
> If you agree will you mark the papers to A.D. and then, if A.D. approves, pass them to C.D. [Sir Charles Hambro] for approval.[10]

However, K.R. Lund, the nurseryman, was aged twenty in 1941.

Another note in K.R. Lund's SOE file from Senter to Colonel G.F. Taylor, Director of Overseas Groups and Missions, Chief of Staff, on 17 July 1942 mentions that Lund had requested that he be sent to India 'in order that he may act as liaison with China, a country which he knows well'. Taylor 'discussed the possibility of sending Captain LUND to India to act as liaison with China, with my people here but I regret to advise you [Senter] that they are quite firmly of the opinion that this would be impossible. They have considered the proposition very thoroughly before this already and they have put it to the field who turned it down.' He suggested that he might be offered to SIS.[11]

Knut Lund's Home Office file states that his wife Beatrice had arrived on the Tyne with their daughter Karin Patricia on 28 August 1939 and stayed with a Mrs Clarke, 9 Eaton Mansions, Cliveden Place, London SW1. 'Ronald Kay (Kaj) Lund' is listed as single in his SOE file. During his SOE training he corresponded regularly with a girl in Dawlish, Devon, and 'It is obvious that their present intentions are to get married as soon as it is possible; she would like to at once, but he advises waiting until the end of hostilities.'[12]

Both Lunds had applied for naturalisation – Knut Lund on 12 December 1940, and Kaj Ronald Lund in February 1940. The latter enclosed a letter from Charles Hambro supporting his application. In early January 1941 Hambro gave as his reasons for Lund's naturalistion as

He is to be employed by the P.I.D under Mr Rex Leeper in certain very confidential matters, and the nature of his work makes it impossible for him to carry on efficiently unless he is able to pass certain documents himself. Such documents can only be passed by a British subject or a naturalized British subject and to pass them from him to somebody less qualified to deal with than them/he is (merely because he is not a British subject or naturalized) not only endangers the success of the work he has to do but adds to the inefficiency and lessens the security.[13]

Merchant banker Charles Jocelyn Hambro was at that time deputy to Sir Frank Nelson, the first head of SOE, and head of the Scandinavian Section; in February 1942 he succeeded Nelson as its head. But the work which Lund would have carried out for PID at the Foreign Office was not the same as being an agent for SOE, which was directly responsible to the Ministry of Economic Warfare.

On 13 January 1942 Senter explained to Guy Liddell that Knute Lund [*sic*] was one of their officers, a captain in the General List, and gave his address and place and date of birth; that he had worked in Switzerland, the USA and the Far East as an engineer, and whose naturalisation was pending. He also mentioned Robert Gardiner, formerly employed by British Graphitised Metals Ltd before joining SOE at the end of 1941. Lund and Gardiner were longstanding close personal friends, as were their wives.

Liddell recorded that Lund was 'dismayed to find Gardiner a member of this Organisation' [SOE] claiming that Gardiner was indiscreet, and 'intimate with one [Metcalfe], the right-hand man of Potznikoff [*sic*] of whose business ethics Lund has a low opinion'. According to Lund, Potznikow was concerned with Industrial Facilities Ltd, and a gun runner. He was also disturbed by the fact that Gardiner 'maintains his contacts with British Graphitised Metals Ltd ... through [Metcalfe] with whom he is said to be sharing a flat'. At that time Gardiner was living at 34 Hampton Court, Brompton Road, London SW3.

When Liddell queried Gardiner's alleged indiscretion Lund said that it was due to his work for SIS in Germany sometime before 1938, but had been 'blown'. However, Liddell's investigations confirmed that Gardiner had never 'at any time worked for S.I.S. and from other enquiries I am told that Gardiner is most discreet and does not talk about his work'. Two issues of concern arise from this: whether there was any truth in Lund's allegations that Gardiner was 'personally undesirable and a man with dangerous associations from our point of view'; and 'whether there is any sinister reason affecting Lund, which actuated him in making these allegations.'[14]

At the beginning of February, Tar replied on Liddell's behalf about Lund and Gardiner. He confirmed that Gardiner was a director of British Graphitised Metals Ltd, and that SIS had denied all knowledge of him, but 'rather a delicate source' had confirmed that he had had to leave Germany because the Germans were suspicious that he was a British spy. Since joining SOE, 'We have, as you know, very definite evidence ... [that] he has been most discreet', which may have led to Lund's confusion. As to Potznikow, he was the owning director of BGM, and whose loyalty to Britain was not in doubt, and had already proved useful to MI5. And while the arms business tended to attract a lot of crooks, 'he is generally regarded as being the best', and that BGM had a good reputation. Nor was Metcalfe's loyalty in doubt. Tar concluded, 'I cannot believe that LUND's denunciation of GARDINER is justified, and his dismay at finding him a member of your organisation may well arise from other motives.'[15]

BALLOON claimed not to know Lund very well, 'but had recently seen him dining at the Hungaria [restaurant Lower Regent Street]. He considered him to be 'reasonably discreet', but 'lacking in tact and quickness of intelligence', so he didn't trust him with any delicate instructions. If MI5 wanted to know more about him they should ask Gardiner, who he did not want to approach himself. Wilson added, 'I rather suspect that in the past BALLOON has sought to get some information from Gardner [sic] and had been rebuffed.'[16] The following day he reported this to Senter.

In spite of positive initial reports from STS 1, Brock Hall, Flore, Northamptonshire in August 1941, it was eventually decided to remove K.R. Lund 'as he appeared incapable of "making the grade"'. His instructors had reported that he had 'shown up very badly in his security/W.T. schemes', and 'doubted whether he was mentally equipped for his role'. Yet he proceeded from RAF Tempsford to Denmark where he was dropped by parachute at Hvidsten on 16/17 April 1943.[17] There he operated as a W/T operator to establish a radio connection with Jutland and England, first working with Captain Ole Christian Tuede Geisler of the Hvidsten group in Aarhus, then Poul Jensen in Aalborg, but was arrested by the Gestapo at a flat in Bruunsgade, Aarhus on 13 December 1943 and sent to a concentration camp in Denmark, but survived. He relinquished his commission on 15 September 1945, having ceased to be employed by SOE since 2 August 1945.

A letter dated 2 March 1944 to Major R.H. 'Dick' Warden of BSS, the Bayswater Security Section of SOE, from Captain Kenneth Strong of MI5[18] states that

> A report from a reliable Danish source which has just arrived states that a blacksmith, Niels LUND, and his wife has been arrested at Brønderslev, Denmark, because their son, Kaj Ronald LUND, has been caught and found to be a British agent who landed in Denmark by parachute. The date of this information is 28th January 1944 ...
>
> This information is perhaps of interest to you since it is noticed that Kaj Ronald LUND was submitted to us for vetting in 1941 for employment by your organisation.[19]

But K.R. Lund's father's name was Christian, not Niels. Kaj Ronald Lund is registered in the Resistance Database in the Nationalmuseet, Denmark.[20] If the Lund employed by SOE was the same one born in 1898, then the information in his SOE file is incorrect.

Particulars	Knut Lund	Kaj Ronald Lund/K. (Kaj) R. Lund
Date of birth	1 February 1898	20 February 1921
Place of birth	Oslo	Brønderslev
Country of origin	Norway	Denmark
Occupation	Consulting engineer	Nurseryman
Marital status	Married	Single
Spouse	Beatrice *née* Heyerdahl	None
Children	Daughter: Karin Patricia	None
SOE PF.	N/A	HS9/949/5
Rank	Lieutenant; Captain	Lieutenant, The Buffs (Royal East Kent) Regiment; Captain
SOE service	Unknown	9 April 1943 – 1 January 1944; Deployed by parachute 16/17 April 1943; WTO aka TANNER, LAMP; POW - Survived
SOE section	L – Intelligence Section	SD – Denmark Section
Applied naturalisation	12 December 1940	February 1940
Address	- Thatched House Club, London, SW1 - 96 Cranmer Court, London, SW3	Holly Lodge, Church Lane, Cheshunt, Herts
Civilian employment	H.A. Brassert	Wished to leave SOE to rejoin H.A. Brassert

Figure 1. Comparison Chart.

Chapter 14

'A sub-machine gun of outstanding design'

In the spring of 1941 BALLOON had learned about the development of a new sub-machine gun, the Vesely 9mm, from a brother officer who told him how the 'Authorities' (Ministry of Supply) had rejected it and 'expresses high opinion of design and criticizes Authorities for not accepting it'. On 24 April he provided MI5 with a report on the gun's genesis:

1. <u>Narrative</u>
    Mr Vesely, a Czech and former designer at the Skoda Works, and the man responsible for the .303" Bren gun and 7.92mm and 15mm Besa guns, is employed in an advisory capacity by the Small Arms Department at Enfield. He has recently designed a sub-machine gun of outstanding design,[1] the chief points of which are:

    (a) The very compact double magazine which has a capacity of 64 shots usually only obtainable in guns fitted with the unwieldy circular magazine.
    (b) Great simplicity of construction owing to the general tubular and round shapes of all parts thus eliminating cross cutting and machining and so making the gun particularly suitable for mass production.

    Mr Vesely immediately offered the design to the British Government and the experts at Enfield with *one* exception [Sheppard] and the Ordnance Board have commented very favourably on the gun from the technical point of view. Colonel Sheppard [sic] late of B.S.A. Ltd who is in charge of the Designs Branch (Cheshunt) near Enfield[2] is the only person who seems to be jealous of Vesely and this, I think, may be due to the fact that one of Sheppard's men (Turpin by name) has invented a sub-machine gun which he (Sheppard) is anxious to push. Further to this Sheppard declined to consider some designs of Vesely's regarding an anti-aircraft single-post mounting for 2 or 4 Bren guns which could be fitted to a Morris Truck to deal with the dive bomber when on the march (I bet the Anzacs wish that they had some!) These facts define Sheppard's attitude.

Accordingly, although Vesely's gun was accepted in principle by all other experts, the Ministry of Supply have turned it down on the score [?] that they cannot consider quantity production of many types even though this gun is designed for mass producing. Vesely was very upset about all this and asked the Chief Inspector of Small Arms if he might have permission to send the drawings through the Censor to a Czech friend in America in order to try and commercialise the gun for him there.

At this stage I and my firm come in to the picture and I wish to state quite clearly that my firm have a financial interest in the success or otherwise of this gun. We consider it to be outstanding and that it would be highly undesirable for this weapon to fall into unauthorised or enemy hands. Realising that a penniless Czech in USA without money or connections might easily get into wrong hands I offered to arrange for my influential and thoroughly reliable agent in USA (himself a Registered Arms Dealer) to get an introduction to a director of Colts at Hartford or some other well-known American firm (Smith & Wesson, Harrington & Richardson etc.). Vesely was delighted and this suggestion and I cabled my man to this effect. He has replied that he can arrange such an introduction and indeed knows one of the directors intimately. My man will also look after the patents etc. and handle the business angle. When the drawings are received in USA he will call on the firm with Vesely's Czech friend and the drawings and generally look after the matter over there so as to safeguard Vesely's and indeed our own interests.

Chief Inspector of Small Arms agreed to Vesely's request for permission to send the drawings to USA and Vesely has been given a written permission signed by Lt Col E. Hooper (used to be in my Regiment 2nd Loyals) to export the drawings. Poor Vesely believes this to be sufficient and I have not disillusioned him. Actually what happened is this:

A junior official in the Ministry of Supply called Gibb (Director of Munitions Production Dept) is against letting Vesely commercialise his gun (any connection with Sheppard I wonder) and Gibb has actually written on the documents concerning the case 'in any case the drawings will never pass the Censor and a good thing too.'[3]

Personally I believe he intends to have them stopped and it is indeed a scandal that a junior official should be in a position to do such a thing and indeed should dare to write such a comment on official documents above his signature.

2. Proposed line of action
   Naturally I cannot tell Vesely about Gibb and his evil intentions so I have asked Vesely to come and see me and to show me his written permission. I then propose to 'fling my arms up in horror' and tell Vesely that his permission is not strong enough. What I want to do is to get a really powerful chit signed by someone at the WO that will ensure that the drawings (already approved by the Director of Artillery and C.I.S.A. Enfield) really pass the Censor in spite of Master Gibb. Unfortunately, I believe that the Censorship Dept who deal with drawings is situated in Liverpool. However, if they have a representative in London I thought that it might be wise to take Vesely along to them with his existing written permission and get their reaction. This would be a good way of breaking the news gently to Vesely that a chit signed by Teddy Hooper is, as I believe, of little value. What we must avoid is a delay and long correspondence between the Censor and the Ministry of Supply and Director of Artillery which would give Gibb a chance to put his oar in. The obvious thing is to get the correct permission and get the drawings out with the minimum of delay.

   I am of course financially interested but quite apart from that I do think that in the National Interest this gun should go to American [*sic*] under authorised control on the lines indicated by me. If you can assist as regards the Censor I would be grateful as I do feel that this whole matter is a bad show as it stands.[4]

BALLOON kept his word. On 25 April he asked his contact, Mathews (Lennox), to 'please do what you can'.

Shortly afterwards Luke wrote to Lennox asking him to obtain the Ministry of Supply's file on Vesely from MI10 – the directorate of the War Office responsible for weapons and technical analysis – and what they knew about him. The Czech section knew nothing about him but Lennox was having his name put through MI5's records.[5] That file, obtained by MI10(a) for MI5 from a Major Shallard, shows that correspondence between the various sections of the Ministry of Supply dated back to 20 December 1940.[6] A note from the Secretary to the Ordnance Board of the Ministry of Supply, dated 23 January 1941, stated that

3. Mr VESELEY's design may, or may not, prove superior to the Schmeisser, but its development to the production stage would certainly take longer than either weapon and may prejudice the chances of a quick decision being reached as to the machine carbine to be adopted.
4. Under present circumstances the Board, therefore, do not recommend that a model to Mr VESELEY's design should be manufactured or any further action taken.[7]

DOUBLE AGENT BALLOON

As Desmond Orr pointed out to Tar Robertson on 5 May:

> M.I.10 have kindly obtained for us M.O.S. File No.A.9593 on the subject, in which you will see at 12 an interesting note signed by Harman! Also see 8.
>
> As M.I.10 are not supposed to have given us this file, it is important that they should not be mentioned as the source of our information, and I have undertaken that we will let them have it back again at the earliest possible moment. They themselves know nothing about VASELY [sic].[8]

8.

M.P.F.

We have spoken A.3, and learn that Mr VEZELEY [sic] is a Czech, apparently connected with the Syndicate* *in which you are interested.* You will note that he wishes to send drawings to USA, and so this file is referred to you in a way corresponding to that in the Sterling Armament Case involving the Schmeisser patents. Doubtless you wish that the drawings should not go.

(Signed) J.F. Stacey
for A.D.S.R.

S.R.3.
12.3.41

(Note written at foot of this minute:
* Officially, yes!
M.P.F. 18/3   A.F.W.B.)

12.

C.I.S.A.

Please see Minute 11. Copies of relevant minutes 46, 47 on 284/D/681 are attached at 12A.

Thus it will be seen that while no objection will be raised to the transmission of drawings, we do nothing to facilitate it.

Presumably censorship will pick up anything sent and submit it to us for examination before allowing it to pass. This will produce delay, but that is no disadvantage to us. Mr VESELEY [sic] will, of course, not be informed of the subject matter of this paragraph.

(Signed) J.R. Harman
for A.D.S.R.

S.R.3/26.3.41[9]

'A SUB-MACHINE GUN OF OUTSTANDING DESIGN'

Major Peter Hope of B21 wrote to Tar on 5 May 1941:

> With reference to my enquiry regarding the HISPANIC BRITANNIC TRADING CORPORATION, the 'no action' slip under your name refers to [BALLOON] who has supplied this office with a certain amount of information concerning the firm.
>
> As, however, in this particular instance the information has been duplicated from other sources, I presume you will have no objection to my going ahead?[10]

Tar told Luke that he should get Hope to show him the file. Luke noted: 'TAR. Have seen Hope and have put a question to [BALLOON] at his request. [BALLOON] knows a good deal about Hispano Corp. Is there any great objection to his passing it on to Hope verbally if [illegible] there?'

BALLOON was interested in the gun's design and knew Vesely by reputation and his association with the Bren gun, so he introduced him to Postnikow. Vesely claimed he had not been given a 'square deal' because the Sten had been given 'undue backing', so together they attempted to get the Ministry of Supply to reconsider. The Sten was a far from satisfactory weapon, 'highly unreliable, prone to jamming, and inaccurate beyond 30 metres ... . But it was easy and cheap to produce, a gun was said to cost fifteen shillings ...'[11] whereas Vesely's gun cost considerably more.

Postnikow's attempts to persuade the Ministry to reverse its decision failed, and therein lay a problem: In spite of BGM being a registered arms dealer, under the Firearms Act (1937) it was still necessary to obtain permission from the Ministry to make and possess fully-automatic weapons.[12] The Ministry refused, but BALLOON managed to obtain permission from 'another Service Department'. Postnikow had two prototypes made up at his expense, but Vesely was proving to be a difficult partner in the whole venture.

Work began at a factory near London, the project completed in February 1942, and the prototypes test fired. Because of a lack of range facilities and difficulties of being able to obtain ammunition in wartime, BALLOON asked a friend at Enfield who had already provided unofficial support and assistance if he could approach the Chief Inspector of Small Arms (CISA)' 'and suggest that Vesely in view of his past services re: Bren gun may be given range facilities'. CISA agreed and Vesely started appearing regularly at Enfield.

Postnikow arranged for production of the guns by entering into an agreement, based on a Licence Agreement with Vesely, and the Farnham Trust. However, as a report points out,

> All these negotiations could have been completed long ago had not Vesely:
>
> (a) Failed to produce complete amended drawings, operations book, lists of tools, etc.

(b) Made extravagant claims as to his importance to the project and asked for remuneration for exceeding that agreed in the Licence Agreement of 12/8/41.

In fact as soon as the guns were made and showed signs of exceptional promise, Vesely kept continually asking for more and more.

Under the agreement Vesely was to receive a royalty of two shillings [ten pence] per gun sold and 'a Service Agreement the terms of which were to be agreed upon'. That agreement in June/July had offered him very favourable terms, but then he changed his mind for the third or fourth time and wanted a lump sum instead, to which they agreed. At his request a meeting was held at 417 Victoria House on 28 July to finalise the settlement, which lasted five hours. Ten days later Vesely's solicitor, Alfred Shindler, wrote to BALLOON and Postnikow informing them that Vesely 'had repudiated his Supplementary Agreement of 31st July 1942 on the grounds of having been "induced to sign" an allegation entirely without foundation', as well as his licence agreement of 12 August 1941, which was still legally binding but which he had not fulfilled. BALLOON and Postnikow met with their solicitors, Simmonds & James, Church Rackham & Co., 425 Staple Inn, London WC1, to discuss the terms Vesely had asked for, but rejected them on the advice of their solicitors.

BALLOON, on behalf of BGM, informed Colonel Icke (CISA)[13] of the dispute, pointing out that the guns were the property of BGM and that he should ensure that Vesely, who had access to the Ordnance Factory, did not remove them from Enfield. Icke agreed to do so and expressed an earnest desire that the dispute should not delay the testing of the guns. A few days later he decided to 'hold the guns impartially until the dispute is settled'. BALLOON's report confirmed this arrangement and stated that it was clear that this 'hostile and greedy Czech peasant' had been 'pampered and spoilt by us' and had brought the whole project to a standstill by acting on the advice of 'undesirable friends and a not financially disinterested solicitor'.[14] He also discovered that Vesely had approached SR4 of DSR (Directorate of Scientific Research) at Berkeley Court, Baker Street, so he instructed BGM's solicitors to write 'informing them of the existence of the licence and its validity as set out by Mr Gerald Gardiner and Mr James Mould (Patent counsel)'. The present position was a 'complete deadlock.'[15]

Simmonds & James wrote to Shindler & Co., 23-25 Eastcheap, London EC3 on 26 August 1942 outlining the more favourable terms which Vesely had attempted to obtain than those originally negotiated and by which he was already bound. Their letter outlined Vesely's other demands, stating that the document they had received was merely a redrafting of the licence agreement and did not mention anything about cash payments, shareholdings, or a seat on the board. It concluded: 'In these circumstances we are instructed to ask you to let us know within seven days whether your Client desires to maintain his repudiation of the agreement of the 31st ultimo. If so, our Clients will accept that repudiation and act accordingly.'[16]

'A SUB-MACHINE GUN OF OUTSTANDING DESIGN'

On 11 September 1942 Cyril F. Simmonds of Simmonds & James wrote to Postnikow updating him on the current situation, saying that on 12 August 1941 'Vesely ... was very depressed regarding the V.A.P. gun in that he felt that it was hopeless to pursue the matter in this country bearing in mind the rejection of the drawings by the authorities'. Therefore, counsel was of the opinion that the offer made on that date was 'not only fair and equitable; but gave to Vesely a hope of reward under the Service Agreement should the gun at any time be reconsidered and accepted.'

Given how the situation had improved regarding manufacture and testing, and his access to Enfield,

> Vesely acquired a state of mind in which he quite possibly believed himself to be the biggest if not the only factor in the success of the gun at the present time. It is, of course, apparent that but for your efforts and those of your Company and associates Vesely could not have succeeded.

In Simmonds' opinion, the terms offered to Vesely were extremely generous and 'It would be a generous agreement for an inventor in any event'. He was 'satisfied that you have faithfully carried out all your obligations under the Licence and we are equally satisfied that in certain points Vesely has failed to carry out his obligations, one point in particular being his failure to hand over to you all drawings showing alterations from time to time in the prototypes.'

Vesely was trying to have any drawings returned to him, but legally Postnikow was entitled to keep them and 'to regard the two prototypes as entirely the property of your Company and further the drawings in Vesely's possession also belong to your Company'. Simmonds stated that the 1941 licence was still binding and valid and 'Vesely really cannot acquire under that any service agreement because the law has held that "an agreement to agree" is too vague to be implemented.' He advised against pursuing litigation at that time given 'the issues and personalities, both official and unofficial, involved'.[17]

On 12 November BALLOON and Vesely attended a test of the V.42 sub-machine gun. Also present were Captain J.R. Stewart, Combined Operations HQ; members of the Ordnance Board; Colonel Edward Hooper, Deputy Director of Weapons at the War Office,[18] and his technical officer Major Phillips; Commander Young representing DNO; officers of Home Forces; CISA department; and Mr G.G. Turner of SR4, Ministry of Supply. The test was conducted by CISA's department, but the officer giving the introductory explanation failed to mention BGM, only Vesely as the designer, and co-designer of the Bren and Besa guns.

Much to their chagrin, the gun failed two of the tests, although the report states that this was simply a case of bad luck rather than any weaknesses in the design. But 'The general consensus of opinion of all present after seeing the tests ... was that the gun is a robust and workmanlike job and far superior to the Sten.' Commander Young requested one of the guns for trial by the Royal Navy, and Colonel Hooper suggested to the Ordnance Board that they should order additional guns for extensive trials at Pendine Range in south-west Wales. Combined Operations also hoped to acquire some of the guns for testing by commandos under training.

BALLOON told SR4 and CISA that BGM would be willing to accept an order for further guns and that their offer would be brought to the notice of the Ordnance Board and the War Office Department. Interest had been shown in the gun, and facilities were made available through BALLOON's brother-in-law, Lieutenant Colonel A.P. Lane, the Deputy Chief Inspector of the Small Arms Inspection Department, and an officer in his old regiment, who had approached Colonel Icke. But it was not until 18 November that Vesely agreed to the terms he'd been offered – a cash payment of £8,000 and a royalty 'in some cases' of 2/6d [fifteen pence] – and a new and final agreement drawn up between him and VAP (Holdings) Ltd, the company formed to promote the guns, which would be manufactured in Britain and India.

Later, on 21 November, BALLOON gave an account of the history of the development of the gun, followed by a description of the difficulties which had arisen, his object being 'to place the facts on record, so that credit may be assessed where credit is due':

I <u>History</u>
  (i) This weapon was designed by Mr Josef Vesely, a Czech National and co-designer of the Bren and Besa guns, who submitted it to the Ordnance Board early in 1941 but the gun was turned down in favour of the Sten.
  (ii) Lieut Colonel A.P. Lane 2nd Battalion The Loyal Regiment and now employed in C.I.S.A. Department Broxbourne Herts drew my attention to the fine qualities of this weapon and being a brother officer of mine and knowing that I was a Registered Arms Dealer, he introduced me to Mr Vesely with a view to helping V in any way possible.
  (iii) The design appeared so good to my Director Mr A. Postnikow and myself that we tried to get the gun reconsidered by the authorities through the good offices of Sir Charles Maclaren [*sic*], Director General of Ordnance Factories[19] and Sir Peter Bennett, Chairman of the Automatic Gun Board [at the Ministry of Supply, from 1941-44].
    This failed and the Director of Artillery declined to reverse his previous decision.

He drew attention to the fact that the gun had been rejected twice, and had it not been for the efforts of Lieutenant Colonel Lane, Postnikow's funding, and his drawing attention to the gun, it would have remained simply as a drawing. He pointed out that it was ironic that the moment the gun was undergoing tests the CISA actively promoted it, given that he was chairman of the Ordnance Board when the gun was rejected in 1941.

'A SUB-MACHINE GUN OF OUTSTANDING DESIGN'

> Facilities for manufacture of the gun, subject to government approval, have been made and I have written to both the Ordnance Board and D.N.O. offering to make up further models free of charge for tests by Service Departments, DDW [Deputy Director of Weapons at the War Office], Combined Operations, and Airborne Troops are also interested and my firm intends to make up at least another 25 guns so as to give the Services a chance of trying the gun operationally.[20]

In his opinion 'if the Services want this gun they will now be able to try it and have it, so that 18 months work will not have been in vain.'

At the end of the year he informed Ian Wilson that everyone was pleased with the gun. He'd been asked to become a director of VAP (Holdings) Ltd, and whether he would be prepared to go to the USA or other countries to open up negotiations there. Wilson commented that he couldn't quite understand why BALLOON didn't want to be a director of the company, given that Postnikow was already one, and if the Germans ever found out about the gun they would assume that BALLOON would know of it. But MI5 would have to give serious thought to his going to America because it would probably involve going via Lisbon, which would mean having to contact the Germans, being obliged to mention the gun, and giving them details of it. They would first require the FBI's co-operation, notably Thurston at the American embassy, and the Bureau would need to keep BALLOON's case in proper shape while he was in the USA; secondly, that the Germans would not be given too many details of the gun.

BALLOON thought that, with the aid of Lane whom he preferred over anyone else, it would be possible to prepare special blueprints, but while Lane would have to be put in the picture, Vesely would not be consulted. The drawings would be

> substantially accurate, but which contain minor alterations, particularly on tolerance which would mean that the blue prints would be a handicap rather than an asset to the Germans, and, if they wished to manufacture the gun from the blue prints, they would hold them up for some months. BALLOON feels that by the time that they had made the necessary adjustments they would in any case have captured some of the guns.

The chief concern was whether they would be sufficient to deceive the Germans without blowing BALLOON's cover, and the errors enough to slow them down until they captured any guns, something which MI5 would consult Lane about. Wilson thought that

> as a way of preventing the details given being too accurate it might well be plausible to say that BALLOON had no justification for carrying out the original drawings as these were already in American

hands through official channels, and therefore he only took with him some small photographs of blue prints which he could smuggle in his pockets. The photographs, being notionally taken by BALLOON himself, need not be too perfect.

Although the definite question of BALLOON going to America may not be very urgent, we ought to decide our policy as soon as possible, because if he is ever to make any reference to the gun in his correspondence with the Germans he ought to do so in the very near future. He can merely state that his firm is interested in the introduction of a new automatic weapon designed by VESELY, of which he could give the Germans details if he gets to Lisbon. BALLOON assures me that there are no useful details which he could in fact give by letter only.[21]

Marriott was all in favour of the idea, but not of BALLOON having copies of the blueprints in his possession. As he pointed out: 'Surely if his firm is at all secret Balloon would never be allowed by Censorship to take blue prints [sic] through a neutral country in war-time.' Under normal circumstances they would be sent by diplomatic bag to the USA. He suggested that BALLOON only talk about the gun in general terms. Masterman agreed, but added, 'It seems to me, however carefully the attraction [illegible] that if the blue prints were such as to give the Germans [illegible] help, they would carefully follow Balloon when looking at [?] some of the actual guns when captured by the Germans.' They all agreed that Wilson should discuss with BALLOON and Lane the technical aspects of the problem.

On 6 January 1943 BALLOON prepared a further report on the gun in which he explained that 'all outstanding difficulties and disputes with the Inventor (Mr J. Vesely) have been settled and all final licences and agreements signed and duly adjudicated'. Together with Postnikow, M. Mackenzie (Director of H.A. Brassert), L. Tufnell, Maurice Cole, and Vesely, he was to be a director of VAP (Holdings) Ltd. The company had also acquired the American rights. Vesely's solicitor, Alfred Burnett Shindler, was denounced as a 'crook' who was being brought before the Law Society 'to prove why he should not be dismissed for unprofessional conduct'.[22] Vesely was persuaded to dump Shindler and arrangements were made with Messrs Freshfields, solicitors to the Bank of England and the Czech Legation, to act for him.[23] An associate of the company, a Mr Bridges Webb, had formed a trust to handle Vesely's financial affairs.

General D.M.C. Clarke, Director General of Artillery, was considering whether to place an order for the gun and had also instructed Lieutenant Colonel Reginald Vernon Shepherd of Designs Cheshunt and co-designer of the Sten to report on production. To that end, DSR had requested that drawings be sent to the Ministry of Supply at Cheshunt. The gun was also undergoing tests with the Royal Navy through Commander Robert Young of HMS *Excellent*, the Portsmouth Gunnery School at Whale Island.[24] A further ten guns were being made for Combined Operations, Airborne Forces, and the Inter-Services Research Bureau (SOE), for which Vesely had already received 'considerable sums of money', and careful arrangements had been made to ensure quality control.

Early in January Wilson wrote to Arthur Thurston, the FBI's legal attaché at the US Embassy in London, about the possibility of BALLOON going to America sometime in the future, which would also give him a chance to contact the Germans in Lisbon en route as the Pan Am Boeing 314 Clipper flew from Lisbon to New York. Thurston 'saw no reason whatever why they should not co-operate in order to assist us, even if the chances of the FBI themselves deriving any direct benefit was not very great.' It was possible, Wilson told him, that the Germans might want to use him as a courier to take money to one of their agents in the United States. While this might assist the FBI, MI5 wanted their assurance that they would not blow BALLOON's cover by any information he may obtain. Thurston assured him that if a German agent were to be identified, 'internal investigation in the United States would provide sufficient evidence so that the agent could be dealt with without involving BALLOON'.

***

The saga of the Vesely gun continued when Wilson and BALLOON met with Lane on 26 January.[25] Lane agreed to make modifications to the drawings so that the Germans would be delayed in deriving any real benefit from them but, he emphasised, this would not prevent the Germans from using them, or from realising after a time that they had been planted once their technical experts got their hands on them. 'From a pure technical side Lane is convinced that minor alterations he could make would require an absolute minimum of two months hard technical effort to be found out and corrected.' In all probability, there was a good chance that due to the Germans' red tape or existing production arrangements, the drawings could get side-lined and they would fail to make use of them, as had happened in England, had it not been for BALLOON's persistence. Therefore, Lane thought that there was no real advantage in providing the Germans with modified drawings two months before they might actually capture a gun. What would interest them, however, was the double magazine, which, even if they didn't adopt the entire gun, might be used to improve their Schmeissers.

Wilson concluded that

> In these circumstances it does seem to me that we must abandon the idea of BALLOON passing these drawings to the Germans unless this event can be timed to co-incide with his participation in some other deception which would in any event result in blowing him after a month or two. If any such scheme were afoot then the drawings would give him a temporary build-up and help any other deception, but the difficulty in using BALLOON in any deception which results in blowing him, is the effect on TRICYCLE and possibly, although I think this is less likely after the lapse of time, upon TATE and the agents linked with him.

Yet in spite of his misgivings he agreed to have Lane make the modifications in case a situation arose when they could be used, even if that meant ending BALLOON's career as a double agent prematurely, but then had second thoughts, saying that 'the exact nature of the modifications might have to vary with the actual plan'. There was also the question of what, if anything, BALLOON should tell the Germans about the gun. As he pointed out,

> He has already, in May 1941, mentioned Vessely's [sic] design for a sub-machine gun, which had then been turned down. If, as seems now highly probable, the gun comes into general use sooner or later BALLOON's interest in the gun may become known to the Germans. A mere verbal description of the gun is of no value to the Germans without drawings, specifications etc. which cannot be given in secret ink. BALLOON tells me that it is now most improbable that any question will arise of his going to America in connection with the commercial side of the business. The Germans have not reacted positively to previous suggestions that they should arrange an arms deal which would take him to the Peninsula, nor have they arranged any other channel for acquiring documents mentioned to them in other cases. The fact that the Germans were informed that BALLOON knew all about the gun would therefore not seem likely to force us into the position of having to pass over drawings. Even if, at a later stage, they come back on the suggested arms deal we could, although it would be a pity to have to do so, invent reasons why BALLOON was not able to take copies of the drawings to Lisbon with him, while if they should suggest some other channel for passing the drawings we would obtain some information for which we have been fishing unsuccessfully for a long time. If you agree I suggest we should submit for approval BALLOON's draft letter which is attached, but omitting the parts I have enclosed in brackets, as I think it is a mistake to emphasise the question of drawings when we will probably not wish to supply them.[26]

He therefore asked BALLOON to instruct Lane *not* to make any modifications to the drawings for the time being.

Towards the end of February Wilson wrote to Ewen Montagu about the gun, drawing his attention to the following points:

1. The story in a slightly different form has been submitted to the War Office, who are not yet ready to approve it but are prepared to reconsider the matter if the Admiralty have no objections.
2. BALLOON is in fact demonstrating the gun in all sorts of circles, and some of those who are interested in either making or getting the gun feel rightly or wrongly that its development is being obstructed

by those whom have vested interests in the manufacture of Stens. It is, therefore, quite possible that in the near future there may be some questions asked in Parliament or other publicity, in which case, even if BALLOON is not mentioned by name, his business associates who are known to the Germans would be mentioned. If he had said nothing about the gun this might be fatal.
3. BALLOON who is quite an expert in these matters is absolutely certain that the particulars proposed to be given do not of themselves help the enemy in the less [sic] degree to produce a similar weapon. Without drawings or detailed specifications their particulars such as heat treatment and the mere fact that one person has made such a gun does not help another person to make a similar gun. This view has been confirmed by the Deputy Chief Inspector of small arms at Enfield unofficially when he was consulted on the possibility of cooking drawings of the gun should there ever be an opportunity of handing them over.
4. I understand that the officer responsible for ordering the three guns for tests for the navy is Colonel Rutledge D.N.O.(L).[27]
5. At the beginning of his career as a double agent BALLOON informed the Germans that Vesely had invented a new sub-machine gun.[28]

Lord Birkenhead had spoken to Lord Cherwell about an allegation that Gibb and Shepherd at the Ministry of Supply had been 'deliberately stifling the production of the V.A.P. gun'. Cherwell had become interested after meeting with Birkenhead and had promised to take up the case. Professor Frederick Lindemann, who beamce 1st Viscount Cherwell in July 1941, was Churchill's principal scientific adviser, but not someone who endeared himself to everyone. Jock Colville, Churchill's private secretary, thought him 'Arrogant, boastful, childishly competitive, reactionary, racist – Lindemann raised the hackles of practically everybody. He thinks he is a mixture of John the Baptist, Maynard Keynes and Lord Leverhulme ... he is really an ingenious but slightly inflated frog with an unpleasant croak.'[29]

Frederick 'Freddie' Winston Furneaux Smith, 2nd Earl of Birkenhead, was a Conservative politician who at that time was attached to the Political Warfare Executive (PWE), the Foreign Office's propaganda arm. Before Cherwell accompanied Churchill to the Third Washington *Trident* Conference (12-25 May 1943) BALLOON arranged for him to view a demonstration of the gun at Enfield.[30] The demonstration was reported as 'the greatest possible success and showed the V.A.P. gun was superior in all respects to the Sten gun'. Cherwell sought the views of Colonel Hooper of the Ordnance Board and 'it looks as though the obstruction by a certain gentleman in the Ministry of Supply will be broken down'.

Birkenhead suggested to BALLOON that the Ministry of Supply might try to exclude VAP (Holdings) Ltd from participating in the actual manufacture or assembly of the gun because Postnikow was a security risk. But Wilson noted that the argument was invalid as Postnikow had known all about the gun for the last two years; had he wanted to tell the Germans about it 'he would have done so long ago.' Birkenhead was going to see Victor Rothschild in B1c, most likely about facilitating any possible vetting enquiry from the Ministry.

BALLOON used subterfuge to get models of the gun made for the Airborne Division, Canadian troops, and the Chief of Combined Operations, Lord Louis Mountbatten. He had also sent one to Canada which, Wilson observed, could be used as a cover for him to pass quickly through Lisbon en route to Canada in connection with the development of the gun.[31]

On 11 July Wilson arranged with Major E. Goudie of MI11 at the War Office for BALLOON to visit 'Hythe', which he took to actually mean Bisley, the location of the Small Arms School.[32] BALLOON reported that he had seen the 'Peart A/T mortar projector' [*sic*] and the Dome trainer.[33] Wilson wondered whether there was anything BALLOON tell the Germans about them.

***

During this time BALLOON also managed to get himself into trouble with the police by placing an advertisement in the *West London Observer* under the name Davidson, an offence under regulation 20(2) of the General Defence Regulations (1939). He was summonsed to appear at Clerkenwell police station, 400 King's Cross Road, where he was questioned about his background and why he had not been called up. (It will be recalled that he had also used the name R.S. Davidson when he approached the Spanish military attaché in May 1941.) With the collaboration of Superintendent Leonard Burt, the Scotland Yard detective seconded to MI5 at the beginning of the war to head B5, MI5's Investigation Staff, the whole matter was cleared up quickly when, on 9 July 1943, the charge was deemed a technical offence, to which BALLOON pleaded guilty, and was discharged.[34]

Exactly why he placed it or the nature of the advertisement is unknown, but through a Home Office warrant (HOW) MI5 learned that he had placed another in *The Times* on 14 October 1943: 'Bachelor, 34 (exempt) seeks afternoon or evening post Companion-Secretary or Valet-Help to gentleman. London area. – Write Box D.843, The Times, E.C.4.'[35] A reply to the advertisement from a Mr W. Fothergill of Prospect Cottage, Cookham, Berkshire, looking to fill that position was dated the same day.[36]

Chapter 15

A thorn in BALLOON's side

The Ministry of Supply continued to be a thorn in BALLOON's side. On 20 March 1943 Claude Dixon Gibb, Director General of Weapon and Instrument Production, sent British Graphitised Metals a tersely-worded letter requesting that they acknowledge his previous letters, and that they understood his current letter. He emphasised that if production of the gun were to go ahead, although they considered it '[m]ost unlikely there will be any requirement for this carbine', they would handle planning and production, without the interference of BGM, and 'We must request that you at once cease wasting the time of manufacturers already fully occupied with the production of urgently required weapons by inviting them to consider production of components for this weapon'.[1] This prompted a reply from D. Bridges Gibb, one of BGM's directors:

> Having regard to the favourable impression created by this highly efficient weapon, we regret that we cannot, subject to higher authority, acquiesce in your suggestions, nor can we agree that the time of any manufacturer has been wasted, except the time wasted through the delay in your furnishing us with the necessary certificate for 330 lbs [?] of iron and steel for which we asked on the 1st February for the manufacture of a simple press tool for sizing magazines.
>
> We do not understand the non-co-operative attitude adopted by you in respect of the development work already carried out on the production of this weapon.[2]

The Special Service Brigade Headquarters in Midhurst, Sussex wrote to BALLOON on 13 August 1943 requesting a demonstration of the gun 'to ascertain if the weapon is likely to be of use to this Brigade'.[3] The author of the letter had been in touch with 'Major Ashford Russell' [sic],[4] described by Cuthbert Bowlby, Head of SIS's Mediterranean Section, as 'a man of extreme (there is no other word) personal ambition which prompts him to aspire to quicker promotion than is the normal practice in this organisation', but was 'extremely able'.[5] On 20 August BALLOON visited Midhurst to give them a demonstration, as well as showing it to the Director of the Ordnance Board on the 23rd.

Major A.J.M. Perkins, RE,[6] Airborne Forces Development Centre (AFDC), Amesbury Abbey, Wiltshire[7] requested that 'the General was asking to see your weapon', presumably Lieutenant General Frederick 'Boy' Browning, as a note from Hugh Astor of B1a stated later that General Browning was 'favourably impressed'.[8]

At the end of August BALLOON received information from Tufnell, a co-director of VAP Holdings Ltd, about an attack on Peenemünde, the location of the launch site and development of the German V-1 and V-2 terror weapons. Given the date of Wilson's report (31 August 1943), this must relate to Operation HYDRA, the first attack of Operation CROSSBOW, on the night of 17/18 August by 596 heavy bombers of the RAF.[9] Someone named Lyell at the Air Ministry had approached Tufnell a day or two before the raid and 'talked about the fact that the Germans had a secret weapon for attacking London, and that we knew where it was made, and that steps were being taken to knock it out', although the type of weapon was not disclosed. But 'As far as BALLOON knows, Lyell was in no way to blame for the leakage and it was only inference on the part of BALLOON and Tufnell after the raid on Peenemünde had been announced that linked the conversation which Tufnell could not help overhearing with the place attacked.'[10]

Group Captain J. Archer of D3 thought that this was Louis Tufnell;[11] Lyell could have been Flying Officer A.C. Lyell in the Directorate of Ground Defence at the Air Ministry. The launch site was only identified on 23 June by Flight Officer Constance Babington Smith, a WAAF photographic interpreter at the Central Interpretation Unit (CIU) at RAF Medmenham, Buckinghamshire. Clearly, there had been a security leak either from the unit or the Air Ministry.

Chapter 16

The Grand, Cliveley and Postnikow Affair

Luke reported on 'THE GRANDE, CLIVELEY AND POSTNIKOW Affair' on 17 March 1942, that sometime towards the end of 1940 Clively, who had briefly worked for Postnikow, returned to the office after lunching with the latter, with more than £2,000 in an envelope. Since then Postnikow had instructed BALLOON to withdraw money from the envelope from time to time or had withdrawn it himself, but BALLOON had never been able to discover to whom the payments were made. He suspected that Clively was 'a wrong 'un' and had come by the money illegally, possibly as a bribe which he had handed over to Postnikow for safekeeping, and also that

> a man called GRANDE was also mixed up in this deal, and it is interesting to note that GRANDE was also employed by S.I.S. and was engaged on the part of their work which has now been taken over by S.O.E.
> There is no doubt that he had at his disposal very considerable sums of money for disbursement to his agents. I believe that he [Grand] has now severed his connection with S.I.S. and is not employed by S.O.E. and of course CLIVELY is also out of it.

It was thought that Gardiner, Postnikow's partner, also knew that the money had been put in Postnikow's safe, and might be able to shed some light on the transaction. He and BALLOON were both convinced that there was something wrong about it. Luke reported

> Fortunately BALLOON took note of some of the bank notes and has given the numbers to me. These were handed over to Sir Edward Reid on 12.2.42 and he is investigating the matter. According to BALLOON both GRANDE and CLIVELY are thoroughly unsavoury characters, and as I know there was some major trouble in connection with GRANDE's organisation, the information which BALLOON has given me, although it is somewhat flimsy, may provide some of the missing pieces in the puzzle which I understand has never really been pieced together.

Tar thought that Vivian at SIS, who was familiar with 'the GRANDE set-up', would be the most suitable person to be told.[1]

Major Richard Constantine Clively MC @ Richard Gearing had been sent to Estonia for the Foreign Office in 1920.[2]

> Born in Russia [in 1892], son of a British diplomat. He was commissioned into the South Lancashire Regiment and then served in the Tank Corps [16th Tank Brigade] in the First World War, reaching the rank of Temporary Major. He became involved in intelligence work against Russia from 1921 and joined Section D in December 1938 at a salary of £600 p.a., becoming head of the Russian and Polish section. He was [one of twenty-five officers] sacked by the new SOE in September 1940 but by 1943 he was head of the Russian section of the Ministry of Economic Warfare.[3]

MI5 presumed that Grand was Colonel Laurence Douglas Grand RE, the subject of a registry file which had now gone missing, who had formed Section D (for Destruction) in April 1938 acting on orders from Admiral Sir Hugh 'Quex' Sinclair, then 'C' at SIS. By December 1939, it consisted of forty-three officers, excluding secretaries and other ancillary staff. On 22 July 1940, along with SO2, it was subsumed by SOE. On 14 February 1942 Tar wrote to Luke:

> The name of GRAND is familiar as in the early days of the war a man named Major GRAND was running a sabotage organisation in S.I.S. It seems quite possible that this may be the same one as referred to in your note of 11.2.42. The man CLIVELY may possibly be identical with a man who was at one time working in the Department of Overseas Trade. However, a look up might help in this direction.[4]

On 28 February 1942 Luke reported on his meeting with BALLOON about Cliveley:

> Apparently CLIVELEY was at one time employed by 'Centrosous England Limited', the leading lights of which were a man called Scriapp and Weiss. Later this company became merged in Russo British Grain Limited of Arcos.[5]
>
> GRANDE [sic] was a friend of CLIVELEY's who operated on the Baltic Exchange and the Stock Exchange. CLIVELEY then married a divorcee with two children, and for some time lived on his wife. He went into business on his own, but lost any money he had on some options which he put on grain in Liverpool.
>
> During the last war he was in Baku and dealt in furs. Both he and GRANDE [sic] are friends of a man called Reynell who is supposed to be half Japanese.[6]

THE GRAND, CLIVELEY AND POSTNIKOW AFFAIR

On 21 March 1942 he informed Vivian about BALLOON, Postnikow and Clively, much of which was taken from his 17 March report. Given that Clively was staying with BALLOON, and that he knew nothing of BALLOON's work for MI5, Luke felt it inadvisable to approach him. He remarked, 'I believe however that he and BALLOON have discussed the affair many times together and that both are convinced that there is dirty work somewhere ... .'

> I am passing this information to you for what it is worth, and am sure you will fully appreciate the particular necessity for secrecy in this matter. I feel that if Grand and/or Clively have conspired in any way, you may wish to make some investigations, unless you feel that the 'affaire Grand' with all its mysteries should now be regarded as dead and buried.[7]

Major R.C. Clively (Russian Section) arranged for the return of Emperor Hailie Selassie to Egypt as a focus for future revolt but in June 1940 Grand concluded that although there had been some success in raising support from local chiefs, it was pointless trying to organise anything on a larger scale unless full support was given by the British government for raising a large-scale revolt against Italian occupation.[8]

Chapter 17

'It is clear that B is in debt.'

Throughout this time BALLOON's debts continued to accumulate, causing consternation within MI5 as he had been dealing with a firm of money lenders. Luke had made enquiries about them but pointed out that 'it is difficult to see how I can worm any further information out of BALLOON himself without revealing the fact that his correspondence is intercepted'.[1] Unbeknown to him, mail sent to 34 Crompton Court, Brompton Road, London SW3, had been intercepted over the past few months under a Home Office warrant.

Based on a letter BALLOON had received from his solicitors, Attenborough's of New Court, Lincoln's Inn, Luke inferred that he was probably in considerable debt. The letter concerned a claim he had made against Air France, 'possibly in respect of his forced landing when he was shot down returning from Paris in May 1940'. Jack F. Attenborough had also sent him a cheque for £15, which was obviously a loan.

Further correspondence between BALLOON and his creditors revealed that he owed one month's garaging of his car, and an outstanding bill from Messrs Ollard & Ollard, solicitors of Wisbech, who wrote, 'Payment of outstanding bills and costs is proceeding. I expect you will be receiving an authority to sign for us to obtain the security from the bank, and when this is done, the matter should be cleared up quickly.' Luke stated that he was unable 'to interpret the implications of this letter'. The same day Ollards sent another letter to William Evans, gun maker of Pall Mall, regarding two twelve-bore shotguns once belonging to Metcalfe's father, giving Evans authority to lend one to him. He also owed £37 11s.1d to his tailor, Huntsman of 11 Savile Row, for two suits they had supplied in April; and the rubber company, Messrs P.B. Cow of Streatham, was pressing for payment of £2 still outstanding.

Lloyds Bank South Kensington Branch wrote on 4 October that his account was in credit, but that cheques were probably outstanding which would result in a deficit, noting that they would be made good the following Monday. On 12 November Attenboroughs wrote again in connection with the 'Balloon' Trust, in which Williamson Hill & Co., solicitors of Bedford Row, asked them why it was necessary to raise such a large sum as £1,500. The fact that the name 'Balloon' Trust had been used suggests that Metcalfe had set it up, and knew his codename, something to which agents were not normally privy.

On 26 November, Bowmakers, a hire-purchase company, sent a letter acknowledging receipt of BALLOON's post-dated cheque for 16 December 1941

'IT IS CLEAR THAT B IS IN DEBT.'

for £8 9s.6d which they would retain as collateral security for the instalments due for October and November; and a letter from insurance brokers G. Poland of Iver, Buckinghamshire, on 4 December revealed that he had had difficulty paying for his car insurance on the date when it was due.

In the New Year Attenborough's enclosed a cancelled promissory note for £100 which he had signed on 30 December 1940 in favour of a Mrs M.S. Doble of 398 Gloucester Road, St Mark's, Cheltenham, saying that even though they were not really in a position to pay off the balance of a loan from her (since Luke presumed that BALLOON had no funds to meet the obligation) they had done so anyway. They had also not been able to arrange the loan they had been trying to obtain for him, as Mr Starling to whom they had written, had expressed a preference to invest his money in Defence Bonds. Exactly who these people were or their connection with BALLOON is unknown.

The Cathkin Laundry pointed out that they could not extend further credit as he already owed £4 10s.1d for an unpaid laundry bill. The next day he received an account from Bowmakers for £4 4s.9d which had been due on 16 December. On 7 January B.S. Lyle Ltd wrote asking that he call on them. He still owed £23 11s.4d to Messrs Offord & Sons, Ltd, a garage in Kensington, to which he had paid £5 towards his account, and Messrs Fox & Nicholl of Surbiton, to whom he still owed £1. As Luke pointed out, 'It will be remembered that on August 22nd, 1941 he had received an account from the same people for £52 12s.1d. It can therefore be assumed that he had made no effort in the intervening time to reduce this indebtedness.' (Note: £1 in 1940 was worth £18.59 in 2021.)

Also in January he received a receipt for £5 from B.S. Lyle Ltd, which had been credited to their account. He noted that he would try to visit them in the near future. The following day Attenborough's wrote thanking him for his cheque for £5, a partial repayment of the £15 lent the previous July. As the report noted, 'They concluded this letter by saying that they would make enquiries as to the best Counsel to engage in the proposed proceedings in Chancery.' Luke discussed the matter with Sir Edward Reid who informed him that it would be extremely difficult for him to inspect B.S. Lyle's accounts, but suggested that he approach Superintendent Burt 'who might know something of the firm'. Luke impressed upon Burt that the matter was 'exceedingly delicate'. Burt assured him that he would do nothing without first consulting him 'and fully realised that under no circumstances should any action be taken which would lead to BALLOON's discovering that enquiries are being made'. It was also necessary to avoid approaching HM Customs & Excise 'who are presumably entitled to inspect the books of money lending concerns of this kind', because it would mean taking someone else into their confidence. Luke's report of 17 January 1942 stated that

> the best suggestion put forward was that someone from Scotland Yard should go to LYLE's and say that they were endeavouring to trace £5 notes which they believed had been paid to a West End money lending concern. It seems likely that BALLOON paid to Messrs

LYLE £5 in cash. In this way his name his name [*sic*] might crop up along with a lot of others at the interview and it might be possible for the officer carrying out the interview to discover the amount of his indebtedness. Even if this part of the investigation was successful I can not see how BALLOON could be approached without running the risk of disclosing the fact that we intercept his correspondence, *and I can not impress upon you too strongly my conviction that this disclosure would react most unfavourably on our future relations with this valuable agent and on his work.*[2]

Luke had repeatedly sought assurance from BALLOON about his financial position, who brazenly told him that he didn't owe any money '[A]nd that with the recent increase in salary we have paid him he can live quite comfortably without running into debt'. Of course, this was a barefaced lie. Luke suggested to Tar that he take BALLOON out to lunch and express their appreciation for the work he had done for them. During the course of their conversation he would impress upon him that their agents needed to be perfectly frank about their financial position so that they might be able to 'help them out of any difficulties they might be in. It is possible that a direct appeal of this kind might bring BALLOON to confess his present straits.' As Tar observed, 'It is clear that B is in debt' but since Luke had already spoken to him about his finances he was not going to bring it up again. But the following day Luke tackled him again, explaining that he expected to be informed immediately if he should run into difficulties. Without batting an eye BALLOON assured him that 'his circumstances were quite easy and that he owed no money'.

On 22 January H.V. Hughes of HM Inspector of Taxes, Covent Garden District, wrote to Attenborough's regarding BALLOON's outstanding tax bill for £27 17s.0d. In February Luke forwarded to Tar information which Wilson had received through commercial enquiry agents regarding BALLOON's financial situation which Wilson noted 'may help you in talking to Balloon about his finances without blowing the H.O.W':

> He has no effects other than personal and is not known to possess means beyond his salary as secretary to British Graphitised Metals Co. Ltd. The company are concerned with the manufacture of a metal mainly used for bearings and to have their equipment at the works of Johnsteads Ltd, Rainsford Road, N.W.10. It is a respectable concern but their activities are only on a small scale ... .
>
> 14 County Court Judgements were registered between 1929 and 1938 against [Remainder redacted] at various addresses at Tidworth, Aldershot, Shorncliffe and Bracknell.[3]

Luke told Tar on 14 February 1942 that he felt it would be better if BALLOON opened up to him of his own accord. He again suggested that taking him to his club some evening and after 'sufficient lubrication' he might elaborate on how

Right: *Dicky Metcalfe, double agent BALLOON.* (Crown Copyright © TNA KV2/1080)

Below: *Dicky Metcalfe, 18 March 1933.* (Getty Images, PA Images Archive)

Above left: *Lt. Col. Herbert Metcalfe.*

Above right: *Loyal Regiment, officer's cap badge.* (Ian Kelly Militaria)

Left: *Vincents of Reading.* (Grace's Guide, 1920s; public domain)

Friedl Gärtner. (Dennis Wheatley Museum; unknown origin)

Fritzi Stottinger (Friedl Gaertner). (Dennis Wheatley Museum; unknown origin)

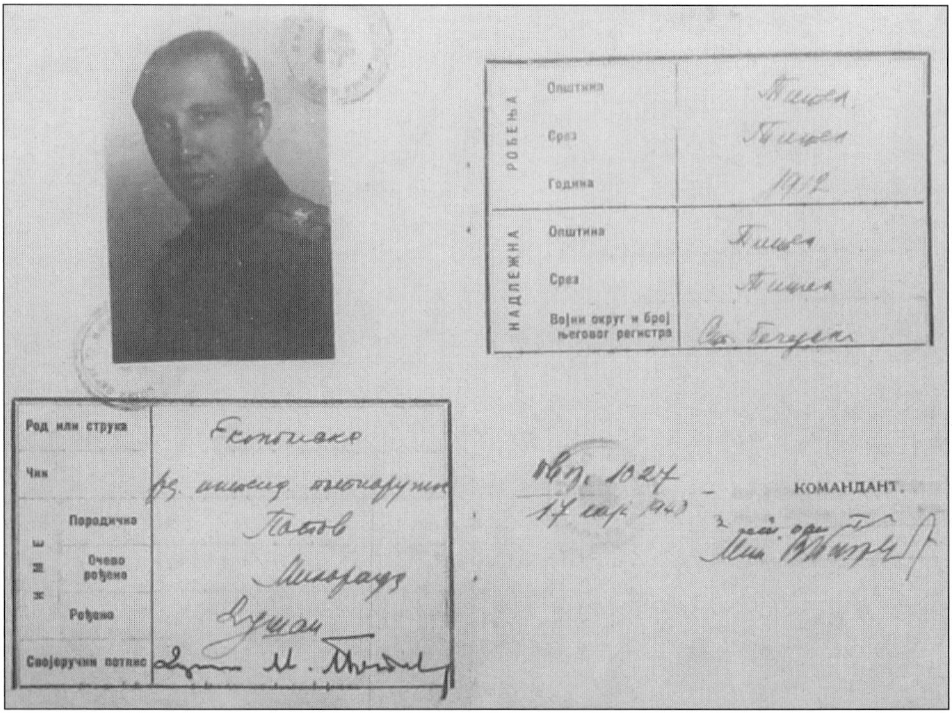

РОЂЕЊА
Општина
Срез
Година 1912
НАДЛЕЖНА
Општина
Срез
Војни округ и број његовог регистра
Род или струка
Чин
ИМЕ
Породично Попов
Очево рођено
Рођено
Својеручни потпис
КОМАНДАНТ.

Duško Popov. (Crown Copyright © TNA KV2/847)

Registration Certificate No. 1022652
Issued at Piccadilly Place. W1
on 5th February 1941
Name (Surname first in Roman Capitals) POPOV Douchan
Alias Dusan
Left Thumb Print (if unable to sign name in English Characters).
Aliens Registration Office Metropolitan Police 7.2.41 Piccadilly Place
Signature of Holder.

Nationality Jugo Slavian
Born on 10/7/12 in Telet Serbia
Previous Nationality (if any) Serbian
Profession or Occupation Representative
Single or Married Single
Address of Residence Cumberland Hotel W.1.
Arrival in United Kingdom on 22/8/1928
Address of last Residence outside U.K. 98, Boulevard Sevastopol
Government Service
Passport or other papers as to Nationality and Identity.
Issued Belgrade 16/11/40.

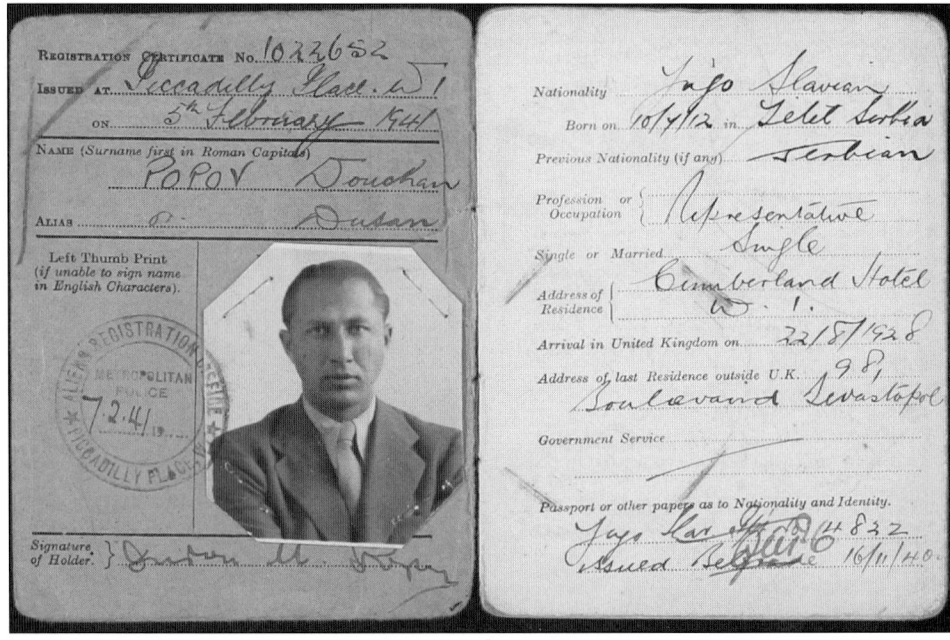

Double agent TRICYCLE, certificate of registration. (Crown Copyright © TNA KV2/862)

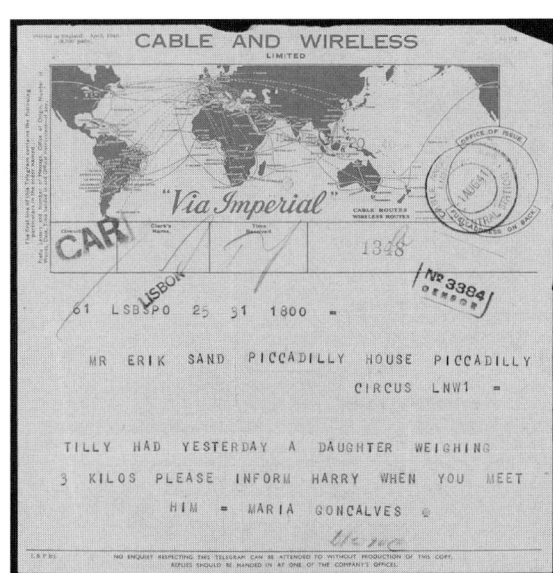

Above left:
R.L. Boissevain.
(John Tepper Marlin)

Above right:
TRICYCLE's telegram. (Crown Copyright © TNA KV2/846)

Right: *BALLOON'S debts.* (Crown Copyright © TNA KV2/1075)

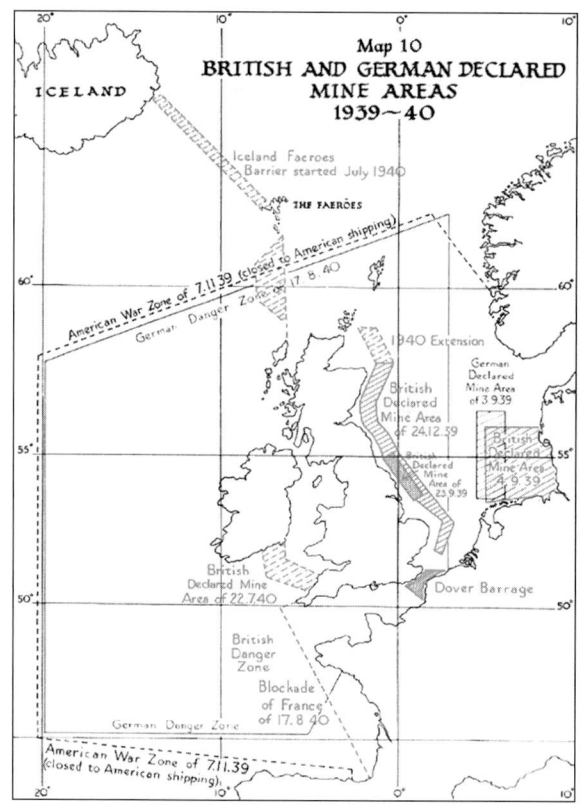

Left: *Minefield.* (Peter C. Smith)

Below: *Vesely V-42 submachine gun.* (Royal Armouries, Leeds); (Small Arms Review)

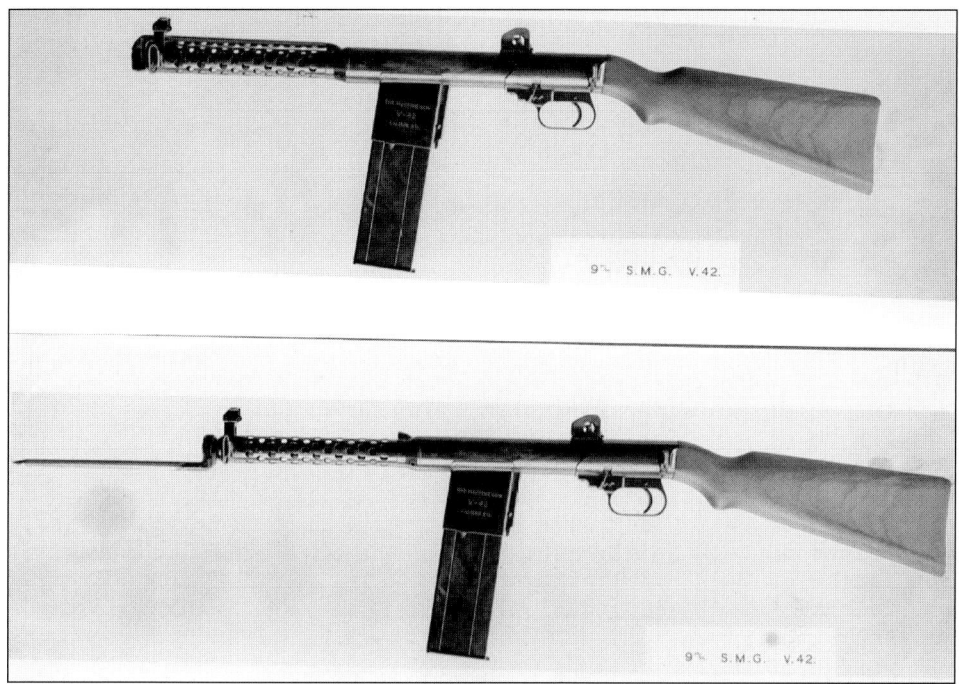

Vesely (02). (Royal Armouries, Leeds)

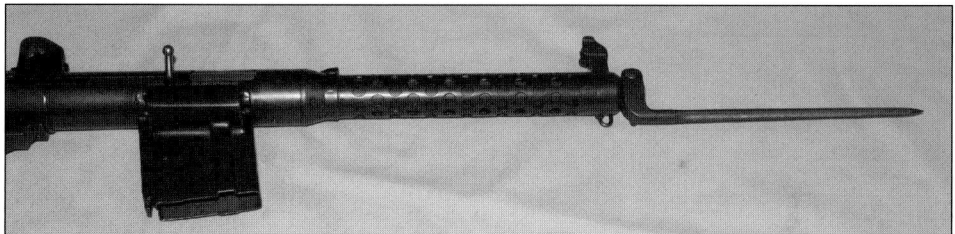

Above: *Vesely (03)*.
(Royal Armouries, Leeds)

Right: *Vesely (04)*.
(Royal Armouries, Leeds)

THE
V.A.P. MACHINE CARBINE 9 M/M.

TYPES

V-42 Infantry Model
V-43 Paratroop Model.

Data

Gun and Magazine:
Length of gun without bayonet	33"
Length of gun with bayonet	41½"
Length of barrel	10"
Length of Magazine	8½"
Weight of V-42 Model with bayonet ...	6 lbs. 14 ozs.
Weight of V-42 Model without bayonet ...	6 lbs. 10 ozs.
Weight of V-43 Model with bayonet ...	7 lbs. 3 ozs.
Weight of V-43 Model without bayonet ...	6 lbs. 15 ozs.
Weight of Bayonet	4 ozs.
Weight of full Magazines	2 lbs. 5⅔ ozs.
Weight of Magazine Empty	13⅔ ozs.
Capacity of Magazine (Box Type) ...	60 rounds.

Rate of Fire (Lower Rate) -   900 rounds per minute.
"   "   "   (Higher Rate) - 1,000   "   "   "

Sights:
Foresight is of the blade type (adjustable laterally)

Backsight is of the open type adjustable to 100, 200 and 300 yards.

These sights are for use when firing from the shoulder, and are accurate up to and including 300 yards.

Ammunition:
The carbine fires British, American, Finnish, German, Italian and other makes of 9 m/m Parabellum ammunition satisfactorily.

P.T.O.

Vesely specs. (Royal Armouries, Leeds)

'IT IS CLEAR THAT B IS IN DEBT.'

he'd managed to get into these difficulties, if he could steer the conversation in the right direction. Failing that, they would have to approach him directly and make reference to Wilson's report.[4]

But it was not until 2 March that BALLOON had come clean and explained what he proposed to do about his finances. He admitted owing money to his tailor, and the hire purchase company for his car, but reiterated that he would be able to pay them off without any difficulty, and was confident that by the following year he could clear himself of his debts so didn't need MI5's help. Luke reminded him that

> it was a confirmed rule in this particular service that agents should always divulge to their masters their exact financial position. I told him that recently I had sent a list of agents and others in whom I am interested to a firm of financial enquiry agents, and had discovered amongst other things that he, BALLOON, had had several County Court Judgements up to and including 1938.

It was an extremely delicate situation, but he was confident that without divulging that his correspondence was being intercepted, he was able to indicate that they knew a lot about his financial position. He hinted that whatever he had estimated of the amount of BALLOON's debt, his superiors might be prepared to pay it off by some salary deductions. He pointed out

> that as long as he had debts of this kind his position vis-à-vis this organisation could hardly be satisfactory, and that for his own sake it would be much better if he produced a completely frank statement of his financial position which would only be seen by myself and if I think it necessary, Major Robertson.

But he remained sceptical that BALLOON would have ready for him the list he'd promised of his personal debts by the time he returned from Cambridge. He was also 'extremely doubtful' whether the amount borrowed from the money lenders would be included, or the fact that he would admit to pawning something recently. He added:

> Any experience I have with this type of person convinces me that in money matters it is quite impossible for them to lay their cards on the table. However we shall probably be able to ease his position very considerable [*sic*], and if we provide him with a little extra money, we shall be able to tell from the products of the H.O.W. whether or not he is clear of his debts to money lenders. I should imagine his indebtedness does not exceed £200, and this being so we might arrange with him that in future his weekly remuneration would be reduced to £5 per week, the balance being used to pay off the amount advanced by us. Any money which he would otherwise have received

from the Germans will also be used to this end. Later on if all goes well, and if the H.O.W. produces evidence that he has not run up further debts, we might raise his salary to the £7 level.[5]

BALLOON told Luke that when his father died his 'affairs were in rather an involved and unsatisfactory state', meaning that he was unable to derive the £200 or £300 per annum from his estate. He expected that in five years' time any liabilities would be paid off, but some of the money would be given to his sister who was not a beneficiary under the will. Luke observed, 'If this is true it is an interesting sidelight on BALLOON's character.'[6] He lived up to his word by providing a note on 16 March showing that he owed £313 19s.8d.[7]

Chapter 18

Correspondence

On 18 January 1942 BALLOON received a letter from Mrs Charles Wilson (signed Gwen) of Place Farm Manor, Tisbury, Wiltshire, enclosing a letter addressed to 'My wicked Dosko', in which she asked 'My dear Dicki' [*sic*] to forward to 'that evil Dosko' in the United States. 'Gwen' or 'Gwennie' was Gwendoline K. Wilson *née* Radcliffe, born in Devon on 22 November 1914, employed as a welfare worker with AEF Clubs (although her letter says she ... was 'now a complete little housewife'), and the wife of Army officer Charles Wilson, as well as one of TRICYCLE's erstwhile girlfriends.[1]

The letterhead bore the cap badge of what appears to be the 4th/7th Royal Dragoon Guards, an armoured cavalry regiment, so it must be assumed that Charles Wilson was an officer in that regiment. Luke forwarded it to Tar on 24 January noting that 'During the course of his visits to this country, and prior to this very attractive and somewhat unprincipled lady's marriage ...TRICYCLE spent a good deal of time with her'. And while her letter to TRICYCLE was 'perfectly discreet', he thought that the following extract to BALLOON was worth noting: 'Hope spying, rum-smuggling, dope-running, white-slaving, gun-selling etc. is paying well.'[2]

Since BALLOON didn't know TRICYCLE's whereabouts and was away for the weekend, Luke proposed having him return the letter to Mrs Wilson. But when Ian Wilson (no relation) saw him on the afternoon of 26 January, 'He made no reference to the fact that GWEN had asked him to forward a letter to TRICYCLE.'

When Wilson saw BALLOON at Imperial House on 7 March he suggested that he write three separate single-page cover letters as he had a lot of traffic; however, BALLOON preferred to write one single-page letter and one two-page letter. Wilson noted

> He has not for a very long time past written a two-page letter, as the practice was discontinued because it might look suspicious to a censor that one side only of two pages should be used, instead of both sides of a single page. As it seemed quite natural that, after a long and apparently successful career of letter writing, an agent might become slightly careless and take that sort of risk, I agreed to the two-page letter, and Major Robertson subsequently confirmed that he saw no objection to it.[3]

Also that day he informed Luke that

> BALLOON handed me yesterday for you the attached letters relating to UZELAI. I don't quite follow their significance.
>
> BALLOON told me that he had asked UZELAI to introduce him to BARRA [Spanish military attaché], but UZELAI had claimed only a slight acquaintance with BARRA and did not seem keen. In fact BALLOON says UZELAI knows BARRA well. He can, however, get an introduction through a different channel.
>
> I again warned BALLOON that his job here was to contact BARRA but not to try and investigate things.[4]

Those letters are not included in BALLOON's files; nor is Uzelai's file available but he may be the Spanish painter José Maria Uzelai who had sought refuge in England in 1938.

The manager of the Midland Bank, Brompton Road informed BALLOON that they had received £375 from Francisco Barroso dos Santos via their overseas branch and invited him to come to the bank and bring his passport 'for identification purposes'. BALLOON handed Wilson the letter when they met on 10 March, which provoked the comment later that it had not been intercepted by the Home Office warrant:

> BALLOON took the view that if he was really an enemy agent he would be terrified of receiving this letter because he would think that the bank manager's request for him to call bringing his passport was intended to trap him, or at any rate investigate his movements as far as ascertainable from his passport. He handed me his passport which as he himself said might well arouse suspicion.

His passport had been issued in 1931 when he was an Army officer, but that description had been struck out and another photograph of him in mufti dated March 1940 had been added describing him as a 'Designer and Secretary': 'The passport shows considerable travel abroad, including the drawing of money in Germany in August 1937; a visit to Holland in March 1940 and again in April 1940, and to France in June, 1940.'

Sir Edward Reid didn't attach any particular importance to the bank's approach, putting it down to either a probable miscommunication by the Portuguese bank, or a different clerk handling the payment. There was also the likelihood that they were poaching customers from other banks by trying to induce BALLOON to open an account at their branch. The bank was unlikely to investigate, so Reid thought that if BALLOON went to the branch nothing undue would happen, and it was unnecessary that the bank's head office be approached. Wilson added that, had Reid not known about BALLOON, the method of payment would have caused him to make enquiries. 'I think when ~~enlarging~~ acknowledging this payment BALLOON should express great terror and should most strongly urge that a safer means of payment should be set up.'[5]

CORRESPONDENCE

Luke commented: 'I feel that Balloon's reaction to this mode of payment should be dictated by reason of expediency & policy from our own point of view. It is not reasonable to suppose that the Germans are aware of the change in mode of payment.' He instructed BALLOON to obtain payment of the cheque by asking that his own bank – Lloyd's Bank, South Kensington Branch, Onslow Square – collect the money for him: 'This seemed to be the most reasonable method to adopt and met with Sir Edward's approval. The latter pointed out that the bank would not make any investigations in connection with the payment from the security point of view, as this would always be left to him.' Reid reported that the payment had been ordered by a telegram sent on 5 March from the Banco Pinto e Sotto Mayor of Lisbon. 'They told me that it was not included in the list of payments which I have received because it was not debited until BALLOON claimed the money. This ought to appear in the next list which I have.'[6]

When BALLOON met Luke on 17 March he again rejected MI5's proposal of help to pay off his debts, saying that by accepting their offer he would be regarded adversely. He wanted to be allowed to 'settle his debts himself ... within a reasonable time' using the money he was paid. Luke told him that 'of course the arrangement really amounted to a funding of his salary and commission, and pointed out that there was every prospect of our being reimbursed within two years ... . It is quite obvious that my proposal to settle his debts is hurting his self-respect ... .' He proposed that BALLOON should be allowed to pay any additional sum he liked from time to time against their advance. And 'if after receiving ten per cent commission of the German payment of which commission we would keep half, he should wish us to keep the whole ten per cent, then he can do so. If in this way he is able to reimburse us more quickly, then it would be to his credit.'[7]

***

Cowgill reported that while TRICYCLE was in Lisbon he'd not told the Germans anything which would have led them to believe that GELATINE knew BALLOON or vice-versa. TRICYCLE was also unaware that GELATINE had been given the address of Maria Gonzalves De Azevedo, Calcado de Desterro 5 IIc, Lisbon; however, Maria had left Lisbon while he was last in England.

> TRICYCLE, who does not know that GELATINE has re-established contact, suggests that he should write to BALLOON who would answer his letter enquiring about YVONNE. TRICYCLE would reply evasively to BALLOON's letter, but at the same time would write to GELATINE giving her one of his cover addresses in Lisbon, viz: LUCILLA MARTINS, Rua da Rosa 164.
> TRICYCLE further suggests that GELATINE should, in the letter she writes to this address, explain in detail how she received it.[8]

Handwritten underneath: 'All this seems unnecessary as Gelatine has regained contact.'

Wilson wrote to Marriott on 24 March about the correspondence BALLOON had received from Portugal stating that the only Portuguese address he had was that of Francisco Barroso dos Santos of Suosa & Campos Lda., 162A Rua da Rosa 164A, Lisbon [sic], who was the antique dealer 'on whose behalf payments are made, and the letters are no doubt written as cover for payments.'[9]

> In the early stages of July 1941, BALLOON received payment through the Swiss Bank Corporation by order of Paulo Pinto-Lima which was another cover address, but no address was mentioned. I doubt if this will be repeated because Barroso dos Santos seems now to be established as the pay-master and all subsequent payments have been made through the Midland Bank at his order. The other communications have been letters or Christmas cards which gave no address of origin, the two Christmas cards being signed by names which do not link up with the cover address, and the letters being signed merely 'Elizabeth'. There does not therefore seem to be very much risk of the name and address of José NUNES appearing on a letter addressed to BALLOON from Lisbon, and therefore blowing BALLOON because from our proposed course of action the Germans will realise in time that we have discovered NUNES' name and address by catching an out-going letter of BALLOON in the censorship.[10]

Marriott instructed Wilson to 'carry on accordingly' and write a suitable letter 'which can be referred to in future correspondence, notionally catching it and putting the addressee on the Security list'. The attached letter dated 24 March 1942 to Masterman via Cholmondeley reads as follows:

> GELATINE and BALLOON do not in fact know of each other's existence, and it was not intended that the Germans should think they they [sic] were in contact. TRICYCLE was instructed accordingly and seems to have carried out his instructions. No action seems to be necessary. GELATINE has re-established contact, and I am by no means sure that the reference to Yvonne in the cover letter to BALLOON from Elizabeth dated 28.1.42 was really intended to have particular significance. At the most it may have been a fishing expedition to ascertain whether BALLOON had heard of GELATINE.

For convenience I set out the text of 'Elizabeth's' letter which is as follows:

> Dear Dickie,
> Yesterday I have been in Lisbon and have posted a letter for you. I hope you will have received it by now. If I write you today once more

it is because I request you a favour. Please be so kind and write me the address of Charly and Yvonne. It is awfull, [sic] but I must have lost it, though they wrote me their in their last letter. [sic] It is too stupid, but it must have come off when I ordered my correspondence last time. Well I have to write to Yvonne at any rate, because I want to tell her to help me settling a lot of affairs.

Many thanks, dear Dickie and let me soon hear some news of you. With hearty greetings and wishes I am always,

Yours sincerely,
Elizabeth.[11]

Masterman noted that 'I think we have got to be careful about this. If this reference was a "fishing expedition" might not Balloon ask what is significant to pay much attention to his other letters? [sic] Are we satisfied that Germany will not be suspicious if Balloon just passes it over without comment?' Marriott agreed with Wilson and thought that 'no further action is necessary or desirable. Balloon pays no attention to the text of cover letters and as he does not know Yvonne [GELATINE] I think it would be dangerous for him to make any show any interest.'

Elizabeth was 25-year-old Elisabeth Sahrbach, Karsthoff's 'beautiful blonde' secretary with whom he was having an affair, and in 1944 became his wife. August Kraatz's file on the personnel of KO Portugal describes her as MAUSI @ LUDOVICA, in her late thirties, with a slightly crooked right shoulder, and a 'Dangerous intriguer' who exerted 'considerable influence on her husband and was mainly responsible for the bad running of the KO'. OSTRO's file gives her name as Sauermann, and that she had a passport in the name of Sarbach [sic].[12] TRICYCLE recorded that, 'Her attitude towards me is very friendly and I am sure she will, the same as KARSTHOFF, always give me her strong support. She has an excellent memory.'[13]

To Marriott's relief, Cowgill told him on 27 March that Cecil Gledhill, the SIS Head of Station in Lisbon, had informed them that the José Nunes of BALLOON's post-box was not connected with José Nunes of 10, Rua dos Fanqueiros, Lisbon, the name and address found on Schatz:

Neither the name nor the address, José NUNES, Rua Conseilheiro, 26, Arautes Pedroso, Lisbon [sic – Arantes], have been used by the Germans in any communications that they have made to BALLOON, and I have therefore thought it preferable to take the seemingly slight risk of this happening in the future and thus casting doubt on BALLOON's outgoing letters had ever been caught in Censorship.[14]

According to Theresa Clay in B1c[15] Charles Herbert Schatz was British born of German parents, and had been living in Portugal since October 1941.[16] There he was in touch with a Miss Ahlers who worked as secretary for Van Der Vliet, 'the suspect K.L.M. Manager in Portugal'.[17] Marriott replied to Cowgill on 30 March 1942:

> Mention has been made at the Twenty Committee ... that in a cover letter to BALLOON the enemy had mentioned 'Yvonne'. We have decided that BALLOON should not show any reaction to the use of the name 'Yvonne' as in fact GELATINE [a]nd BALLOON do not know of each other's existence, and it would seem from your letter of the 21st that TRICYCLE has carried out his instructions to indicate to the Germans that they were kept apart.
>
> I am by no means sure that the reference to 'Yvonne' in the cover letter was intended to have a particular significance, especially as the cover letter asked for the address of 'Charly' and 'Yvonne', and 'Charly' seems to have no meaning. Even if the letter was a fishing expedition to ascertain whether BALLOON had heard of GELATINE, the correct policy seems to be to take no notice of it.[18]

In December 1941 José Nunes, a clerk (i.e. sales assistant) in a fabric shop,[19] had been added to the Censorship Black List. According to a list of addresses in TRICYCLE's file, his Rua Conseilheiro address was a cover address used by LUDOVICO @ Major Albert Ludovico von Karsthoff @ Kremer von Auenrode, *Leiter* III, KO Lisbon.

Marriott told Cowgill that he had come to the conclusion that TRICYCLE was under suspicion:

> Anything which affects the position of TRICYCLE as an agent is obviously likely to have repercussions on BALLOON and GELATINE, and I think therefore that Wilson, the case officer who is now handling these two cases, should be given all material which might influence him in forming a correct estimate of the extent, if any, to which their position may have changed. I hope therefore that the efforts to get the FBI to produce complete copies of the TRICYCLE traffic will yield quick results.[20]

Wilson reported that BALLOON had written to the Francisco Barroso Dos Santos cover address on 31 March, but before the letter was sent to the GPO the following points needed to be dealt with:

1. Approval should be obtained at the Twenty Committee to the Statement included at the D.G.'s request that BALLOON had heard that Chiang Kai Shek has built up a very large reserve of petrol in China.[21]
2. BALLOON was always very anxious to include some detailed particulars of MTBs because he said the Germans might know

that his firm had been agents for British Power Boats Limited and would therefore expect him to have access to detailed specifications, even though these might not be completely up-to-date. BALLOON submitted particulars and these were approved for use, but I understand that Lt-Commander Montague [sic] commented that the particulars were very inaccurate. I therefore discussed the matter with BALLOON on the basis that it was essential that these particulars should be accurate because there was always the possibility that one of these boats might be captured and he ran the risk of blowing himself if he was found to have given false information. He said he was prepared to stake his life that his particulars were accurate, as they were taken from specifications his firm had had from the makers in or about 1939. He was convinced that the Germans were likely to have similar documents which they would have captured in Holland. He added that the British Power Boat models were now being made in America and Canada, whereas manufacture here was mainly of Vosper boats which might be different. Possibly this may account for the details he gave not being accurate, as his figures may have been compared with the Vosper figures. I think it would be as well to discuss this point with Lt-Commander Montague [sic] before the letter is despatched.

3. The information about MTBs on the cover letter to Santos breaks off in the middle and ends with the word 'Cont.' It is suggested that the rest of the particulars should not actually be despatched, but should in theory have been written on the back of a letter to José Nunes, also dated 31st March. A previous letter to Nunes has in theory been intercepted in censorship, and Nunes' address placed on the Security List. The fact that the continuation of the message would not reach the other side would indicate to them that a letter has been intercepted, and in time when no letters reach Nunes they will presumably discover which address has been found out.[22]

***

BALLOON had come up with a scheme for building a wireless transmitter, something he had sufficient knowledge to do if he had instructions and drawings, and suggested that he should ask the Germans to supply him with drawings and instructions sent by means of 'duff'. Having a wireless set would enable him to send at intervals 'blind', very short messages 'from different places on matters of supposed urgency', but not two-way traffic or long messages, which would be dangerous. Wilson thought the idea was a good one which they could make use of, but should be postponed 'until it would become apparent to BALLOON that the Germans had spotted the fact that one at least of his cover addresses had been blown'.[23]

Chapter 19

The BALLOON Traffic (Part 1)

MI5 received the following urgent telegram from Felix Cowgill on 13 April 1942:

> WE HAVE JUST HEARD THAT TRICYCLE HAS RECEIVED INTIMATION THAT BALLOON IS WORKING BADLY. HE (TRICYCLE) HAS BEEN ASKED IF HE CAN PUT PRESSURE ON BALLOON FROM HIS END.
>
> IF YOU WISH TO INFLUENCE TRICYCLE'S REPLY TO THIS SUGGESTION, WILL YOU PLEASE LET ME KNOW AS SOON AS POSSIBLE WHAT YOU WANT HIM TO SAY?[1]

Marriott replied the same day regarding the TRICYCLE traffic, pointing out to Cowgill that it was essential that they receive daily updates on him:

> In fact it is hardly too much to say that TRICYCLE is a vital link in our entire organisation. As you know there is not only the direct link with GELATINE and BALLOON, but as a result of Plan Midas there is a connection with TATE, and through TATE with most of the other double agents.

He telephoned Cowgill and asked him for the exact text of the 9 April message to which he was referring, which had been in Cowgill's possession since the previous day. It read as follows: 'IVAN 2 works badly. Can you put some pressure behind him from there?'

After Marriott had discussed it with Masterman and Wilson he suggested to Cowgill that the SIS representative in the US should be asked to arrange for TRICYCLE to transmit a message to the effect:

> Disappionted [sic] and surprised at IVAN 2's bad work. If you will tell me how his work is bad I will write and encourage him if you think it wise, but you should know that I have not written to him for sometime.

He told Cowgill that MI5 had drafted the message on the proviso that nothing relevant had taken place subsequent to the messages about IVI of 10, 12 and

THE BALLOON TRAFFIC (PART 1)

13 March.[2] Cowgill's information undoubtedly derived from the following decrypted ISOS traffic:

> 7.4.42. Berlin – Lisbon. LUDWIG – ANDREAS to LUDOVICO 1) IVAN II reports 66. very canty. More enerjetic [*sic*] approach most urgently recommended. Request comprehensive written opinion on our last communication. 2) Is W/T comminucation [*sic*] with IVAN I working? ...
>
> 9.4.42. Portugal – N.America. IVAN II works badly. Can you put some pressure behind him from there?
>
> 16.4.42. N. America – Portugal. Am disappointed and surprised with IVAN II bad work. If you will let me know what is wrong and if you think it wise I will write and encourage him. I have not been in contact with him for some time.
>
> 8.5.42. Portugal – N.America. Try to suggest IVAN II to work better. Informations are in-precise and bad to read.[*sic*]
>
> 14.5.42. N.America – Portugal. Have written to IVAN II very strong letters. Please tell me if his work does not get better.
>
> 20.5.42 Lisbon – Berlin. LUDOVICO TO LUDWIG for ANDREAS. Ref. your 139 of 7/4. IVAN replies 'Ref.1) I have written IVAN II a letter couched in strong terms. Please tell me whether his work is improving. Ref.3) I do not understand your message about Jonny. Please clarify at once, as I am probably making an important journey soon.[3]

On 17 April a peeved Marriott expressed his concern to Cowgill with the way communications had been handled between SIS and MI5:

> In view of the very delicate stage which has been reached in the TRICYCLE case, and in view of its close connection with the cases of BALLOON and GELATINE, I think it absolutely essential that we should be supplied at the earliest possible moment with copies of the messages received by and sent to TRICYCLE.
>
> In this connection, I am a little disturbed that the recent message about BALLOON, which was dated 9.4.42, did not come to our knowledge until 13.4.4.2, and, if I understood you correctly, did not reach you until 12.4.42. As this message was intercepted by R.S.S., it seems to me that it ought to have reached you much earlier than it did, and ought to have been available for our consideration correspondingly sooner.
>
> Since, for the time being at any rate, our interest in the TRICYCLE case is of paramount importance, do you not consider that it would

be preferable for particulars of TRICYCLE's code to be supplied to us and for the intercepts as and when received to be sent by R.S.S. direct to us?[4]

Cowgill replied the following day that 'the message first reached us from New York where no action was taken on it pending our advice. The R.S.S. copy did not reach us until later but there are many reasons why R.S.S. cannot get their material out more quickly than they do.'[5] He then quoted the text from the ISOS decrypt of 16 April (above). As he told Marriott on 19 April:

> Our representative in New York reports that, in a recent conversation, TRICYCLE stated that he himself gave to GELATINE the address of Maria GONCALVES DE AZEVEDO. It is clear, therefore, that the first sentence of paragraph 2 of our letter under reference [CX/ of 21.3.42] is incorrect, and, as you suggested, that TRICYCLE's memory is not as good as it might be.[6]

One indication that perhaps BALLOON's performance was not quite up to par was on 24 April when Wilson had discussed with him the various questionnaires he had received between 30 December 1941 and 14 March 1942. He pointed out to BALLOON that the information was useful for his own use, but much of the rest of it lacked focus and did not concentrate on answering the questions he had been asked. BALLOON accepted this criticism and 'promised to do his best to provide information which had a bearing on the questions'. Wilson attached copies of the questions to his report, and noted that 'the Service and other Departments have made only one suggestion towards answering these very numerous questions'.

> Lt Commander Montague [sic] did provide some information about the transports mentioned in the questions received on the 13th February. On the other hand certain of the information which has been obtained on these questions has been deleted by the approving authorities.
>
> Apart from the difficulty of keeping the agent well regarded by the Germans, without more assistance from the Departments in providing information, are they not losing opportunities of deceiving the enemy by their failure to put up suggestions? In this connection I draw particular attention to the question about the Night Fighting Device received on the 30th December 1941. Is it not possible for a technical expert to put up a story which would be at first sight reasonable, and which might cause the Germans to spend a great deal of time on useless research? This was regarded as a good objective in Plan Stench.[7]

In this context Wilson's comments made on 28 April regarding the document 'Concerning the POLICY STATEMENTS of the Various Departments' provide

THE BALLOON TRAFFIC (PART 1)

some useful insight into how the Double Cross Committee handled information requests to double agents:

> In the first place there are certain general aspects of the matter which have always to be in the mind of the case officer and which are not expressly referred to in the Policy Statements, although they may be borne in mind by those responsible for approving traffic.
>
> 1. The agent must report what from the nature of his position or movements should come into his personal knowledge. There are obviously bound to be times when this principle must yield to the vetoes imposed on certain subjects. In the case of a letter writing agent this difficulty can occasionally be overcome by the device of having his letter notionally stopped in the censorship, but this get-out does not apply to a wireless agent, and cannot be used to excess even by a letter writer, as to do so would blow all his cover addresses. In such circumstances is it not better that the agent should give false information than that he should render himself suspect by omitting all comment on a matter on which he ought to have been able to report?
> The War Office lay down that false statements should be avoided except when specially authorised for some important and particular reason. I am not sure whether the exception is meant to include the necessity of an agent reporting what he ought to be able to see.
> 2. When an agent is asked a question he should either answer it or there should be a good reason why he fails to do so. In the case of TATE difficult questions have largely been avoided by restricting his opportunities for travel etcetera. In the case of BALLOON this excuse does not apply, but some answers can be caught by the censors. However, I think it is better that a certain amount of false statements should be made in answering questions rather than that by one device or another the giving of an answer is avoided *systematically*. [added, handwritten]
> 3. As Mr Harmer [Major Christopher Harmer, B1a] pointed out on 14.4.42 as a result of what he learned from S.I.S., the intelligence value of details far exceeds any important general statements which on the face of them would appear to have very much more significance. There seems to be a distinct tendency on the part of the approving authorities to cut out factual details, while leaving in the vaguer and more general parts of material submitted for approval.
> I think consideration should be given to some of the questions which BALLOON has been asked since Christmas in connection with certain parts of the Policy Statements. The Air

Ministry now desire to impress upon the enemy our increased strength. BALLOON received a question on 9.2.42 asking how large was the out-put of aircraft in a given month or for several months separately. He proposed to answer this by saying that as far as he could find out about 2,300 aircraft of all types are made per month in this country. This figure in the course of being approved wa[s] stepped up to 4,000. BALLOON himself did not like using the figure 4,000 which he considered a great over-estimate, and as I was not aware that there was any particular desire that this piece of information should be given, BALLOON did not use it. The figure of 4,000 was approved on 3.3.42 and as the Air Ministry might like to alter the figure if it is now to be used, I suggest they should be asked if they now wish a figure to be given by BALLOON, and whether as part of their policy they would like regularly to give some stepped up production figure in the future.

BALLOON has not answered the questions he received on 30.12.41 relating to particular squadrons and groups. The Air Ministry might like to suggest an answer to some of these questions for the purpose indicated in paragraph 3e of their Policy Statement.[8] I appreciate the reluctance of the War Office to approving information of movements of forces from one theatre to another. In commenting on the questions received by BALLOON on 13.2.42 Colonel Graham said he would see what rumours he could release about embarkation leave having been granted to units. It would be useful if some such rumours could be released for BALLOON. The War Office says that normally our armament production, food stocks etcetera should be written up, and it would I think be better to give written up figures than none at all in reply to the questions BALLOON has been asked with reference to the out-put of tanks and in particular the 18 ton tank. *They can be given as hearsay.* [added, handwritten]

I see it is the policy of the H.D.E. [Home Defence Executive] that as much as possible is made of the factory dispersal scheme. Many of the questions received by BALLOON on 9.2.42 were directed to this matter and it would be most helpful if H.D.E. could suggest answers to some of these questions.

With deference I suggest that the questions received by BALLOON do present a suitable case for diverting bombing off to decoy factories, food dumps and similar erections, the possibility of which H.D.E. is always 'bearing in mind'.

In general it would be most helpful if the authorities concerned could indicate when questions are received whether,

THE BALLOON TRAFFIC (PART 1)

(a) they can be answered in a reasonably straight-forward manner,
(b) they must not be accurately answered, but are a suitable opportunity for passing misleading information,
(c) an answer must be avoided altogether.

Where technical information is sought such as the questions put to BALLOON about night fighting devices there may well be opportunities for causing the enemy to waste time on ineffective experiments by giving misleading information which could be done without much risk to the agent, because in such cases he can only be reporting hearsay.[9]

Wilson felt that BALLOON had been remiss in not providing enough true or false information when answering TRICYCLE's questions, citing as an example a question about iron and steel production 'but he has not even been given permission in replying, to refer to the Times Trade and Engineering Monthly Supplements'.[10]

On 2 May Marriott wrote to Cowgill about a message TRICYCLE was to send, suggesting that 'your representative' (Stephenson) be cabled with a request that TRICYCLE should:

(a) write a letter to BALLOON in the following terms:

I have heard from my buisness [*sic*] friends to whom I introduced you that they are not at all satisfied with the attention you have been giving to their buisness [*sic*] and that your advice has been both bad and vague. You must please pay particular attention to these people since the buisness [*sic*] has great possibilities for you and is even more important to me. It will be very unfair to me if my buisness relation-ships [*sic*] suffer because of your having failed to take full advantage of the opportunity I gave you.

The rest of the letter should be couched in ordinary personal terms.

(b) send over a message saying he has written a letter.

We think it desirable that an actual letter should be written but suggest that this be not posted but sent over by bag.[11]

When he met with Wilson on the evening of 5 May BALLOON admitted that there 'had been a falling off in the quality of his traffic in recent months'. Wilson re-read the traffic but didn't think that the quality had been affected, just that the reports sent in February were perhaps rather more of '*a gossipy character than his previous and subsequent traffic*'. Therefore, the Germans might be justified in complaining that his answers to questions before Christmas were not as detailed as the ones which TRICYCLE had given him in August 1941. That being said, the questions were more difficult for him to answer, but 'I still think however that the approving authorities and in particular H.D.E. ought to assist us far more than they have done in dealing with the unanswered questions'.

They discussed at length how BALLOON should answer TRICYCLE's 'letter of complaint'. Wilson warned him that 'possible indications' suggested that TRICYCLE might be under suspicion of being a controlled agent, but the Americans were treating him as a successful agent and not 'blown'. BALLOON agreed to write a very indignant letter in his own words 'refuting any suggestion that his work had been vague or bad', saying that if the Germans thought they had cause for complaint they should have rebuked him indirectly through TRICYCLE instead of writing to him directly.

Wilson thought that maybe BALLOON should suggest to the Germans that the reason why his work was 'not as good as expected' was because some of his letters were not getting through, possibly because British censorship was picking them up. That being the case, he might suggest that he would 'try and construct a transmitter if they would send him the necessary drawings'.

> When BALLOON receives TRICYCLE's letter he should I think answer it in case any trick questions are put to TRICYCLE asking whether TRICYCLE has received a reply. BALLOON questioned the wisdom of certain insertions made by the Admiralty in his information about torpedo bombers. I arranged with him that I would hold up his letter while I endeavoured to ascertain if the information proposed was likely to be so obviously false that it might jeopardise his position. I telephoned Lt Commander Montague [*sic*] about this point this morning and suggested that we should endeavour to obtain more technical information, which is being done.[12]

TRICYCLE's original letter sent to BALLOON from 530 Park Avenue, New York, dated 6 May 1942, was forwarded by W.H. Blyth, Section Vx of SIS, to Tar on 21 May and followed verbatim the text provided by Marriott on 2 May (see above), but without the typos. Signed 'Sincerely yours, DUSHAN', it concluded: 'Write me soon and let me know and all about you and what steps you intend taking to amend the bad impression you made in business.'[13] But when TRICYCLE wrote to BALLOON on 6 May he waited until the 14th to inform the Germans, which Tar assumed was because of the message he had received on 29 April. The Germans

> would naturally assume that he had. When, however, he received the further message of 8.5.42 he thought it as well to confirm that he had written to BALLOON, I am assuming that the outgoing traffic of 14.5.42 is intended to refer to TRICYCLE's letters of 6.5. and that he has not written a second letter as a result of receiving the message 8.5.42, consequently as far as BALLOON is concerned he will not have received a complaint that his reports are 'bad to read' but the complaint will appear to b[e] [dir]ected at the substance of his traffic.
>
> These points are I know somewhat trivial but it might be as well to inform New York of the position as we see it, so that they will not act inconsistently.

THE BALLOON TRAFFIC (PART 1)

Before I discuss TRICYCLE's letter with BALLOON himself I would like to disc[uss] with you at what date or on what lines he should refer to it in his correspondenc[e] with the Germans.

I understand from the G.P.O. that with the new summer Clipper Service operat[ing] twice a week airmail letters from New York are being delivered much more quickly than before. It might be wise therefore that BALLOON should write to the Germans before the end of May, although we had provisionally decided that he should cease to write for a period after writing a normal letter which it was intended should be dated about the end of this week.

Before the doubts on the position of TRICYCLE become acute it had been decided that the line BALLOON was to take on receipt of TRICYCLE's letter was to be indignation. We should perhaps discuss whether this line should be revised in the light of more recent information.[14]

But a teleprint Cowgill sent Marriott on 8 May 1942 was cause for concern:

WE HAVE JUST RECEIVED FROM AMERICA A CPOY [sic] OF A MESSAGE FROM BERLIN TO RIO DATED MARCH 20th (REPEAT MARCH 29TH 20TH) WHICH STATED THAT THEY (BERLIN) SUSPECTED TRICYCLE TO BE WORKING FOR BOTH SIDES AND RECOMMEND EXTREME CAUTION WHEN DEALING WITH HIM.
    SIMULTANEOUSLY WE HAVE HEARD FROM ANOTHER SOURCE THAT BERLIN DEFINITELY DECIDED ON MAY 5th (REPEAT MAY 5TH) THAT BOTH TRICYCLE AND BALLOON HAVE BEEN UNDER CONTROL SINCE THE FORMER ARRIVED IN AMERICA.
    THEY HAVE ORDERED LISBON TO SEND TO BERLIN ALL QUESTIONNAIRES ISSUED TO TRICYCLE OR BALLOON INCLUDING DUFF AND W/T, SINCE TRICYCLE SENT TO AMERICA. WHILE THIS INVESTIGATION IS PROCEEDING NO FURTHER AIR QUESTIONNAIRES ARE TO BE SENT EITHER TO TRICYCLE OR BALLOON. WE DO NOT KNOW THE REASONS FOR THIS DECISION BUT WE KNOW THE GERMANS IN BERLIN THINK THEM SOUND.
    WE HAVE WARNED OUR REPRESENTATIVE IN NEW YORK AND HAVE ASKED HIM TO REPEAT TO US IMMEDIATELY ANY FURTHER COMMUNICATIONS WHICH TRICYCLE MAY RECIEVE [sic] FROM LISBON.
DATE 8.5.42.
SENT AT 12.07[15]

BALLOON had not yet seen a copy of TRICYCLE's letter although Wilson had already warned him about the Germans' complaint of his work being 'bad and vague.' Therefore, the wording of his letter to Lisbon would have to be altered somewhat to be consistent with the wording of TRICYCLE's letter. He doubted whether it was wise for BALLOON to ask for specific instances, 'particularly as this is what TRICYCLE has done when they complained of inexactitude in some of the TRICYCLE reports'. He felt that BALLOON's vagueness in his reporting was actually in the Germans' best interest, since filling in the details might have made the reports read better, but would have been misleading.

In preparation for the forthcoming meeting between MI5 and SIS on 11 May Wilson wrote a report on 'TRICYCLE/BALLOON/GELATINE' in which he stressed that his conclusions were not final but were intended 'to set out for ... consideration ... certain interim opinions I have formed.' Many of them referred to TRICYCLE, but the references to BALLOON are worth mentioning:

> 3) Berlin do not seem, at least so far, to have come to the conclusion that BALLOON is also a controlled agent but they are suspicious of that possibility ... .
> 5) If the Germans believe that TRICYCLE only became controlled after his arrival in the USA it seems reasonable that they would not expect the FBI to have extracted from TRICYCLE information about BALLOON and GELATINE until the existence of such agents was indicated by the Traffic passing between the Germans and the FBI operator who is transmitting for TRICYCLE. For this purpose the dates of the relevant messages in the TRICYCLE Traffic are 10th, 12th, 13th and 21st March, 9th, 16th April, and (?) 1st May.[16]

In subsequent points, he stated that it was reasonable for the Germans to assume that information extracted from TRICYCLE by the FBI would be passed on to the British which would then enable them to arrest BALLOON and GELATINE. Any delay in following up on this may be as a result of a lengthy interrogation of TRICYCLE by the FBI, a lack of co-operation between the FBI and Britain, or 'incomplete clues having been extracted from TRICYCLE in the first instance, or the British having temporarily held their hand in arresting BALLOON or GELATINE for a period in the hopes that by watching them without interfering with their traffic, other members of the same spy ring might be identified'. Therefore, it was important that the Germans not realise that TRICYCLE's earlier traffic and also BALLOON's was controlled, causing them to re-evaluate their conclusions on their contents or giving them an insight into how British intelligence ran the traffic of controlled agents:

> 9a) There has been no obvious break in the continuity of BALLOON's Traffic since its inception; therefore if the Germans reach

THE BALLOON TRAFFIC (PART 1)

the conclusion that he is already controlled they are likely to conclude that he has been controlled from the beginning. Sooner or later they are likely to come to this conclusion if BALLOON's traffic is allowed to continue in its present style. We must therefore create a break in the traffic so that they may think that he became controlled only when the break took place. To protect ISOS BALLOON should ~~further~~ write at least one more normal letter before the break ... .

9d) If the BALLOON traffic is interrupted there should I suggest be a period of silence during which BALLOON is being broken, and when the traffic is resumed it should be completely different in character and obvious errors in the machinery of running the traffic should be made. For example some or all of the following steps might be taken.

The substance of the traffic should be what we would like the Germans to believe without much regard to whether they were likely to swallow the alleged facts. The style when setting out information should be completely different. There should be no indication that the contents of BALLOON's questionnaires were known. We might use an address already notionally blown in censorship. BALLOON might write from his own address instead of from an address extracted at random from the telephone book. He might use different note-paper. The post office might be instructed to use always the same censorship label which should not of course bear any of the numbers previously used. We might fail to hold letters for reasonable delay in censorship etc.

9d) iii The Germans would be likely to conclude that when GELATINE became a controlled agent BALLOON also became controlled if he had not previously been so; whereas for reasons indicated above it seems better that BALLOON should write at least one further letter before the break in his case ... . [see also below]

9f) It also has to be decided whether BALLOON should produce any reaction as far as the Germans are concerned to the letter of rebuke which TRICYCLE is supposed to have sent to BALLOON. In any case no such letter could have been received for some days yet so that one or more letters in the old style could be sent out first. Any reference to the indirect rebuke should be held over until after the temporary suspension of the traffic during which BALLOON is supposed to have been broken. Further, ~~that~~ BALLOON's reaction should not I think be indignant which was the policy intended before it was known that TRICYCLE was blown, Instead when the rebuke ~~might well be~~ is referred to in BALLOON's ~~letter about~~ 'blown' traffic he might be very apologetic and give promises to make up for his past bad vague reports by sending better reports. In fact his reports as a 'blown' agent would no doubt be worse than his previous reports; but he would naturally have tried to persuade us that he had sent nothing of importance before he came under control.

9g) ... Obviously if they [GELATINE and BALLOON] are to disappear from their normal activity we would have to provide for their future.

In the case of BALLOON at least, I do not think it would be too difficult to set him up under an assumed name, in some entirely different part of the war effort, and I am sure that he would at whatever personal inconvenience, co-operate in any scheme whatsoever, which might serve to assist, among other things, in protecting TRICYCLE's family in Yugoslavia.[17]

Masterman considered this 'an excellent analysis of the position in the light [?] of our present handling. It will have to be studied with great care at the conference.'

The same day BALLOON wrote two letters, one to Wilson, the other to Francisco Barroso Dos Santos in Lisbon, regarding the negative report he'd received from TRICYCLE (IVAN I). In his letter to Wilson he defended the quality of material he'd been forced to send saying that he found it 'rather disturbing' about the message which Ivan I received in America.

He, personally, has so much to lose if this set up is 'blown' and I sincerely trust that the message does not represent an awakening on the part of our German friends. I agree that it certainly looks like some sort of test on their part, but nevertheless my own personal opinion is that they have some justification for their changes of 'bad working' and 'vagueness". I know that your department and the powers that be have to look at the picture as a whole and adhere to a predetermined policy, but and as against this I can only judge within the confined limits of my own little sphere of activity, but I can say that I am definitely of the opinion that we have sent the Boche some very poor material for several months past. I am sure that if you compare what we are sending now against that which we were sending 9 month[s] ago, you will find a marked difference. Certainly, we can claim that it is now more difficult to get about the country and that internal security has improved? but we do not seem to have answered many of their questions. Surely it is possible to send correct information which is just suffic[ient]ly out of date to prevent enemy intercept action, and information about such things as night fighter techniques which has been so dealt with by our scientists as to cause more trouble than assistance. Also, I cannot believe that they really have any check on 'long term policy' questions such as special steel production which could be answered optimistically

THE BALLOON TRAFFIC (PART 1)

thereby causing despondency and alarm! After all the greater part of what I do collect is not passed and presumably the Germans are entitled to expect a standard of information which in point of fact they would actually be receiving if I was a spy.

He enclosed a copy of his proposed 'indignant reply to my Lisbon friends' for Wilson's consideration, saying that 'I do hope that you do not mind my writing like this but I do really believe what I have said.'[18] His 'indignant reply' to dos Santos read:

> Today I have received a letter from Ivan I from which it is obvious that you are complaining about my work and accuse me of working 'badly and vaguely'. I resent this most strongly and I consider your charges ~~most uncalled for~~ quite unfounded. Also, I am most annoyed that you should go behind my back to my friend and complain. Surely, the proper thing to ~~do is to~~ have done was to have written to me direct if you are not satisfied with my work.
>
> I have sent you much good material and I have always written regularly, never less than once a week and sometimes more. After all I risk my neck for £300 per quarter which is not wealth, and with the present petrol restrictions it is not so easy to get about as it was. Also it may not have occurred to you that I have a job to hold down and if I do not do this efficiently I might be called up.
>
> The least you can do is to write and give specific instances of what you call 'bad work', obviously much of my information must of necessity be incomplete but you have had plenty of hard work out of us. It does just occur to me that you may not have received all my letters. There has been talk in the press recently about tightening up Censorship, and the referen[ces] to secret inks in the American papers describing their spy trials over there may have resulted in more careful investigation of letters over here. If you have not been receiving my letters for Heaven's sake say so as I had better lay off for a bit if you haven't. At any rate the least that you can do is to write to me fully about the matter and you had better cable me if you have not been getting my letters. Just send a cable saying 'Money for silver not received' or something like that. But do let me know at once if you think that anything has gone wrong.[19]

The following day a meeting between MI5 and SIS to discuss the 'TRICYCLE/ BALLOON/ GELATINE' took place. Present were Cowgill and Foley of SIS and Marriott, Masterman and Wilson of MI5.

> It was agreed that future policy must depend on the correct interpretation to be placed upon the message which gave rise to the

teleprint dated 8.5.42. It transpired that this teleprint was an inaccurate report and that the statements that Berlin definitely decided on May 5th that both TRICYCLE and BALLOON had been under control since the former arrived in America and that the Germans in Berlin think their reasons for this decision sound, were far more definite than the facts justified. In the first place the reference in this context should have been to TRICYCLE only and not to TRICYCLE and BALLOON. Secondly it appeared that the true picture was that those dealing with airforce intelligence matters had reasons for suspecting that TRICYCLE had become a controlled agent rather than that they had decided that this was the case. The intentions of SIS were to continue and in fact improve the TRICYCLE traffic with a view to dispersing those suspicions, and they were averse to immediate adoption of a policy which made TRICYCLE irretrievably a blown agent, and which also caused BALLOON to become blown at least from a date in the comparatively near future. SIS emphasized the fact that the members of the German service responsible for running TRICYCLE and BALLOON would fight hard to persuade Berlin that they were still genuine German agents. There was additional evidence that BALLOON was at least not yet blown as it seemed that the Germans on 8.5.42 were alive to the fact that BALLOON's ink was compromised, were considering ways to give him an alternative means of communication, and in the meantime were going to send him no more punkt [microdots].

Major Masterman on the other hand stressed the importance if the Germans had in fact either already concluded or were going in future to conclude that TRICYCLE was blown, of taking all possible action to ensure that they would not come to the conclusion that TRICYCLE and BALLOON had been controlled from the beginning.

In the end the following decisions were come to:

1. TRICYCLE should for the time being proceed with his traffic as before, and if possible improve it.
2. The letters which GELATINE had written should not be dispatched.

As regards 2, the idea was that whether or not it was necessary to assume that TRICYCLE was blown, BALLOON ought to write at least two more letters. If after that he was to be run as a blown agent, a period of silence while he was being broken would be desirable, and if he was to be continued as a genuine agent the silence could be explained by illness or even left unexplained, leaving it to be assumed that a letter had been caught in censorship. In either case he would not refer to the letter of rebuke he is to receive from TRICYCLE until after this period of silence as it seemed likely that they found it necessary in America to have the instructions to send this rebuke repeated on the 8th May, presumably owing to the mutilation of the original instructions.[20]

Wilson concluded that they would reconsider the position within a couple of weeks by which time they might know what conclusion the Germans had reached.

***

GELATINE and TRICYCLE had a mutual friend in Maria Gonçalves de Azevedo. When TRICYCLE was last in Lisbon he stayed at Lucilea Martens' cover address at 164 Rua de Rosa, Lisbon, which was then a brothel area. Maria was described as 'a girl of 15 or 16, who is supposed to be Skoot's girl friend' [*sic*]; however, it was her mother who received the letters without Maria's knowledge.[21]

There was reluctance from MI5 to send GELATINE's messages to the new cover address supposedly obtained from TRICYCLE, because she couldn't have given TRICYCLE's new address unless she was controlled. They suggested that this had occurred immediately before the date of her letter to the new cover address 'which might react on ISOS'. Furthermore, the Germans would conclude that if she was controlled *ergo* BALLOON was too, if he hadn't been already. For reasons already stated 'it seems better that BALLOON should write at least one further letter before the break in his case.'

> If GELATINE does not write to the new cover address the Germans may find out it difficult to come to any definite conclusion and may think that the FBI did not bother to send over the cover address in spite of the statement in the traffic that they had done so, or that they did cause TRICYCLE to write to GELATINE with the new cover address and that we let this letter go through and caught GELATINE's resulting letter to the new cover address in censorship in order to provide evidence against her.[22]

On 22 May Tar wrote to Foley regarding his CX sent the previous day and the enclosed copy of TRICYCLE's letter to BALLOON. He presumed that TRICYCLE's message number 64 'is identical with the un-numbered message sent 2110 GMT 14.5.42 reading "Have written BALLOON very strong letter. Please tell me if his work does not get better".' He also referred to another unnumbered message, thought to be number 25 in the traffic dated 29.4.42, which read 'Wish you to write BALLOON his reports bad and vague', and number 27 dated 8.5.42 which read 'Try to sugge[st] BALLOON to work better. Informations [*sic*] are imprecise and bad to read.'

A report on a KO Portugal conference held in Lisbon on 26 May 1942, taken from the CSDIC interrogation in December 1945 of Oberleutnant August Friedrich Franz Kraatz @ George @ Krais, *Leiter* I T/Lw (Technik Luftwaffe) of KO Portugal in Lisbon in 1942, offers the following opinions of TRICYCLE (IWAN I) and BALLOON (IWAN II):

Note 1. <u>IWAN II</u>	The cover-name for a V-man of KRAEMER-AUENRODE's network, operating in LONDON and reporting chiefly on troop movements and camps in the neighbourhood of LONDON. He also sent some messages on South Coast defences. Prisoner [Kurrer] can give very little information about him, but he believes that IWAN II may have been a Serb. He does not think that IWAN II was very successful and did not regard his methods as being at all clever; for instance he used Ponal for secret ink, and sent his messages to MIETLITZ [*sic*] via accommodation addresses. According to Prisoner, MIETLITZ himself was probably working for the Allies too ... .
Note 2. IWAN I	Another V-man of KRAEMER-AUENRODE, operating in NEW YORK; not a single message came through from him during Prisoner's stay at LISBON. Prisoner believes he may have been a Yugoslav.
Note 4. WT contact.	The contact in America was IWAN I, mentioned above.[23]

Hauptmann Otto Kurrer was *Leiter* I/H Madrid in April 1941, before becoming *Leiter* I/H Lisbon in May 1942. He was replaced by Oberstleutnant Aloys (Alois) Schreiber, *Leiter*, Referat I/H, KO Lisbon because of inefficiency. Later he worked as a liaison officer between the SD and the Vichy government. According to OSTRO, he was 'well educated, from a very good family, but unfit for his task. Personally very agreeable ... [but] more unreliable than even the Portuguese.'[24] OSTRO stated that 'He [Kurrer] had a very disagreeable time with LUDOVICO, for LUDOVICO wanted to have him sent back to Berlin. But somehow he had excellent relations through his family with CANARIS ... . Eventually he had to go, because LUDOVICO ordered it, that he was not to take any further part in KOP [KO Portugal] work ... . Eventually he was called back to Berlin.'[25]

According to a 1946 interrogation report on Schreiber, 'At the time of SCHREIBER's arrival, the personnel of the KO were leading a rather loose and immoral life in LISBON, with little concern for their duties as members of an Abwehr organisation ... . KREMER-AURENRODE [*sic*], generally known as KARSTHOF, a young Austrian, who set the example for their gay existence.'[26]

***

THE BALLOON TRAFFIC (PART 1)

On 23 May BALLOON came up with a couple of tests 'if after you have weighed all the evidence you still are doubtful as to whether or not the Ivan I & II set up has become a source of grave suspicion to the Germans ... in order to satisfy ourselves as to the Germans' feelings about the matter'.

The first of these was Acting Pilot Officer William Lethbridge Cotesworth,[27] who he had known on and off for many years, having been at preparatory school with him. Aged 34, he had enlisted in the RAFVR as an aircraftman, then commissioned into the Administrative and Special Duties Branch on 18 July 1941.[28] His chief faults were drink, women and money. He had been posted to Bomber Command headquarters at High Wycombe, where he became acquainted with operational technique. He fell foul of his squadron leader, exacerbated by his returning to duty blind drunk, and Air Vice-Marshal Graham recommended that he be dismissed.[29] He had also received an 'almighty rocket' from his cousin, Air Marshal John Slessor, to whom he appealed.[30] Currently he was awaiting call-up as a private soldier in the Army. BALLOON proposed writing to his German masters about 'this ex officer' who he was prepared to bribe for £1,000 as he was 'disconsolate and hard up' and ideally situated to obtain secrets of Bomber Command – 'The Germans reaction to this might well give us some indication of their true opinion and feelings.'

Wilson reported that 'BALLOON was confident that the man was entirely loyal and, much as in BALLOON's own case, was suffering from some foolish act of which too much had been made'. He was not entirely in favour of Cotesworth becoming BALLOON's sub-agent since he was in a delicate position, but thought that the suggestion should receive due consideration. If the proposition were put to the Germans their reaction might help them to come to a conclusion about BALLOON's standing with them. But MI5 would first have to approach the Air Ministry to see to what extent they would be willing to provide any information about the workings of Bomber Command.[31] After speaking with Tar they agreed to take no action.

BALLOON continued:

> (2) Another test might be to complain bitterly about their complaint to Ivan I regarding my work (when his letter arrives), and to say that it is quite obvious that many of my reports must have been caught in Censorship – (a good point since the tightening up of censorship has been written about recently in the Press) – and suggest that: (a) they send me a wiring diagram for a transmitter set which I will make up. (b) Better still, they do what they were going to do, i.e. create some sort of arms offer from say the Star Sub-machine Gun Company, Spain,[32] which will enable me to fly to Lisbon to inspect the goods and so discuss all matters with them or go on to Madrid or Berlin if they so require, in the event of the Lisbon man not being enough of a 'big shot' to really discuss matters with me. I could pretend that I obtained a quick priority and Exit Permit on the grounds that I have offered the

arms to the Ministry of Supply for the Home Guard on Factory Defence, who accorded me every facility, I can then tell them that I will return and say to the Ministry that the arms were not new and so many failed on test that I rejected the whole consignment.[33]

Wilson felt that suggestion (a) about the wiring diagram appeared like a 'fishing expedition', and (b) BALLOON going to Lisbon as an illustration of his courage. He didn't doubt that he would be prepared to make the trip if his bluff were called, but there was a grave risk of becoming blown – '[I]f at the last minute he made excuses about permits or the like it would look extremely bad.'[34] Tar agreed. Wilson thought that it might be worth considering whether BALLOON shouldn't use attack as the best means of defence, such as when he had concrete material for them, e.g. about the gas mask and photographs, the Germans made no effort to enquire what he had to offer.

Cyril Mills drew Wilson's attention to his concern that censorship labels used on BALLOON's outgoing letters were not varied enough. During this time GELATINE had written two letters, bearing the same numbers on the censorship labels as two of BALLOON's. Wilson observed, 'I do not know how many different numbers are in fact in use on the air mail to Lisbon, but I suspect that it must be much higher than the number of labels used by Colonel Allan's Department.'[35] He asked Alan Grogan of B3d (Liaison with Censorship) to look into it and provide a list of numbers used by the Port and Spanish Sections in Censorship. Grogan reported that hundreds of different numbers were being used on Iberian mail 'and that further [?], as the pressure in various sections varies, so may the user of any particular label be shifted from one class of mail to another. He adds that Colonel Allen [sic] was provided with far more labels than he would appear to have used.'[36]

On 1 June BALLOON provided Wilson with a draft of the letter he intended to write, a copy of which was sent to Foley. Wilson noted that 'Although, in fact, the answer will be sent over by special channels, it is intended that the wording shall be such as could have passed through the Censorship'. While overall it was a good letter, it would be better that 'he felt indignant that the complaint had been made to TRICYCLE and not to himself, and he has expressed this indignation to their 'mutual friends'. He also wanted to know whether, if there was any foundation to Cotesworth's loose tongue, he ought to be cautioned.[37] The revised draft would be discussed at the XX Committee meeting on 4 June 1942, and that 'He might add the Admiralty's request for photographs'.

***

In May BALLOON had written to nine different cover addresses in Lisbon, one of which had been cancelled by the Germans, while another had not been used since 25 February 1942, and a third not since 3 April. Those unused were discontinued, working on the supposition that Censorship would have intercepted them:

THE BALLOON TRAFFIC (PART 1)

The Germans know that BALLOON's secret ink is one well known to us. In practice BALLOON supplies a large part of his traffic and moreover reports to us a good deal more than he is permitted to use in his traffic. As far as possible we see that his letters are written in his own way and he prepares and typewrites his own cover letters selecting the name and address of the sender which appears on the cover from the London Telephone Book. He usually writes about three times a fortnight and as he has never been asked to number his letters he does not do so. If the Germans study the traffic carefully, they must see that there are a number of letters missing which have been notionally caught in the censorship and it is hoped that they will assume that his answers to some of the questionnaires which he either cannot or is not permitted to answer were contained in the stopped letters.[38]

Tar had already sent Foley an explanation of BALLOON's set-up and *modus operandi* in London, with a promise to send him copies of all their traffic; and William Stephenson of BSC had received a copy of a 'carefully edited' sixteen-page summary of the TRICYCLE case with not only information about him, but also how he had recruited BALLOON and GELATINE.[39] Tar described BALLOON as

A man of considerable ability and both personally and because of his business has access to many people from whom he might obtain information, particularly about all kinds of military equipment. He is supposed, by the Germans, to be harbouring a grudge against this country, because of having been forced to leave the Army in disgrace which makes it impossible for him to obtain a commission in spite of the war.

His communications were sent written in secret ink, and questionnaires were received in 'punkte' [microdots].[40]

***

Many of the payments BALLOON had received from the Germans had come through the London office of the Swiss Bank Corporation and the Banco Espírito Santo e Comerciale de Lisboa, by order of Paulo Pinto da Lima.[41] Tar requested that Foley transmit BALLOON's letter to Stephenson, adding that 'It might be as well to warn New York that although BALLOON's letter to TRICYCLE is dated 1.6.42, his letter to Lisbon on the matter was dated 23.5.42'.[42]

On 23 June Marriott reported that BALLOON had informed him that he was designing a new type of armoured car, and collaborating with Commanders R.E. Conder and Reggie Parish at the Admiralty; it was now at the stage when armament was being discussed. He thought that the two officers would probably make enquiries about him through NID.[43] Therefore, he was anxious that 'the Admiralty should ... not be given any indication that he is doing any work for the War Office'. Marriott suggested that Montagu talk to ADNI 'and get this point fixed up';[44] Tar spoke to Montagu about it the same day.

The following day Victor Rothschild told him that the previous evening Parish had telephoned 'on a most urgent matter' and told him that he and Conder

> had for some time been studying the application of Naval methods of war to tank warfare, and had come to a number of interesting conclusions on the subject. In working out what was the best tank to use in this war, they had solicited the services of a very brilliant engineer called [Metcalfe] They were now at the stage in their work where it would be necessary to tell [Metcalfe] certain secrets and Parish felt he would like to have [Metcalfe] 'checked' before going any further. He said that Condor [sic] and he had put up their idea to a certain General, whose name I forget, but whom he described as Lord Louis Mountbatten's General at Combined Operations Headquarters,[45] and to certain Generals such as General Martell [sic],[46] who had been very enthusiastic about this new tank and had referred them to Mr Lucas of the Ministry of Supply.[47] Mr Lucas had not been uninterested, but had put certain queries and virtually they were going to re-design their tank, and it was for this reason that the brilliant engineer [Metcalfe's] closest assistance was needed, and they would like to tell him secrets.
>
> At this stage, Commander Parish said, 'Have we already been naughty boys? I would rather come and ask you about it than anybody in London.' I said that if they had divulged any secret information about naval tactics or tank matters to [Metcalfe] they had been naughty boys. Parish said that they had not, but they very much wanted to.

Parish thought that Metcalfe had been engaged in arms racketeering before the war and was associated with Hodgson of BSA, telling Rothschild, 'What a pity that HODGSON has gone in with STRAUSSLER.' Rothschild replied that, given Metcalfe's 'slightly doubtful career ... it was a pity perhaps that they had found it necessary to use him instead of one of the many engineering experts available in the Service Departments. Parish agreed but said that it was chiefly Condor who had done this, but emphasised [Metcalfe's] brilliance.' Rothschild said he was unsure why Parish had come to see him, speculating that

> It might have been sincere security-consciousness, but on the other hand, the association with HODGSON, STRAUSSLER and POSNIKOFF [sic] makes me wonder whether he felt that he had not gone a little bit too far and was coming round to try and ensure himself against repercussions. I said that I would let him know about it in the course of the next few days.[48]

THE BALLOON TRAFFIC (PART 1)

Nicholas Peter Sorrel Straussler was a British-Hungarian engineer who had devised a flotation system for Allied amphibious Duplex-Drive tanks (nicknamed 'Donald Duck' tanks) first trialed in June 1941 at Brent (Hendon) reservoir and which would later be used on D Day of Operation OVERLORD.[49]

In Wilson's note to file on 30 June he explained that BALLOON had kept them apprised of his involvement with the design of the armoured car and that Parish and Conder had overstepped the mark by involving him at all by taking him to Farnborough and introducing him to 'various other people who should be kept away from spies' making him privy to 'some most secret information, and he asked for and obtained permission not to include anything learnt in this way in his reports to this section'.

Only the previous day there had been talk of 'including some rocket devices of a very secret character in the design. It is no doubt that this has led the Commanders to become security minded.' BALLOON had suggested to them that he didn't need details, just the dimensions of the space required for his design and to store the ammunition. Wilson was satisfied that he had 'acted with complete propriety'. He had spoken to Rothschild 'and told him my end of the story'. Rothschild proposed submitting his letter to Parish to B1a.[50]

When Wilson saw BALLOON on 26 June he reported that he

> mentioned in passing that he had some normal business which he thought would be sufficient to justify his obtaining a permit to visit the USA. I have not told BALLOON of the German's [sic] suggestions that TRICYCLE might be paid through him. It is worth while [sic] bearing in mind the possibility of BALLOON going to the USA and offering to take currency with him.

Tar wrote a note at the bottom saying, 'Yes. We might draw them on this. But first let us wait for the letter to B and see what that contains, then we can take a better decision. I don't think at the moment that we want to encourage this as a means of paying Tricycle, as it is in fact far easier for them to pay direct from Portugal.'[51]

Chapter 20

The TRIBAGE Organisation

On 10 May 1942 Charles Cholmondeley provided an account of the Double Cross committee's views on the so-called 'TRIBAGE Organisation' (taken from the first few letters of TRICYCLE, BALLOON and GELATINE), and what their future strategy should be.[1] From the evidence the committee had obtained so far, the Germans did not trust the organisation as they believed that TRICYCLE had come under control once he had arrived in the USA:

> In these circumstances it appears desirable that we should salve what we can from the wreck. For this purpose it must be taken for granted that we cannot continue the case as heretofore since it will be impossible for us to decide whether or not our information is being believed. The alternative is, therefore, to try and supply the enemy with the relevant facts which would confirm in their minds what they would like to believe.

Cholmondeley noted that the traffic would need to be reviewed. GELATINE's traffic was 'practically useless', but that of TRICYCLE-BALLOON sent from England, had given the Germans 'a considerable amount of accurate and interesting details'. He added,

> The only deceptions to which this traffic has been made party are Plan MACHIAVELLI (which failed), Plan OMNIBUS (to a very slight degree), Plan MIDAS, Plan BIRD WATCHER and 'Anson in the Far East'. Of these deceptions it is only necessary to make serious consideration of Plan MIDAS since none of the other plans implicate agents; hence the action which we take must, if possible, cover the Plan MIDAS period and induce in the German's mind that TRICYCLE's seduction took place after that date, namely August 1941.

Even though BALLOON had not been inclined to answer questions the Germans put to him, what he had provided was 'interesting and in some cases valuable information'. Therefore, he assumed, 'BALLOON must rank comparatively highly in their esteem.' As for TRICYCLE, whilst not being as outstanding an agent as BALLOON, he had introduced BALLOON to the Germans

THE TRIBAGE ORGANISATION

and also carried out that excellent financial feat whereby the Germans obtained £200,000 sterling in this country. In these circumstances, I think it may be accepted that the German case officers running the TRIBAGE Organisation must be very loth [sic] to reach the conclusion that they have been led up the garden path from the very start and will certainly review the case to try and establish from what date the case went wrong. A further spur will undoubtedly reflect on their own efficiency and hence their pride will receive a severe shock.

With this in mind the following plan would suggest itself and for the purpose of clarity, will be dealt with from the German end. The following it is hoped would form the essence of the report which would ultimately be put up to the German cheifs [sic] by the case officers, and would be dated about the middle of June.

TRICYCLE only went wrong after going to America. Prior to that date he was a bona fide German agent and his operations in connection with Plan MIDAS were apparently unknown to the enemy intelligence. On arrival in America, however, owing to some mishap, he was apprehended by the FBI who subjected him to cross-examination and ultimately elicited the fact that he had two sub-agents in England who were writing in secret ink to José NUNEZ. This information was passed by the FBI to the British Intelligence Service with the usual delays and the British were only able to stop two or three outgoing letters which they could in no way connect with either of the two suspects, BALLOON and GELATINE. The FBI then tried by means of the 'IVY' message to implicate BALLOON through mentioning that they had a safe and easy contact with IVAN II. Nothing came of this rather crude attempt to draw information. The inference was, therefore, that the British were watching BALLOON and GELATINE in order to try and locate further members [o]f the spy ring.

Their operation was not, however, successful and they only continued this unproductive operation for approximately two months. It then appears that both GELATINE and BALLOON were arrested and interrogated. However, apparently at the request of the FBI, the British decide to turn BALLOON into a double-cross agent since, as the FBI no doubt pointed out, his sudden demise would react unfavourably upon the TRICYCLE case which was now working well.

The reason for this supposition is the obvious change in style of the BALLOON communications between the letter of May 27th and that of June 15th when ... no communications were received. Up to June 15th financial matters had formed a very small part of BALLOON's correspondence and the arrangements made for paying him had caused him very little serious inconvenience. His vehement requests that the money should now be sent, not by draft, but by some other safer route in a letter giving next to no information seemed to point to the British decision that the BALLOON case should anyway for the time bieng [sic] be run for counter espionage purposes only.

No further word has been heard from GELATINE but it is to be assumed that the British squeamishness prevented them from interrogating her suitably and hence they felt unable or unwilling to attempt working her as a double-cross.

He suggested the following 'window-dressing':

1. BALLOON and GELATINE should both be absent from their formal circles of life for a fortnight at least.
2. Cables should in fact be exchanged between the FBI and the American Embassy over here referring to the TRICYCLE case and possible repercussions which maybe [sic] expected by BALLOON and GELATINE's arrest. There should be further replies stating the British propose to cover this by running BALLOON as a double-agent.
3. The TRICYCLE case should be run as heretofore with no change in its operation.
4. The possibility of a leaky source in New York referring to recent successful cooperation between the FBI and the British Intelligence has led to several captures in England of enemy agents.[2]

Tar had noted that on 6 February the Twenty (XX) Committee had agreed that a plan of the East Coast minefield barrier should be passed to the Germans by SKOOT (TRICYCLE). The plan, proposed by Montagu, just needed an excuse for how SKOOT had obtained it. What they proposed over lunch was

> Montagu being a Jew is anxious to have some sort of pass which will enable him in the event of a successful German invasion of this country to go free. He is a man who cannot be bought with money and this is the only way one can really get at him. He will indicate to SKOOT that the only terms on which he will part with this plan are those stated above. This means that SKOOT will have to get in touch with Lisbon and inform them of his achievement by a letter in secret writing, and state the exact terms which are wanted.
>
> It is considered that this plan will appeal to the German mentality enormously, and it is proposed to implement it as soon as possible.[3]

On 13 February 1941 TRICYCLE, writing in secret ink as 'John Danvers', had referred to the minefield plan in a letter to Paolo Simões. He had used

THE TRIBAGE ORGANISATION

Cholmondeley's address, 18 Queens Gate Place Mews, London SW7, as a cover address, although another document stated incorrectly that it was Masterman's. But Masterman's autobiography states that he lived first at the United University Club, then the Oxford & Cambridge, from which he 'migrated to the Reform and there it was my inestimable good fortune to be allowed to live until the conclusion of the war'.[4]

The letter referred to 'An English Naval Officer friend, who is a Jew', who had drawn up a chart for the Admiralty 'showing the secret clear passages of the English East coast minefield for the ~~trawlers and small~~ boats in the Humber to pass through and back if there is an invasion by Germany' which he had kept 'in return for his safety if he was made prisoner.'[5] But, according to Nigel West, 'the matter was pursued no further, apparently because the Germans believed the document to be out of date.'[6]

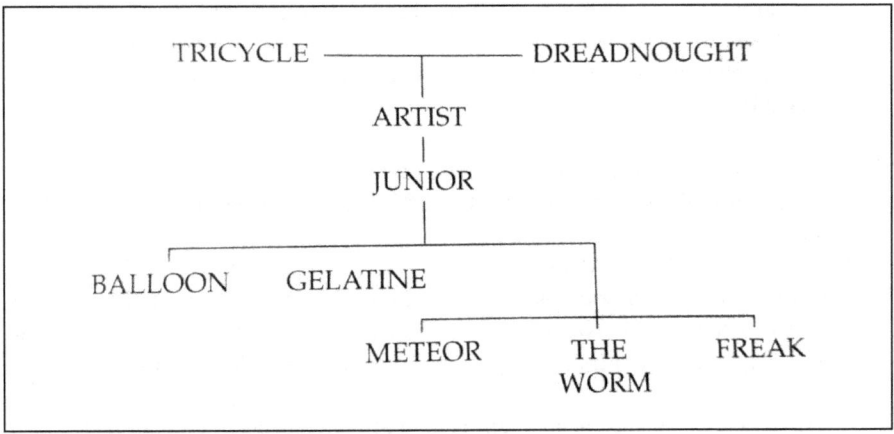

Figure 2. Yugoslav network (from West, Nigel, *MI5*)

Chapter 21

The BALLOON Traffic (Part 2)

Guy Liddell wrote in his diary on 10 October 1941:

> On looking through BALLOON's traffic, I found that he had reported on an ammunition dump situated on Lord Swinton's estate. This had apparently escaped notice both by the Air Ministry and the Home Defence Security Executive. BALLOON was communicating in secret ink but had not sent the letter off. The necessary amendments have been made.[1]

During the war Harrogate Ladies' College had been evacuated to Lord Swinton's estate at Swinton Park, Masham, North Yorkshire, which seems like an unlikely arrangement.

During August 1942 BALLOON's traffic was examined, primarily to ascertain his known contacts and sources of information. It struck Marriott that 'certain unsatisfactory features' between autumn 1941 and spring 1942 had given rise to German complaints about the quality of his information. In his opinion

> BALLOON's status as an agent is, and always has been, a great deal lower than we for a long time supposed. I have never believed that the Germans would classify an agent whom they had never seen as being in the first class and, for such an agent to be regarded as being as high as second class, it is necessary that his information should be very good.

It surprised him that the period 8 August 1941 to 23 July 1942 covered a wide range of contacts: officers and enlisted personnel in the Admiralty, RAF, Army, and civilian positions. Yet, in spite of being a former Army officer with no naval background, the majority of BALLOON's contacts were naval officers, particularly given that 'naval officers are notoriously very much a class apart from the rest of the community'. But he thought that speculation was pointless; of more relevance was 'the quality of the information he contrives to supply'.

It irked Marriott that the information BALLOON should have been supplying should appear to be from a man who knew what he was talking about, but instead, was rarely any better than 'that of an intelligent layman and is often not as good as that of an ordinary soldier'. It was also apparent that a large proportion of his information was of interest to the 'ordinary English man in the street who is anxious for news about the progress of the war, but is not the sort of information which the Germans require from a spy for the reason that it is, on its face, information which becomes available to the Germans simultaneously with its becoming available to the British.'

He cited several instances of the type of information BALLOON had supplied: a letter to João Maia on 12 January 1942;[2] a fighter pilot's views on the respective merits of Spitfires and Fw 190s in combat; and the introduction of catapulted fighter aircraft to merchant ships which had made the task of German long-range bombers more difficult; and on more than one occasion, the effect that air raids on occupied territory had on the Germans. As he pointed out, the Germans must have known all of this in a more accurate form than BALLOON had supplied, and in a timelier manner.

BALLOON's allegations of what the English believed to be German intentions were occasionally useful, but were only valuable if he was quoting 'sources of the very highest grade'. He agreed with the assertion that much of the information was very vague and 'even ... information about such things as tanks, consists ... of a list of their alleged defects and contains practically no facts at all'. But he was also critical of 'our approving authorities' who 'ruthlessly blue-pencilled' a lot of the good information that BALLOON actually produced, and his tendency to produce 'gossipy material which is of interest to the English as opposed to the Germans', or as F.H. Hinsley, the official historian of British intelligence in the Second World War put it, 'political tittle-tattle'.[3]

Marriott conceded that since BALLOON's traffic had improved considerably in recent months, he

> should be allowed to give what appears to be good and detailed information upon the sort of topics which a person in his position would be bound to know about. In his case this is clearly equipment in all its forms with particular reference to arms and to a great extent small boats.[4]

Tar agreed with Marriott's 'extremely illuminating' report, adding, 'It seems that if he is to concentrate on putting over information about armament matters, he will have to open up on this line with new contacts.'[5] However, Marriott didn't entirely agree, as he felt that BALLOON was perfectly capable of talking from his own experience.

***

In July 1942 BALLOON informed Wilson of two cases of careless talk which he thought might be worth investigating. The first was Willi von Neurth [sic],[6] a former Viennese banker who had been interned earlier in the war who claimed to BALLOON's cousin at Brown's Hotel on 2 July that 'a high official in the Ministry of Supply [had told him about] a ferry service of heavy bombers to carry military stores to Egypt had been started and that 2,000 bombers would be sent'.

The second was about Commander Robert MacDonald[7] whose job was to prepare reports for the Cabinet. He was at a dinner party given by Brigadier General Stewart M. Anderson[8] and his wife at 1 Buckingham Mews, SW1, together with the Swedish naval attaché, Johann Oxenstierna, and BALLOON's cousin. MacDonald proceeded to read out extracts of a secret draft report, from which he allegedly quoted Sir Miles Lampson,[9] who had claimed that King Farouk's palace was heavily guarded, and that the king 'was very upset and could not make up his mind whether to flee with the British and regain his throne lat[er] or to remain and meet the Germans in a friendly spirit'.[10] The king was also rumoured to be a kleptomaniac and his attendants had to follow him around replacing things which he had picked up.[11] Wilson decided that no look-up on von Neurath was necessary, but included a card in the B1 registry.[12]

***

What was causing MI5 some concern was a payment for £500 that BALLOON had received through the Midland Bank from José Augusto de Castro, a name hitherto unknown to them, and SIS had no trace of him. The only de Castro MI5 had on file was a name given to Nancy Cunard on 1 March 1934 connected with the *Diario de la Marina*, a Havana newspaper,[13] in a list of journalists who might be interested in her book *Negro Anthology*, but Wilson thought that 'Identity seems unlikely'. He queried why this payment had been made through de Castro instead of through Francisco Barroso dos Santos.

It was agreed that BALLOON would write to dos Santos and also send a long letter to one of his other cover addresses, giving all the approved information which had accumulated during his period of silence, but deleting certain items which he regarded either as useless or out-of-date.[14] The reference – 'Furniture sold shall transfer first instalment pounds 500 five hundred stop letter follows. Francisco BARROSO' – was contained in the cable sent by dos Santos which BALLOON had received on 16 June. At the beginning of May Wilson had pointed out: 'It is to be noted that 162A-164A Rua da Rosa is the address of Francisco Barroso dos Santos of the company Sousa and Campos Lda., antique dealers, who is one of BALLOON's cover addresses, and his paymaster. TRICYCLE suggested to the Germans on 28.3.42 that money should be sent to him (TRICYCLE) by Santos as payment for the sale of antiques.'[15]

In September he prepared a list of BALLOON's contacts for Cyril Harvey in B1a. He noted that Mrs Barton kept a list of seven cover addresses which he used, although that of José Nuñes 'has not been used for 6 months and is actually on the Censorship List. The Germans are left to assume that he has been writing to this address but the letters have been intercepted.' He also noted that Antonio de

THE BALLOON TRAFFIC (PART 2)

Almeida's address was not on the list but had been inoperative for several months, 'although one letter has recently been sent to this address on the theory that, even if this address was known to the Censors and some letters had been intercepted, an occasional letter would be missed and would go through'.

BALLOON continued to use Artur Soares' address simply because he hadn't been told not to; however, all letters sent to that address were returned as 'Addressee unknown'. One outstanding letter had been sent from Wilson's home address, but 'if it is returned it will not cause trouble'. Wilson noted that 'We know, because letters have been acknowledged, that the cover addresses Barroso Dos SANTOS and José MAIA [*sic* – João] are working properly, and we have no reason to think that letters to Pinto de LIMA or MATIAS do not get through.'

Some outstanding issues which BALLOON dealt with were about the Blackburn Aircraft factory, about which the Air Ministry had been asked to provide information, and MTBs.

There was also a story about depth charges 'which Montagu wishes to have put over verbatim' and needed approval. Other approved material which wasn't all 'Source BALLOON' could be 'altered verbally in such a way as he thinks fit'. He was due to be paid in September, but if he wasn't he would complain to the Abwehr. They had also asked him about gliders, but Wilson complained that the Air Ministry had been sitting on it, 'which, if they knew their job, they would improve upon'.[16]

All names had been placed on the GPO's IB (Investigation Branch) List. Wilson noted on 29 July that the Germans had told TRICYCLE to stop writing to Soares 'as the poor man is dead'. Letters written to him had been returned to the Dead Letter Office of the Post Office as 'addressee unknown'. Since 'BALLOON also wrote to this address, he added that 'it will be interesting to see how quickly he is told to discontinue using it'.

One letter was allegedly from Walter James Dexter of 10 Astell House, Astell Street, London SW3, a director of Atlas Publishing Company of 18 Bride Lane, Fleet Street, London EC4, to whom Soares had allegedly written on 28 February and the subject of a Special Branch report on 12 August. Dexter had gone to Special Branch with the letter, upset that someone had obviously used his name and address and used W.T. instead of W.J. 'possibly with some ulterior motive in view'. Soares had allegedly placed an order with Messrs Johnsteads for diecast white metal bearings. Special Branch reported that Dexter knew nothing of Soares, Johnsteads, or engineering, and there was nothing in their records of either W.T. or W.J. Dexter, Johnsteads or Artur Soares. The only possible explanation was that Dexter's name and address had been obtained from the telephone directory and used as a code. Both the managing director and the secretary of Johnsteads confirmed that the company did no export trade with Portugal, nor did they know either Soares or Dexter. A former employee of Johnsteads sacked for unsatisfactory performance was suspected of writing the letter, but the evidence was largely circumstantial, and he had disappeared.

Wilson sent copies of the report to Alan Grogan in B3d (Liaison with Censorship) and Captain Derbyshire in E2a (Finns, Poles and Baltic States Nationals), as well as a note to Colonel Allan at the GPO and Foley at SIS. He told Allan that another letter to Soares had allegedly been sent on 15 July by Victor Oliver of 66 Westminster Gardens, London SW1.[17] This was comedian Vic Oliver, born Victor von Samek in Vienna in 1898, who had married Winston Churchill's daughter, actress Sarah Churchill, in 1936. As Wilson pointed out:

> It would seem a possible trick for an agent to write an innocent looking letter from this country upon which the recipient abroad would write a message in secret ink and which he would then return, alleging that the letter could not be delivered. It may be very unlikely that this would be done in practice, but it is perhaps just worthwhile suggesting that censors should not assume that because a letter which is returning through the Dead Letter Office bears an outgoing censorship label it needs not attention on its return journey.[18]

A further letter had been sent on 22 November from M. Ashby, 4A Moore Street, London SW3 regarding a damaged shipment of bales (of wool?). In January 1943 Tar wrote to Allan regarding this letter and one ostensibly sent on 29 December 1942 from B.L. Pavey, 10 Minehead Road, London SW16.[19] Postal & Telegraph Censorship stated that 'The Lisbon postman's note on the envelope says there is no 5th Floor at the address given, and that nobody in the building knows of any ARTUR SOARES'.

Wilson requested that Major Langdon,[20] the MI5 Regional Security Liaison Officer (RSLO) London Region speak with Superintendent Albert Foster of Special Branch and have him destroy all records of the enquiry 'with the minimum of publicity'. Foster told him that destruction of the papers would cause 'undue comment' but he had collected them and locked them in his safe. 'This procedure has been adopted in several of their cases, with the knowledge of the deputy Assistant Commissioner, and will I hope meet your requirements.' Grogan reported that he was not surprised that no secret writing had been found, 'unless the letter in question should have aroused the examiner's suspicions by reason of its contents, lay out or general character'. Wilson confirmed Grogan's query as to whether the latter had been sent out through the GPO, and lent him the letter, which unfortunately is not included in the file.

An undated note from Cyril Harvey states that Paulo Pinta de Lima's name and address had been included on the Statutory List published under the Trading with the Enemy Act (1939): 'that is to say, LIMA is demed [sic] to be an enemy and any person who "has any commercial, financial or other intercourse or dealings" with him is guilty of the offence of trading with the enemy (Act s.1 (2)).' He noted that BALLOON had corresponded with him between May and December 1941, all of which were 'of a commercial character', as well as other letters in 1942, including 'again today (as of the 22.9.42)', making this the date of Harvey's note.

Harvey also outlined how TRICYCLE had exchanged telegrams with Lima, noting, 'I was informed some time ago by Major Hutchins (in connexion with PLAN

PISCATOR) that any letter to a name on the Statutory List ought automatically to be stopped in Censorship.' Furthermore, the payment BALLOON received for £358.4s.2d. via the Swiss Bank Corporation on instructions from the Banco Espírito Santo e Comercial de Lisboa 'by order of Paulo Pinta de Lima' should not have been paid without the Board of Trade's approval. The error was put down to the bank not spotting the name on the Statutory List owing to it being too long. The British Consulate General in Lisbon had warned Portuguese traders that if they traded with anyone on it they would be blacklisted.

Harvey questioned whether they should continue to use Lima's address, but 'If no further letters addressed to him arrive, the Germans may start wondering why not and may wake up to the fact that he has been on the List all the time and that therefore BALLOON has all the time been controlled.' Conversely, there were other addresses which BALLOON could use 'and I doubt whether the fact that we have made the same mistake 18 times is a good enough reason for making it a 19th time.' He pointed out that the Germans had become suspicious of TRICYCLE which had led to BALLOON's and GELATINE's credibility being questioned; however, they had re-examined their cases and found them to be all right. But should they decide to re-examine them again they 'might think of the point about the Statutory List'. Therefore, he suggested that BALLOON should stop writing to Lima in the hope that the Germans might forget that they'd ever written to him in the first place.[21]

Also in September 1942 BALLOON informed Marriott that he'd received a call from Duncan Shaw MacLennan, a trooper in the Royal Armoured Corps, and a director of Hispano-Britannic Co. Ltd; two other directors were Spaniards named Antonio Valverde Gil, the ex-British vice-consul in Zaragoza, Spain,[22] and João Palomero Cantos. The company was involved in negotiating deals with Spanish firms but had a pretty low reputation and were fined £27,000 in February 1942 for breaches of the Limitation of Supplies Order (1940). MacLennan was apparently on very good personal terms with Gil, currently in Spain, and wanted BALLOON to put him in touch with British intelligence there so that he could work for them. Lojendio, the Spanish consul, had told him that Gil could 'fix a Spanish visa very easily' and 'there would be no difficulty about his entering Spain"; all he had to do was ask.

MacLennan, a native of Glasgow, had served in the Indian Army but, according to BALLOON was 'flung out' because he was 'the most appalling drunkard'. He was wealthy owing to money derived from a trust settlement, which to a large extent financed the company, and was 'trying to get to South America in respect of a big timber impregnation scheme devised by that old rogue Irsa de Irsay with whom he has been staying at Marlow Bucks'. He was currently stationed at Bovington,[23] and was also going to approach Colonel Arcy (or Ace) of the Free French Marines.

Maclennan claimed to have genuine business reasons for going to Spain: his friends there could supply unlimited quantities of wolfram (tungsten) and other products to anybody he cared to nominate, and thought BALLOON's company might be interested in the business. A company named Volpa Ltd was involved in doing such business, and Cantos, one of its directors, had been responsible for

Volpa taking business away from Hispano-Brittanic. Therefore, Maclennan wanted to 'do Cantos a bad turn if he can'.

BALLOON was alarmed that Maclennan should think that he had anything to do with British intelligence and quickly assured him that he knew no such people, although he knew a solicitor who worked for the Foreign Office, to whom he would pass his proposal. Wilson didn't attach any importance to the offer. He reported:

> Maclennan's reason for supposing that BALLOON might help him was based on the fact that when BALLOON's company was attempting, about two years ago, to extract £150 from Hispano-Brittanic the latter received a visit from Scotland Yard, and Maclennan apparently thought that this had been arranged by BALLOON. With regard to any chance of using Maclennan BALLOON himself says that he would not trust him to buy a packet of cigarettes. He is a sick man and is obviously dissatisfied with army life and is anxious to get out of it.[24]

Chapter 22

'Plan A'

On 11 September 1942 Luke and Tar met with Lieutenant General Laurence Carr, the Ministry of Supply's Senior Military Advisor,[1] to outline a draft of 'Plan A' – to send BALLOON to Lisbon. Carr indicated that the Ministry would supply a letter authorising BALLOON to inspect arms in Portugal and Spain, providing MI5 could contrive to get a suitable offer to his firm from a neutral firm. However, Tar thought that it was premature to ascertain whether an actual deal could be effected consisting of the purchase and resale of 40,000 Mausers to the Turks. They agreed that BALLOON should ask the Germans in Lisbon to make an offer to his firm and that the real negotiations be left until it was determined what terms they were offering.

In order to initiate the plan BALLOON suggested that he should write in secret ink, but cautioned that it would be better if any letter received did not go through his firm as Postnikow might try to get involved. Therefore, he suggested that the Ministry of Supply inform him and Postnikow that this offer had been intercepted in Censorship (which it would have been), and could he verify the existence of the goods offered? He felt sure that Postnikow would jump at the idea of his going to Lisbon to follow up. BALLOON would explain that his firm had been approached about the offer as the result of his previous discussions with the former Spanish military attaché.[2]

The objects of the plan were (a) to 'set up' the Ivan I and II organisation by proving the existence and bona fides of Metcalfe @ BALLOON; (b) to thoroughly mislead Kasteroff [sic] and the Abwehr by taking over bogus plans and out-of-date information; (c) to exploit Kasteroff's susceptibility to bribery and to extract as much information as possible from him about his organisation and names of other agents; and (d) to study the methods employed by the Germans to execute the deal, and the individuals and firms involved.

> II <u>General Idea</u>
> To create a scheme which, by the very nature of the business concerned, will allay the suspicion of all the parties concerned and which if carried out to its conclusion would be self-financed.
>
> From the security point of view it would appear that only three outside persons need be employed i.e. Postnikow, a senior official of

the Ministry of Supply, and a senior official of Economic Warfare and Treasury. Of these only the last two mentioned would of course be taken into our confidence.

The Germans knowing that C.M. [Metcalfe] is a registered arms dealer should not be unduly excited by the type of business suggested.

III The Plan

(i) Narrative

So far as C.M. can ascertain the Turks still have extensive credits available in sterling in London owing to their inability to purchase material with the funds from the British Credits made to Turkey in 1940.

Although the Turks were badly let down on several arms offers (Norman Cooper etc.) they have always been interested in acquiring 7.92mm Mauser units. In the early days of the war they chased several bogus parcels of arms in various western European countries.

C.M. from direct enquiries which he has made believes that they are still interested in obtaining Mauser Units, and expresses the view that the only genuine parcel which ever existed was German owned – by the Göring A.G. [Reichswerke Hermann Göring] – and that the Germans have at all times been willing to sell arms to obtain foreign currency.

(ii) Method

It is suggested that C.M. should write in secret ink to Lisbon in reply to the last 'spot' letter dated 1st Sept. which asks for plans of MTBs etc. and details of Blackburn works, and say something on the following lines:-

'that the other day he and his employer were sent for by the Ministry of Supply (as per May 1940, details of which the Germans might have assumed in Paris) and were asked if in their opinion there was any possibility of obtaining Mauser Units. The Ministry went on to say in the strictest confidence that these were for the Turks and would be paid for out of the Anglo-Turkish Credits in sterling either in London or a Neutral Country. The Ministry intimated that they were anxious to put the business through a private arms firm in case at any later date there should be questions in the House as to the Country of Origin of these goods. C.M. quickly seeing an opportunity to help his German friends said that he thought that it might be possible to obtain some in Spain via Portugal, but that it was very difficult to get anything these days and that previous requests for offers of arms from Spain made through the late Spanish Military Attaché (they can check this) had not met with much success, but he would get in touch direct with some Spanish Arms firms as there must be some Mausers left over from the Civil War. The Ministry expressed a desire for new rifles if possible and went on to say that all facilities in respect of visit permits and air transport booking would be made available to either Mr Postnikow or Mr [Metcalfe]. It was agreed on the spot that C.M. would be the one to go. The Ministry said that proof of availability of funds would be made by the Treasury or E.W. [Economic Warfare] in the [...] Bank Lisbon and that the cash would be made available as soon as C.M. had reported on the suitability of the stock. The interview closed with C.M. promising to inform the M of S as soon as he received replies from his enquiries in Spain and Portugal.'

[One page redacted]

[Metcalfe] should then suggest in his secret ink letter to Kasteroff that this would be a golden opportunity to meet and to bring over the plans asked for. Also, to go into the question of the unanswered letters as C.M. is not entirely happy that K. is getting all the letters despatched. The [sic] should then ask K. to get in touch with Berlin pointing out to them that they have so much to gain i.e.

(a) Sell rifles of which they have a surplus
(b) Obtain foreign currency
(c) Meet their agent Ivan II
(d) Get plans and first hand information

A further inducement to Kasteroff might be a hint that there would be 'something in it for him'.

[Metcalfe] believes that the Germans could produce a quantity of Mauser Rifles quickly even if such numbers do not actually exist in Spain at the present time, and that the Germans (especially not entirely financially disinterested traders) would welcome the prospect. If and when notification is received by C.M. in the form of an official letter from a Spanish or Portuguese arms firm (selected by Kasteroff) who would have tipped off C.M. in a secret spot letter what firm to approach for a tender in the first place, C.M. would show this offer to the Ministry and would then proceed to Lisbon by air after an exchange of cables with the 'firm' re: prices, specifications, inspection facilities etc. He would contact Kasteroff on arrival in

Lisbon and make it clear over a glass of wine that there was 'a bit in this deal for both of them'. After this one of two courses should be adopted:-

(a) To respect the stock on inspection or to report home that it does not exist being still in Germany and advising the Ministry not to buy

or

(b) Actually consummate the deal as the Government could make a profit on the resale to the Turks which would cover the expenses, loss of exchange, bribe to Kasteroff (C.M.'s 'share' would be brought back with him) and a small wartime commission to Postnikow for allowing the deal to be put through his firm.

At all times the funds in Lisbon would be in the hands of a Bank or Economic Warfare as C.M. would only require a document giving proof of availability, so that except for expenses, tips, and the final 'pay off' (duly divided between K & C.M.!) [Metcalfe] would *not handle* any large sums of cash.

As regards the Turks they would probably ask for delivery F.A.S. or F.O.B.[3] Lisbon and might like their representative to make inspection there. Alternatively, it would probably be better to let the goods come to this cou[ntry] and be reshipped here by United Kingdom Commercial Corporation. [Metcalfe] appreciates that this is only a broad outline and that there are many details to be fixed.

He is however convinced that old Postnikow would fall for the M of S request and the number of people actually involved in the scheme is very small ... .

[Metcalfe] is prepared to go at any time and considers the project practicable and well worth while, he also feels that there are many other useful functions, about which he does not at present know which might be performed while over there.

Alternatively, he feels that if the Mauser project is considered too big a similar request for a much smaller quantity of say Schmeisser or Spanish mark sub-machine guns (Sten) could be substituted.[4]

Chapter 23

'I regard this as very naughty of BALLOON'

In late October 1942 BALLOON informed MI5 that the secretary of a friend of his had learned at a dinner party that the Germans' secret weapon

> was a 90-foot rocket, fired from a cradle hidden underground like a coastal battery position. The rocket contains 10 tons of high explosive and would be directed against London which is well within its range. Apart from its devastating explosive effect it would undoubtedly cause a mass evacuation with its attendant blockage of transport services at a time when they might be most wanted. He did not know how many of these rockets existed, and in any case they were too well hidden to be neutralised from the air. Accordingly the only answer the authorities could think of at present were strong Commando raids on the areas from which the rockets come or are known to be concealed.
>
> I am not myself quite sure how far the above statements go beyond what has in fact been published in one or other of the newspapers, or may have been contained in German broadcasts, and you will of course realise the possibility that any actual remarks made by Mortimer may have become greatly exaggerated on their way to me.[1]

The news had come from Raymond Mortimer, the editor of the *New Statesman*. If this was the V-2 rocket it was between forty-five- and forty-seven-feet long.[2] Its first test flight had taken place on 3 October 1942, but did not go into operation until September 1944. Exactly how Mortimer had learned this information was not explained.

In November 1943 BALLOON obtained further information from an official in the Ministry of Supply who reported that the rockets were installed in concrete emplacements 15 kilometres inland from the coast. He reported that: 'Special A.P. [armour-piercing] bombs are being forged at Woolwich for use against these points. Professor Crowe [*sic*] advises the War Cabinet that in his view the rockets will break up before arrival but this is considered by other experts to be unlikely as they will reach sub-stratosphere heights and fall like bombs.'³ The armour-piercing bombs were undoubtedly the Tallboy designed by Barnes Wallis and first used by 617 squadron during Operation CROSSBOW beginning on 19 June 1944.

***

On 25 October 1942, after consulting with Masterman the previous day, Marriott decided to tell BALLOON that TRICYCLE had returned from America. Almost immediately, BALLOON contacted him and invited him to dinner the following day, even though Marriott had not given him TRICYCLE's address. He regarded this as 'very naughty of BALLOON, who ought not to do this sort of thing without consulting us. He should, in my view, be rebuked the next time he is seen'.

In November BALLOON was asked in a long secret letter whether he could buy copies of a War Office history of the Abyssinian campaign and also to regularly collect gazettes, periodicals and newspapers issued in London on behalf of the Allies, such as *La Belgique Indépendente*, and post them to Tenente (Lieutenant) Fernando Eduardo da Silva Pais, Rua Mocambique 52-1D, Lisbon.⁴ MI5 reported that they had no trace of Pais and asked SIS whether they did; if so, there is nothing on file. There was only a listing for him in the Lisbon directory as an engineer lieutenant, but J.F. Cahan, a Principal in the Blacklist Section of the Ministry of Economic Warfare at Berkeley Square House, told J.G. Craufurd in B4b that the MEW was unable to check who else lived in his building.

Cyril Harvey followed this up with Craufurd – 'He is told not to write to this man but to send him packets of newspapers and official publications etc.' – and asked for any information about him. In December Roland Bird in B3a (Censorship) requested that Colonel Allan add Pais's name to the IB List. Marriott contacted Richard Butler, the DG's personal secretary, asking him to find out from the Ministry of Information whether copies of the War Office publication *The Abyssinian Campaign* had been sent abroad. The MoI sent Butler a list of those countries' consulates and legations which had received up to three copies of the publication, a total of 20,000 copies in all.⁵

On 19 November 1942 Desmond Orr requested BALLOON's presence at Room 055, the War Office, as soon as possible to help them with an unspecified matter. Harvey reported Orr's request to Tar saying that BALLOON was asked about 'a certain man whom he ran across, or may have run across, on his last visit to Holland in 1940' (possibly Boissevain). BALLOON passed on what information he had and also the name of another (unnamed) man who would be able to provide more. Both he and Harvey felt that Orr was stepping on the latter's toes by contacting him since he and Harvey were in regular contact. Harvey also thought that BALLOON should stay clear of the War Office if at all possible and suggested to Tar that he take up the matter with Orr⁶ which he did in a politely worded letter on the 23rd:

> Dear Desmond,
> I understand that you interviewed C. Le S. [Metcalfe] the other day at Room 055. We have been in touch with [Metcalfe] for some

considerable time and were in fact in touch with him early on in the war through Gilbert [Lennox] when he was at Room 055. I wonder it [*sic*] would be possible in future, if you want any information from him, to adopt the method of approaching me in order that I can get the information for you from [Metcalfe] as it is rather undesirable that he should be seen going to the War Office in view of the rather delicate work which he is at present doing for me.[7]

The following day Orr offered a somewhat conciliatory reply:

Let me say at once that I entirely agree with you as to the undesirability of [Metcalfe] being seen calling at the War Office when he is engaged in delicate operations for you. But how were we expected to know this?

[Metcalfe] has been known to me personally for the past 2½ years and at one time was a frequent visitor to Room 055. It was therefore quite natural that when Simmons of E.1.a wanted information about a man named Messerschmidt, who might have been identical with an individual mentioned by [Metcalfe] in one of his earlier reports, that I should have been asked to send for [Metcalfe] and question him on the subject. This in fact was what I did, and although [Metcalfe] himself was unable to help, he indicated a fruitful line of enquiry.

As you may be aware, we keep an up-to-date Card Index here of all M.I.5 regular employees and their pseudonyms. Without it we would be unable to perform our postal and liaison functions. On a number of occasions in the past we have asked also for a secret list of agents, in order to avoid such incidents as the one now in question.

While I do not know whether you will now be any more responsive to this request, I am making a note on [Metcalfe's] personal card that he is only to be contacted through you, but this only covers the case of [Metcalfe] himself and will not prevent a possible slip-up in some other direction.[8]

Chapter 24

Cover Addresses

On 12 December 1942 Harvey mentioned that now that CARELESS @ Clarc Korab, a Polish airman, had been caught, FEDERICO[1] based in Madrid may come to realise that he had been under control from at least 5 September 1942. Given that the Germans had posed questions about barrage balloons to both he and BALLOON recently, it almost looked as if their intent was to check one agent against the other which may cast suspicion on BALLOON:

> from what we know about FEDERICO's character he would be very reluctant to confess to the fact that one of his best agents had been under control for so long and in so far as the blowing of CARELESS might react on BALLOON, it is to be remembered that BALLOON is working for a different organisation. Nevertheless, there seems to be a link between them as BALLOON's last payment was received from Arthur CARRALHO, who may well be identical with the Arthur CARVALHO from whom £220 was received for CARELESS early in September.[2]

The Germans were using the same bank to pay both agents. The questions about barrage balloons in July 1942 were about the number of stationary and mobile balloons on the ground; the number on merchant ships and convoys; how many balloon squadrons in Britain; and how many personnel in Balloon Command.[3] Cyril Mills was going to pass on these questions to Air Commodore D.L. Blackford, D of I (S) at the Air Ministry.

There was now concern that some of the cover addresses in Lisbon given to BALLOON, TRICYCLE and other agents might have been compromised or blown. Harmer added a footnote to his report on FATHER @ Henri Arents on 21 December[4] which he copied to Wilson and Tar, asking Wilson for his comments on the possible notional blowing of the 56 Rua Passos Manuel address used by FATHER, one of the few remaining used by BALLOON and TRICYCLE, in order to preserve the FATHER case, which he admitted was a mess.

Of the six letters BALLOON wrote, only half got through: two were sent off but didn't get through, and one didn't get through because it wasn't actually sent. If they were to blow the Rua Passos Manuel address then only two of BALLOON's letters would get through. Wilson wasn't keen on the idea, but acknowledged that 'the desire to do so for the purposes of FATHER may well overweigh my desire not to do so for the purposes of BALLOON'. And while he admitted that this might not be a disadvantage, presently there was a lot more information that BALLOON could use than any of his other agents:

> [T]herefore if BALLOON only were involved I would be strongly averse to blowing this address. On the other hand, if the address must be blown it will not be altogether a disadvantage, because there will be even greater gaps in the numbers of letters received by the Germans and they will be encouraged to send further cover addresses to BALLOON.
>
> I think if the address is to be blown it should be blown for both agents, although the addressee's name differs slightly; Maia Silva in one case and João Maia in the other. There is, however, sufficient similarity in the names that one must expect both sets of letter to be intercepted.[5]

However, TRICYCLE was not overly concerned as it was not one of the addresses he was supposed to use after returning to England.

Wilson explained the position of BALLOON's various cover addresses:

a) A fairly recent letter from the Germans indicates that they have received all his letters over a period of over 3 months [*sic*] sent to three cover addresses, including the above mentioned address.

b) The Germans did not acknowledge letters sent during that period to a further two cover addresses. In one of these cases letters have sometimes been returned, in the other case there is no sign of any returned letters and the Germans may or may not be deceiving us in failing to acknowledge these letters. We therefore continue to send letters to these two addresses, though there is grave doubt whether such letters arrive, and these two addresses are never used for items we really want the Germans to get.

c) Another cover address was put on the Censorship list over a year ago. We do not, in fact, write any letters at all to this address but we have, since we have started numbering our letters during the last six weeks, skipped a number, on the theory that it has gone to this address.

d) BALLOON had one other address which was discovered to be on the M.E.W. Black List and which has not been written to since the 13th August, (the letter of the 13th August was acknowledged). We do not skip numbers for this last mentioned address, because the story is that BALLOON happens to have noticed that it was on the Statutory List and thereupon gave up using the address entirely.[6]

DOUBLE AGENT BALLOON

Kim Philby replied to Tar on 3 April 1943 about enquiries that SIS had made on MI5's behalf about some new addresses:

RUA DA ROSA 59 A-3° This is the residence of Carolina da COSTA, divorced from Julio BERNARDO CANDIDO, who is employed by the firm of Abel PEREIRA DA FONSECA as a counter-jumper.[7] CAROLINA is stated to be an illiterate woman and is a [f]riend of EMILIA DA COSTA, governess to a rich foreign family in the RUA DO SALITRA. CAROLINA is said by our source to receive letters for EMILIA.

TRAVESSA DO CONVENTO DA ENCARNAÇÃO 15, loja.

ANTONIO DE ALMEIDA, who is a decorator in a small way, left this address about a year ago. His address is now stated to be LARGO DO OUTEIRINHO DO MIRANTE 76-2°.[8]

This prompted Roland Bird in B3a to ask Wilson whether or not BALLOON had been given Almeida's address and if there was any point in listing it; whether he'd been told not to use the Travessa Do Convento Da Encarnação address, 'or whether his correspondence has been returned undelivered from it?'[9] Wilson thought that the new address should be added to the IB list as a precaution, 'although I have no evidence that any agent who was using this man's old address has been given his new one'. BALLOON had not been told not to use the old address, but one letter had been returned undelivered, while others were not acknowledged. The fate of these letters was unknown to him.[10] Bird remarked, 'I take it that you will be suggesting to Section V [SIS] that they too should list the new address Largo Do Outeirinho Do Mirante 76-2°, on the Western Hemisphere List.' Wilson noted that it had been added in London but since the information was from SIS it should be left up to them to deal with the List 'if they think it justified'. Bird then requested that Almeida's name and address be added to the IB List.[11]

The Germans had requested that a telegram be sent about an invasion, suggesting that if it contained an offer it would mean that an invasion would definitely take place in September. It had to contain indications of the exact date and specific words in a plain language code to show where the attack was likely to take place, in this case, car-related terms. BALLOON's letter of 28 December 1942 about a car, addressed to Almeida and signed 'Henry' (the letter gives an address of H.L. Collins, 91 Riverview Gardens, London [SW13]), suggests that it may contain part of a code to which Alan Grogan in B3d would refer on 22 October 1943 when he requested a copy of the telegram BALLOON was supposed to send 'if the agent learnt the date of operations against the Continent' so he could pass it on to Censorship:

Italy: cylinder
Corsica: piston
Sardinia: h.p.

Greece: spare wheels
France (Mediterranean part): tyre
France (Atlantic part): front drive
Belgium: Coupe
Holland: roadster
Denmark: fuel consumption
Norway: hydraulic brakes

'Any other word used could mean "landing to be expected in Germany or on German coast". Any order could mean "invasion is not to be expected this year", any offer "invasion will definitely take place in September"':

> I have, however, since I returned, rung up old Gibson who says that he has not received your letter and that he has no instructions regarding the sale of your car. I ha[ve] told him to get in touch with Sutton & Co. as the Ministry of War Transport will buy cars of this horse power and indeed have advertised this in the Press.
> In view of the fact that it is a late [19]39 model and is 14 h.p. I do not think that there will be any difficulty, and with a mileage of only 13,000 to its credit you should get about £300 for it.[12]

The brief mention of 14 hp in the letter suggests that Sardinia would be the target for the Allied invasion, which did indeed take place on 14 September 1943. However, the letter was returned to the Dead Letter Office with a pencilled note in Portuguese: 'They say he has moved and they do not know where.' Wilson was uncomfortable passing this information on to Censorship without risking blowing BALLOON's cover, so he suggested that before saying anything to Censorship Bird first discuss with him how he intended to tell them.[13]

John Gwyer's note to Wilson on 4 December 1942 reported that:

> Most Secret Sources [ISOS] now show that Eins Luft Paris have complained that the Emilia de COSTA address [Rua da Rosa 59A 3°, Lisbon] (which has also just been given to GELATINE) [on 18 November 1942] does not work, and that an agent of theirs in South America has reported by another channel that he had written repeatedly to the address, although none of his reports had arrived.[14]

Wilson reported on Tar's behalf,

> Here again we have seen no rebuts, but the Germans, while acknowledging letters to other addresses, have failed to acknowledge BALLOON's letters to this address ... Jarvis will of course appreciate that any enquiries about these addresses must be discreet, but it will be interesting to know if possible the reasons why letters to these addresses are not getting through.[15]

Tar's message to Foley at SIS on 8 February 1943, added, '[A] little later Lisbon replied that the address was reliable and had worked well in other cases.' Wilson appended a note saying, 'Gelatine will write to this address and it will be interesting to see if her letter gets through or not.' Bird then requested that Colonel Allan add Emilia de Costa's name to the IB List.

***

Plan SHOTGUN

In mid-April 1943 the Double Cross committee intended to involve BALLOON in Plan SHOTGUN, devised by the London Controlling Section (LCS). They proposed to pass to the Germans 'a forged document of a technical nature on the state of equipment of the British Army exaggerating its manpower and war potential'.[16] Harmer noted, 'by that time we should have a detailed plan to put up to the members covering the manner in which BALLOON will use the document. At the last meeting it was agreed that BALLOON was the most suitable channel, and that there was no objection to the document being sent over in the form of messages.'[17] He asked that Wilson give it some thought so that it could be discussed with Tar and, if necessary, John Drew, the Cabinet Office's chief of deception during and after the war, who acted as controller over all deception operations and campaigns.

On 14 April Wilson showed BALLOON the original document of Plan SHOTGUN and explained to him the identity of the author:

> We discussed in general terms how he might have persuaded CHANTLER [Identity unknown] to produce the document to prove points which he was seeking to make in argument, and BALLOON strongly expressed the view that whether he had merely managed to secure the document for a short time or had stolen it for good, he would not keep by him a bulky and incriminating document, but would photograph it and conceal the small films.
>
> BALLOON drafted a letter announcing his possession of the photographs to the Germans, and agreed that it would be a good thing if at a later date he met CHANTLER personally and discussed with him the exact means by which BALLOON secured the document. There was no hurry for this to be worked out in detail, as space would not permit of his writing at length to the Germans about it, although clearly he ought to have a story ready in case he ever meets the Germans.[18]

Early in May Wilson noted:

> We know from Most Secret Sources [ISOS] that on 29.4.43 Berlin told Lisbon to stop BALLOON's payments with immediate effect

COVER ADDRESSES

and until further notice ... . This letter, the contents of which might have been received in Berlin by 29.4.43, informed the Germans that BALLOON had photographs of the Plan Shotgun document.[19]

29.4.43.
762. Berlin – Lisbon. HERKULES to LUDOVICO. No.156. Please discontinue payments to IVAN 11 untill [sic] further orders with immediate effect. HERKULES 46542.[20]

On 24 September 1943 Wilson updated John Drew at the Home Defence Executive on the sixth floor of Norfolk House, St James's Square, on what BALLOON had told the Germans about SHOTGUN:

> On 11.4.43 he wrote that he had in his possession photographs of a very long document, with graphs attached, giving the detailed state of equipment of the British Army. The photographs were of the final draft copy, marked 'Most Secret', which had been prepared for the Lord President [Sir John Anderson] by a statistical officer in the Economic Section in the War Cabinet Offices. BALLOON mentioned that the document gave, in the greatest detail, such things as 'Overall State of Equipment', 'State of equipment by Theatres', 'Reserves and Transit Stocks', Completion of Equipment', 'Ammunition' 'Requirements for 1943', and graphs of man-power details.
>
> On 8.6.43 BALLOON complained that nearly two months ago he had reported that he had acquired photographs of this document but he had received no acknowledgement, and he did not propose to keep these incriminating photographs indefinitely: 'So please let me know what to do with them as otherwise I think you will agree that I should destroy them, but before doing so I will wait until I have heard from you.'
>
> He had heard nothing further so if we desire to I think we can assume that he got tired of holding the photographs and has burnt them.
>
> If the document or the source are to be transferred to another agent, then we must obviously make sufficient alterations so that they will not be identifiable with BALLOON's references as set out above.[21]

It is unclear to which address BALLOON sent his letter (not included in the file), so either the Germans never received it, or they decided to ignore it as another example of his less-than-useful intelligence. Plan SHOTGUN was never carried out.

***

DOUBLE AGENT BALLOON

In a letter from Lisbon dated 10 April 1943, received on the 16th, BALLOON was given new contact names and cover addresses: Herberto Aguiar, Veronica Aguiar, and Emygdia de Aguiar. It suggested that he 'drop the address to which you had addresses the lost letter [*sic*] and continue to write to the ones that have so far proved O.K'. Two of those new addresses were:

Emygdia de AGUIAR,
c/o Banco National Ultramarine,
Sucurial Cais de Sodre,
LISBON.

and:

Antonio M. SANCHO,
Rua Ilha S. Tomé 14,
LISBON.

To the latter you'd better write about technical matters only as he is an engineer in the automobile business.[22]

John Noble in B4b reported on 24 April 1943 that there was no other information on Sancho.

Bird drew Tar's attention to the fact that, of the three cover addresses given to their (unnamed) agent who was to operate in the Azores under SIS control, two – de Aguiar and Sancho – were of considerable importance to B1a as they 'are in active use as cover addresses for our agent BALLOON, and SANCHO is also a cover address of the agent METEOR'. (Eugn Šoštarić) He wrote to Ian 'Tim' Milne in section Vd at SIS on 20 April referring to Milne's CX to Herbert Hart of B1b on 23 December 1942 that Antonio M. Sancho had now been given to BALLOON for future use. Therefore, it was very important that the Germans wouldn't realise that either of these addresses was known to British intelligence. Sancho's address was placed on the IB List in London, and a watch kept on his name at 'Any Address' in Lisbon for another three months.[23] 'I hope therefore that it is intended to run the agent in the Azores on a long term basis as it might have disastrous results for us if he is run for any purpose which might involve his becoming blown after a period.'[24]

On 22 April Wilson noted that 'The name Antonio M. SANCHO (but without an address) was known from Most Secret Sources when Nest Cologne were informed on 28.11.42 that letters to this man were, so far as possible, to be signed by Spanish or Portuguese names and not German'.[25]

Tar wrote to Philby about the cover addresses on 1 June. Sancho and Aguiar were first investigated in April 1943 when Bird contacted Colonel Allan at the GPO regarding two letters dated 21 April which were intercepted, and requested that Aguiar's name be added to the IB List: 'This man [Sancho] is presumably identical to the person of the same name already listed on the I.B. List at "Any Address,

COVER ADDRESSES

Lisbon"', and asked that he be listed under his full postal address. Philby replied that 'There does not appear to be much prospect of the [Redacted] case developing as he has been refused permission by the police authorities to travel to the Azores. We will bear in mind the fact that two of the cover addresses given to [Redacted] are used by B.1.a. agents and will do our best to protect them.'[26]

Herberto Aguiar sent a telegram to Veronica Aguiar c/o Miss Wellington, Silverdale, Lynton Road, Burnham-on-Sea, Somerset, on 7 June 1943 saying: 'DARLING RECEIVED LETTER AND MONEY VERY ANXIOUS TO GO WAITING VISA ALL MY LOVE.' Bird's memorandum to Wilson on 14 June asserted that 'There is no indication that Herberto AGUIAR, sender of the attached telegram, has any connection with Emygdia de AGUIAR,[27] one of BALLOON's cover addresses. If, however, you think that enquiries should be made to satisfy ourselves about Veronica AGUIAR perhaps you would pass the telegram to B.1.G. for this to be done.' B1g was MI5's sub-section dealing with Spain, Portugal and South America. Bird's memo stated that 'Herberto A is a Portuguese of *British origin*! in the Lisbon orchestra who is believed to be coming as clerk to the Embassy. His wife Veronica is British.' One reference states that he was a violinist who had performed at the Teatro Nacional de São Carlos – Lisbon's national opera house – in 1932; another describes him as a 'Madeiran' and a 'first-class scoundrel'.[28] BALLOON was instructed to write to Aguiar on bank matters or about plants, as he was fond of gardening.[29]

Chapter 25

Going nowhere

In September 1943, in preparation for BALLOON's possible visit to America, Wilson suggested that he send a message to the Germans saying that his firm wanted him to make a business trip to America and, if he should pass through Lisbon en route, it would be a good opportunity to bring information which was too detailed to put into a letter. However, BALLOON requested that the Germans respond to his questions and pay him first.[1] He also felt that it would be better if someone from a government department rather than his own firm were sending him to America, but didn't know the exact date or route; it would also appear more natural if he were to travel by the northern route, and that if he were to land in Lisbon it would be on the return journey. He suggested that MI5 might want to fake his passport to appear that he'd left England before TRICYCLE returned.

Wilson remained sceptical of any advantage to be gained in suggesting to the Germans that BALLOON might go to Lisbon, noting that recently he had been complaining about non-payment and lack of acknowledgement, but

> I cannot help feeling that the Germans do would not place any real trust in information given by BALLOON. If this is correct, then the position as shown by the recent letters seems to me favourable for a fade out without any explanation. If on the other hand the Germans are still interested, then surely they will take advantage of TRICYCLE's return to put fresh energy into BALLOON.

He felt it was safe to assume that, since Jebsen knew that TRICYCLE was controlled *ergo* BALLOON must also be controlled, having managed to conceal from Berlin TRICYCLE's true position, 'but it is not clear that he is pretending to Berlin that BALLOON is also all right'. In terms of getting information from the Germans,

> TRICYCLE's personal contact with JEBSEN provides a better field for exploitation than anything BALLOON can do. In so far as our objective is deception, if the Germans really disbelieve in BALLOON I doubt if their views can be changed merely by BALLOON visiting Lisbon, but the mere fact that he did this might frustrate JEBSEN's policy of concealing from Berlin the fact that TRICYCLE is working under control.[2]

GOING NOWHERE

ISOS transcript No.1014 for 11 August 1943 notes:

> Lisbon – Berlin. No. 58. LUDOVICO HERIBERT to ANDREAS for HOEFLINGER. Ref. you 367. IVAN II received from April – August 42 50,000 escudos, September to December 75,000 January – April 43 inclusive 74639, 95. Sums paid before April 42 cannot be traced at this end as files have been destroyed, and some sent to PALAIS.

But it was not until 26 September 1943 that ISOS transcript No.1206 noted:

> Lisbon – Berlin. HARRY to HIOB for HOEFLINGER No 312. 1) Please sanction by W/T payment 125000 escudos to IVAN II for months of MAY, June, July August and September.[3]

Wilson felt that nothing should be done until TRICYCLE returned from Lisbon on 14 September and reported back; then they would make a decision. Failing that, BALLOON should write another letter complaining and enclosing 'one or two high-grade and reasonably accurate items of information'. He indicated that his views, which were not particularly strong, were likely to change following his meeting with Tar, Marriott and Masterman on 2 September:

> It is, of course, illogical for Berlin to believe in TRICYCLE and at the same time regard BALLOON as controlled, but unless that is their attitude I cannot understand why TRICYCLE was not asked to bring a new secret ink, money, and cover addresses to BALLOON last time he passed through Lisbon. One of the arguments which appears to impress the Germans in favour of TRICYCLE, is that if he were controlled he would not be allowed to go to Lisbon, and we do not want to put it into their heads that it would be our policy to send a controlled agent to make personal contact.[4]

In his follow-up report on 3 September 1943[5] Wilson expressed that should BALLOON pay a visit to America it was essential that MI5 obtain the FBI's agreement before suggesting anything to the Germans 'even if in fact nothing comes of it'. He would speak to Arthur Thurston, the FBI legal attaché at the US embassy about it, but 'If BALLOON actually, or even notionally, gets to the USA then clearly he must give some traffic about what he sees or hears in the States'. He suggested that BALLOON should write a letter mentioning that the Ministry of Supply was supporting his visit, which would ensure that he received his Exit Permit, subject to when the censorship position permitted it, around 6 September. Should he pass through Lisbon, the letter requested that the Germans provide him with a means of contacting them so that he could pass on information which was too long to write, but they must respond immediately as his trip might be imminent. There being no reply, he would send a cable to Santos from England or the USA signed 'with a surname the first letter of which will indicate the day of the month on which I expect to arrive in Lisbon, e.g. a cable signed "Edward Brown" will mean that I expect to be in Lisbon on the second day of the month'.

Wilson preferred that BALLOON's visit to the USA be connected either with the Vesely sub-machine gun, still under consideration by the British authorities, 'or in connection with the armoured car, which, as far as I know, has been turned down'.[6] The War Office had not yet allowed MI5 to provide any details of either of them, but he would try them again. Failing that, he and BALLOON would have to concoct another reason for his trip. He agreed about BALLOON not going to Lisbon en route to the USA 'as it looks less like a journey on our instructions'. In reality, given the issues he was having with the Ministry of Supply over the Vesely sub-machine gun, it seems unlikely that they would have actually supported his visit to the USA.

It was also unlikely that if BALLOON were to use Sancho's address, currently held in reserve in case either of METEOR's two cover addresses had ceased to function, he would be compromised in any way in his 'letter No.40 [which] should notionally have been written during the Censorship period to Sancho'. He would write a letter 'in case it is desired to produce evidence of what the Censorship is supposed to have caught'. And if he were to get to Lisbon he should adopt the attitude with Karsthoff that 'You haven't a hope of winning the war now chum, unless you can produce some stunning new weapon, but as long as you pay I will do what you want'.

Thurston replied that the FBI would have no objection to a notional or real journey to North America, but it would have to be cleared with Washington first. Mills would be able to obtain from Washington a certain amount of traffic to support BALLOON's notional journey if required. But a tactful approach needed to be adopted

> as all the FBI references to BALLOON are in the TRICYCLE file, and the FBI would therefore not welcome BALLOON even as a temporary guest until it had been fully explained to them that BALLOON's connection with TRICYCLE was almost fortuitous and BALLOON was in the first place a British nominee and was not brought into his present position with TRICYCLE except upon British instructions.

He felt that it would be far better if Mills spoke to Washington directly rather than writing a letter. It was also essential that if MI5 were to receive any assistance that this be handled through the MI5 representative in Washington and the FBI, but on no account through British Security Co-ordination [7] (undoubtedly because J. Edgar Hoover, the Director of the FBI, was decidedly prickly about the presence of British intelligence in the USA, particularly Stephenson at BSC). Wilson felt that it was important to keep SIS's Section V informed of BALLOON's 'visit', and agreed with Thurston that all discussions with the FBI be handled by their own representative and not by SIS.

Wilson explained to BALLOON that Censorship had notionally intercepted one of his letters, so that in order to prepare for an *actual* trip to Lisbon 'if this seemed desirable when we had TRICYCLE's report, and partly to account to the Germans for his not having been caught through the interception of a number of his letters ... he should notionally proceed to North America'. He pointed out that 'if he were really a German agent he would want to inform the Germans of his journey and discover the possibilities of making a contact in Lisbon on his return journey'. If his letter got through uncensored the Germans would be suspicious; therefore, to get around the Censorship restrictions he should only write to them once he arrived in Canada on Canadian hotel notepaper.[8] But Mills pointed out that there was 100 per cent testing of mail from Canada to the Iberian Peninsula, so it was decided that 'it would look just as bad, if not worse, if BALLOON's letter announcing his journey was sent from Canada instead of from this country'. Instead, the letter would be written in England and sent through unstriped as if it had slipped through the net.

The next day Wilson discussed his ideas with Tar and Mills. They agreed with Thurston's suggestions about keeping Section V informed, and censorship of BALLOON's letters. They would obtain two passports, exit permits, and US visas in BALLOON's name, one of which Mills would take to Canada so that all the necessary stamps and dates were applied; the other would be the one which BALLOON would actually use, then surrender to Mills once he arrived in Canada, in exchange for the one already in Mills' possession. Tar duly obtained the co-operation of J.W. Stafford of the Passport Office 'who was delighted to assist in this little fraudery'. Hugh Astor also arranged with Stafford that BALLOON's passport would be validated for America as well as the British Empire (the norm at that time), thus avoiding his having to get a special endorsement so that he could travel back via America and Lisbon. To add verisimilitude, BALLOON would notionally follow the day and route actually used by Mills.

When TRICYCLE was in Lisbon Karsthoff and Kammler @ Hauptmann Otto Kurrer had asked him whether he'd seen BALLOON very much. He told them that it had only been occasionally but he had avoided talking to him. Both Jebsen and Kammler believed that no one could have written all the letters BALLOON had written without being caught.[9]

Astor and Captain Herbertson at the Air Ministry discussed the logistics of BALLOON's proposed trip to Canada.[10] The regular flying-boat service from England would be suspended in the middle of October with only the pilot ferry service remaining; however, this required a very high degree of priority, so Herbertson recommended that BALLOON be sent during the first week of October. Obviously this would affect his return journey from Canada, but there were two routes which would remain in service – the bomber service direct to England, and the Boeing service from Canada via Bermuda to Lisbon. Astor noted that in order for BALLOON to get a seat on the Boeing service and avoid being put on the bomber service Herbertson would need to send a telegram to the air attaché in Canada pointing out BALLOON's high priority. This would be apparent when he arrived in Lisbon, but 'it would be quite plausible for him to say that this had been arranged by the Ministry of Supply or any other Government department which you may wish to nominate'.[11] Both services were free, but if BALLOON were to return to England from America on the Boeing Clipper service via Lisbon this would cost £170, to which SIS raised no objection.

***

BALLOON reported to Wilson on 4 October that production of the gun was still being obstructed, 'although a very heavy requirement had been put in for it by the Airborne Division and others, and arrangements for its manufacture in Ordnance factories etc. could readily be made'. He had discovered privately where the hold-up lay and there was 'clear evidence that his gun had been deliberately omitted at the last minute from certain trials which took place at Pendine of all similar weapons of 9 mm dimension.'[12] Therefore, he had sought a meeting with ACIGS, Major General Sir John Evetts, and Desmond Morton, Churchill's personal assistant and intelligence advisor.[13]

The mail he'd received on 9 September had contained 'duffs'; the letter dated 2 October, postmarked 4.10.43, had contained three. As Wilson remarked,

> It is a little difficult to understand why this letter was despatched at that time, as on 9.9.43 BALLOON wrote stating that he was shortly leaving for Canada on a business trip, which would probably last for several weeks ... adding that it was no use writing to him as he might have left by the time the Germans could get a letter here.
>
> I am inclined to think that the first two 'duffs' were prepared a long time before they were sent off, while No. 3 is a last minute substitution for what had previously been intended.[14]

Tar commented, 'Very interesting. They obviously either don't get B's letters or if they do don't regard [?] them. I think he should be assumed to have gone to Canada to ~~have~~ get this letter on his return.'

The Germans complained about not having received from him a 'long and detailed account of gas weapons, etc.', but as Wilson pointed out, BALLOON had already clarified that it was too long to write, and the Germans had failed to provide him with a means of transmitting lengthy information – 'the Germans talk about seeing him, and in the same sentence, say they have not yet heard from him where and when a meeting might take place. This presumably was written before BALLOON's letter of 9.9.43 ... was received, or of course that the letter may have gone astray.' Surely they had also realised that BALLOON's ink was far too elementary for Censorship purposes:

> We will have to consider carefully whether he is to pretend to have left for Canada before receiving this letter, or whether we are to say that his journey had been postponed so that he was still in London when it

arrived. At present I favour the former course, because unless he had left for Canada shortly after 9.9.43 the Germans will think he ought to have written further letters, which, because of the Censorship position at that time, he did not in fact do. We can also, if we so desire, pretend that the letter was forwarded on to him in Canada.[15]

BALLOON was pleased when shown a transcript of the three 'duffs', because, as far as he was concerned, it indicated that the Germans were still interested in him. Wilson noted,

As the Germans have not sent BALLOON a telegram to indicate which of his suggestions they prefer as regards contacting him in Lisbon should he succeed in getting there, and in view of the fact that TRICYCLE is returning to Lisbon, BALLOON and I at present feel that it is probably better that he should not make an actual visit. In due course he should notionally return from Canada, and if, as seems probable, he has not by that time been given a new secret ink, he should perhaps write an open letter explaining his movements, and consideration might also then be given to whether he should try and make use of the plain language code for telegrams.[16]

That response did not come until 29 October, signed Sousa Campos, the business where Francisco Barroso dos Santos worked, presumed to be

as a result of Berlin expressing their agreement to the proposals in a letter from SCHREIBER[17] to Berlin of 15.10.43 in which he [BALLOON] announced his proposed visit to Canada, and indicates that if BALLOON manages to return to England by way of Lisbon they prefer that as a means of making contact he should call on SANTOS and ask if he has any suitable jade for Mr IVAN's collection. The Germans are supposed to have arranged for SANTOS to hand BALLOON a letter telling BALLOON how to make contact with the Germans.[18]

***

By 16 October it had become clear that BALLOON's actual trip to Canada was not going to happen. Wilson wrote to Mills c/o RCMP Commissioner Stuart Wood saying that since TRICYCLE was heading off to Lisbon in three weeks' time it would have to wait as he didn't want the pair to overlap. BALLOON had received a letter telling him not to write until he received a new ink. Wilson mused that it would be interesting to see how they would try to get it to him:

If, and when, they give him a new ink he has a lot of material to send over on technical gas matters, of which he gave them the headings some time ago, and in which they are now showing great interest. As, however, BALLOON is notionally in Canada at the present time, I would welcome it if you could send me something which can, if necessary, serve as traffic, describing your journey out and any information you may be able to obtain about the manufacture of small arms in Canada.[19]

In his note on 22 October 1943 he reported:

> The FBI memorandum dated 5.10.43 giving a general account of TRICYCLE's activities in the USA, discloses to us for the first time an open letter in the hand-writing of KARSTHOFF's secretary, Elizabeth SAHRBACH, dated Lisbon 24.10.41 and received by TRICYCLE on 8.11.41. This letter contained the sentence:
> I was very anxious about Dicky, but he is really a nice chap. I got a letter from him some days ago. I would be so glad if we could arrange to meet us altogether in some nice place.[20]

A staff list of KO Portugal in August Kraatz's file describes Elisabeth as:

> Age late thirties; height medium; face narrow; fair hair; eyes dark-grey; figure slim; right shoulder slightly crooked, but disability well concealed. Since 1944, wife of KRAEMER-AUENRODE. Formerly KRAEMER-AUENRODE's secretary. Very intelligent. Dangerous intriguer. Persuaded KRAEMER to get a divorce and marry her. Had considerable influence on her husband and was mainly responsible for the bad running of the KO. Extremely well informed on all matters.[21]

When BALLOON met Wilson again on 25 October 1943 he suggested that, in order to convince the Germans that he had actually gone to Canada, a telegram should be sent from there acknowledging receipt and saying that he was returning to England immediately by the northern route but was still unsure as to whether it could be via Lisbon. However, Wilson and Tar decided that a genuine agent wouldn't risk sending a telegram, and that no action should be taken. Only if he were asked would TRICYCLE be instructed to tell the Germans that he had not seen BALLOON on his current trip but heard that he was in Canada. He was under strict instructions not to mention any of the other agents. Then, when BALLOON had notionally returned, he should send an open letter confirming the exchange of cables and acknowledging the Germans' letter of 2 October because, as Wilson pointed out, 'he has been instructed not to use secret ink until he is given a new type'. The open letter, addressed to Santos, would explain that he had been unable to travel back via Lisbon and that 'in view of the terms of the letter he has received he can do nothing more until he hears further from SANTOS'.

On 3 November Wilson wrote to Mills again c/o the RCMP in Ottawa saying that it was 'high time I let you know what is happening about BALLOON':

> As you know, he notionally travelled out to Canada with you, having informed his masters by letter dated 9th September that he was going to Canada. In his letter he told them not to write, but asked for a cable to indicate which of two suggested methods of making contact, contained in his letter, was preferred by his masters. He told his masters not to write as he might have left before he could get the letter.

He told him about the Germans' letter of 2 October and the 'duffs', and their instructions not to write until BALLOON had received a new ink: 'This was presumably the result of Lisbon realising that letters generally had been striped, and possibly also realising that one of BALLOON's letters was supposed to have been caught by the striping.' The Germans' preference for making contact, he said was, 'I sent you a cable, on which you will have acted long before you get this letter, asking you to send off a cable in BALLOON's name from Montreal.'

> Our present intention is that at some future date not yet determined, BALLOON should notionally return by way of the northern route. He will then find the letter which tells him not to use his secret ink but to wait for a new one. He would then write an open letter saying (1) that he was unsuccessful in getting home via Lisbon and therefore had no chance of meeting the addressee SANTOS, and (2) that in view of the terms of the letter he found waiting for him on his return he would do nothing further until he heard again from SANTOS. The case will then be in abeyance unless and until BALLOON's masters succeed in giving him a new ink.

TRICYCLE would be returning to Lisbon in the near future and ARTIST (Jebsen) had been in contact with SIS in Madrid and Lisbon:

> If BALLOON has to start writing again he has a good deal he can say on gas matters, as a long time ago he gave the headings of certain information he had available and he has now been asked for details on a number of points. It is very doubtful if he will ever have to use traffic relating to his proposed visit to Canada but as a matter of precaution we should be glad to know of anything which happened on your journey which might form the basis of traffics, and to have your ideas of any possible traffic in connection with armaments generally and particularly small arms, which BALLOON might be supposed to have come across when in Canada.[22]

Mills promised to send Wilson an account of his journey to Canada the following week which might help with the BALLOON traffic: '[Y]ou, of course, will have to have the material cleared through the XX Committee except that referring to the s.s. Lafayette (Normandie) which will go no further than the American Press has gone.'

On 12 December 1941 the US authorities had seized the French ocean liner *Normandie*, converted it to a troopship, and renamed it the USS *Lafayette*. In February 1942 it suffered a major fire, with the loss of one life and many fire- and smoke-related injuries. Mills wrote: 'I don't know how the dates of my journey will fit in with BALLOON's notional voyage but if you have to date the journey back to the QM's [*Queen Mary*'s] previous voyage, I should imagine that what I shall have to say about the journey will fit equally well especially since the visible state of affairs in connection with the Normandie was about the same in the middle of September as it was when I saw her on October 4th.'[23] On 16 November 1943 he provided some notes to Wilson in which he described his 29 September voyage on the *Queen Mary*.[24]

Acting on a new tip from BALLOON, Wilson informed Major E. Goudie of the Inter-Services Security Board (ISSB) at the War Office about it:

> A new device invented by Mr STRAUSSLER to make tanks of all types amphibious. The device also provides a sort of deck on which troops can be carried. This arrangement is now in mass production.
>
> Also there is a new mobile gun mounting being made at Woolwich and designed by the same man. It is called the MONITOR and is in effect a 5.5" Haw. [*sic*] on a mobile self-propelled mounting.[25]

However, he was 'rather doubtful whether it can be used by anybody but perhaps you will let me know.' Headed by Colonel Edmund Combes, ex-MI(R), the ISSB was established in February 1940 by the JIC 'to co-ordinate and improve both the provision of cover for British operations and the prevention of leakage of information about them'.[26] It liaised with the JIC, the London Controlling Section, and A Force in the Middle East, aka Advanced Headquarters A Force, the deception operation based in Cairo established by Brigadier Dudley Clarke.[27]

On 19 November Mills thanked Wilson for the update on BALLOON and apologised that his lack of more information about the arms industry was because 'it would be impossible to get anywhere without taking the matter up with the Minister of Munitions and Supply [C.D. Howe] and he, I am afraid, is a thorough gas-bag and I would not for one moment dare to disclose to him why I wanted the information'.[28]

Wilson sought Tar's opinion on what instructions TRICYCLE should be given about his future dealings with various agents such as BALLOON, GELATINE, METEOR, The WORM, and VELOCIPEDE (identity unknown), all part of

TRICYCLE's 'Yugoslav Ring' (Figure 1). Should the Germans ask TRICYCLE to co-operate,

> he should show great reluctance, but if he is very strongly pressed he should agree to co-operate either by bringing messages or material such as a new secret ink for them, or agreeing to arrange to let them make use of his wireless connections if these become established. As far as the Germans are concerned TRICYCLE is not to be aware of the fact that any of the others, except BALLOON and GELATINE, are working for them.[29]

***

Operation STARKEY

In early November BALLOON was feeling completely run-down, 'no doubt as the result of having fallen out of an aeroplane in France in 1940 and working continuously since, with only one break of a week', Wilson surmised. BALLOON told him that he might be able to persuade the Canadians to send him to Canada in connection with the VAP sub-machine gun being manufactured there as the Canadian Department of Munitions and Supply had written to him in March about supplying a sample of the gun at a cost of £10. That being the case, he would combine it with a holiday. Wilson expressed no objection but informed him that he would require a new passport, not the one they had already obtained 'in case he has to produce the passport showing that he went to Canada in September'. As he pointed out to Marriott on 12 November

> It is perhaps worth recording in connection with Mr Harris' [Tomás Harris, B1g] note on the steps taken in connection with the GARBO addresses to which letters were intercepted during the Censorship tests which accompanied Operation STARKEY, that one letter from BALLOON and one letter from GELATINE were also notionally intercepted during that period. No enquiries have been made by S.I.S. at the addresses concerned. At first sight it is somewhat illogical that they should have interrogated GARBO's cover addressees and should not have approached the addressees of the intercepted letters of BALLOON and GELATINE.[30]

According to SHAEF'S Historical sub-section:

> Operation STARKEY was the threat against the PAS DE CALAIS area of Northern FRANCE. The object was defined as being to convince the enemy that a large scale landing in the PAS DE CLARIS

[*sic*] area was imminent, and thereby to compel the GERMAN fighter force to engage in air battles of attrition in circumstances advantageous to us.[31]

STARKEY was one of three components of Operation COCKADE, a deception operation to take place on 9 September 1943, staged by British and Canadian forces, the others being WADHAM and TINDALL. As Wilson continued:

> Whether at the time the reasons for not doing so were good or bad, or resulted from pure oversight, is now somewhat immaterial, as it is clearly too late now to interrogate the addressees of letters caught by the end of August. In the unlikely event of the Germans realising that letters to BALLOON's and GELATINE's cover addresses failed to get here, and that, notwithstanding what happened in other cases, no enquiries were made of the cover addresses, the Germans might, if they were completely logical, reach the conclusion that we did not make enquiries in these cases because the spies concerned did not code their secret ink messages, and we therefore hoped that if we left the cover addresses alone we would pick up subsequent letters, the secret text of which would contain material through which we could identify the writers.[32]

Astor discussed with Wilson whether they should interrogate BALLOON's and GELATINE's addressees during Operation STARKEY. Since neither BALLOON nor GELATINE encoded their texts:

> It was then decided that ... the most satisfactory method for identifying them would be to intercept their future correspondence in the hope of identifying the writers from the secret text. In this respect BALLOON and GELATINE differ from GARBO, who is in the habit of enciphering all incriminating material.

They were unconcerned about BALLOON since he had been instructed not to write until he received new ink and cover addresses, but GELATINE's position was not so satisfactory. Susan Barton had informed Astor that 'already three letters to the blown cover address have been notionally intercepted and if any more letters are intercepted it seems certain that we would be in possession of sufficient material for even the most thick-headed security officer to identify GELATINE ... .'[33]

***

The assistant naval attaché in Lisbon, Lieutenant Commander Tony Hugill, reported that César Pacheco's friend ran an antiques shop, Sousa & Campos Lda, at 162 Rua da Rosa, Cunhal das Bolas, Lisbon, which he'd taken over before the war after the previous manager had died. The manager had been approached by a German (see below) who'd persuaded him to act during the war as a receiver and transmitter of letters to England, the USA, South America and Axis-controlled countries. Pacheco's friend 'took on this traffic without asking too many questions, as he was aware of the financial indebtedness of the firm to the above-mentioned German.' Hugill reported the identity of the friend as Mario Joaquim Martins who had

> decided to come clean, though somewhat doubtful of his reception, or of whom to come and see. I imagine he has used Pacheco as a sounding device. Full details are not as yet available, but it seems that the letters are received under one set of names, of which one is:
> Francisco Barroso Dos Santos, and sends them on under another. He has never tried to examine the letters but will do so surreptitiously, if he can, from now on. The following is a copy of a telegram he received recently:
>
> 'DAR40 MONTREAL 25/24   8.
> NLT. Barroso dos Santos 162A-164A Rua Rosa Lisbon
> Your cable received stop still uncertain when and how I shall be returning.'[34]

Letters from England passed through the Censor 'so that they must be superficially harmless'. Besides forwarding letters, Martins had been sending about £200 every month to Friedl Gartner's account at the National Provincial Bank Ltd, South Audley Street, London W1 which Hugill presumed must have received Treasury approval.[35] Pacheco had promised to keep him informed of any other details and would arrange with Martins to transmit to him details of future letters. Hugill requested instructions on what action MI5 wanted him to take. Wilson commented:

1. This involves GELATINE's cover address of Lucilia MARTINS, as well as BALLOON's paymaster and cover address.
2. Mario MARTINS will have to be thoroughly interrogated as if we were urgently interested in all details and had no previous knowledge. He must be instructed to hand to us any future letters which we fail to intercept and to maintain the utmost secrecy.
3. Self-interest should prevent him from disclosing to the Germans that he has been in touch with us.
4. This makes a visit here by BALLOON impossible unless the Germans arrange some other means of contact as BALLOON was to have called at the address concerned for instructions.
5. We must get ARTIST to persuade the Germans that they must eliminate the firm in question and everyone connected with its address both as paying agents and receivers of letters.[36]

Lieutenant F. Stilwell RNVR, also an assistant naval attaché and Passport Control Officer in Lisbon, wrote a note on 13 November, referring to Hugill's report and providing more information from Pacheco about the German, whose name was Teodoro Mielitz:

> MIELITZ lives [...] but has a room above, or next to (the informant was not sure [...] the a[n]tique shop. He is reputed homosexual and to use this room for orgies. At one time he owned a house at Aveiro, this was closed by the [...] as clandestine meetings were being held there. The police were unable [to f]ollow up with arrests due to the intervention of 'powerful people' and [becau]se MIELITZ had, at the request of the German Legation, been granted diplomatic [immun]ity!! MIELITZ has now acquired a house at Cruz de Pau near the Alfeite [...] [*Note: The Alfeite was the location of the main naval base for Lisbon and its shipyard.*]
>
> Bef[o]re the war MIELITZ made his living by dealing in rare books, he [has] given th[em] up now and to all intents and purposes lives off the air! He has grown far [more] generous and affluent lately.
>
> On [one] occasion he was observed talking to someone in a CD car who [gave] him a[n] envelope.
>
> He re[c]eived a friend of Baron de Keyler (spelling phonetic). [*sic*]
>
> The s[u]ms mentioned in the letter under reference as being remitted [to?] England and are not sent monthly but about every two months. They are always [illegible] thro[ug]h the owner of the antique shop who takes them to the Banco [Espirito] Santo while the bank in England to which they are credited is always [...] sume the n[a]mes of the benefiters vary. In July and October they were [...] Friedel Ga[rt]ner. Pacheco is trying to find out some of the previous names.
>
> All l[et]ters come addressed to Portuguese names which vary continually. He will try to obtain a list of them.[37]

Pacheco promised to return the following week with any further information he was able to obtain.

According to Michaela Gräfin von Keyserlingk, from another branch of the family, 'Baron de Keyler' was Klaus Freiherr von Keyserlingk:

> [H]is father was an Admiral in the German navy. Klaus was a lawyer and had to leave Germany in a rush during the Nazi period. He immigrated to the US, re-did his legal exams so as to work in the States. Returned to Germany with the Nürnberg Trial. After which he stayed in Germany helping German Industry to rebuild their business connections to the US.[38]

Theodor Mielitz (also written as Militz) was a Portuguese national in his late fifties and well-known to Kurrer who did not use him very much as he believed he was working for the Allies. Mielitz pretended to be a journalist, and had a homosexual relationship with Francisco Lopes da Fonseca whom he had recruited prior to the Spanish Civil War.[39] Fonseca's address, Rua São Mamede 50-51, Lisbon, would also be used for messages sent by Eddie Chapman (ZIGZAG) to his case officer, Baron Stephan von Gröning.

Lucilia Martins was Mario Martins' sister. On 24 November Mario was interrogated by the SIS representative in Lisbon, Cecil Gledhill, the SIS Head of Station. The report confirmed how, in September 1942 Mielitz had approached the widow of the owner of the antiques shop and suggested that they become partners and remove Martins. Initially, the widow accepted, but the creditors refused because Martins was familiar with the business and worked there part-time.

When Mielitz asked Martins about receiving any letters he denied it, neglecting to mention one from Greece which had arrived while the shop was closed between January and March 1943. About ten days before his interrogation by SIS Martins gave the letter to Pacheco to pass on to the British authorities. Gledhill had phoned Stilwell about it saying that he'd seen it and intended to get in touch with Pacheco and retrieve it. His report continued:

5. About four months ago the I.P. [International Police] called on the shop and asked if MIELITZ was a partner in the business. The employee there replied 'no' and told MARTINS about the incident.
6. *All* letters addressed to the shop were for Francisco BARROSO dos SANTOS although the sender varied.
7. Other letters were sent to the widow addressed either to Maria José dos SANTOS or Maria José de Espirito Santo SANTOS, the latter being her maiden name. The address of course was hers, Rua do Embaixador 158 – 1º.
8. Letters from Engla[nd], Brazil and the USA were addressed to MARTINS' [...] [resp]ectively Lucilia MARTINS and Paulo SIMON [...] name is Spanish as Paulo's grandfather was a Spaniard) the address, was Bartolomeu da Costa 43, 1º D, being that of the sister who lives with her mother.
9. The sister had been receiving these letters without comment as she was doing it at the request of her step-father, the deceased ex-owner of the shop. However, round about August 1943 a letter was received bearing the Setubal post mark and as it was addressed to Paulo who was at sea, Paulo's mother-in-law (MARTINS' mother) opened it and on reading it found it gave detailed information about British shipping (arrivals and sailings in Portuguese ports). MIELITZ came round to collect this letter the next day. The mother showed this to MARTINS

and his sister and they all smelt a rat. The letter had some address in the Rua dos Fanquieros. The result was that when the letter arrived from England in September addressed to Paulo she refused to give it to MIELITZ and returned it to England.

10. <u>Resumé of addresses</u>

From England	Francisco Barroso dos SANTOS, Rua da Rosa 164a.
From England, USA and Brazil	Lucila Martins and Paulo Simon of Rua Bartolomeu da Costa 43, 1° D
From [Engla]nd	D. Maria José dos SANTOS of Rua do Embaixador 158 – 1°

11. [Ot]her information on MIELITZ. He lives in Paco d'Arcos with a marrie[d co]uple who act as his servants. The woman is a servant-cum-hou[se-keeper]… and the man, her husband is a confidential messenger of MIELITZ's [to] the extent of taking and receiving messages for him to the Hun C[o]nsulate.
12. This couple have a son – one Francisco – in his twenties who lives with a mulato girl in Parede at MIELITZ's expense. MIELITZ at first used to say [t]his chap was his son, but now admits it is the house-keeping couple's son. About six weeks ago this 'son' and the black girl moved to a ho[u]se on the other side of the river which is in a place called Vale de Gatos. The property belongs to MIELITZ.
13. The 'son' has been to Germany and possibly abroad to other countries with MIELITZ several times.
14. MARTINS once heard MIELITZ phoning to Parede asking if any letters had arrived. He has promised to try and find out the address or addresses concerned.
15. On the day of the clipper crash in the river MARTINS on hearing the [aerop]lanes remarked to MIELITZ 'it sounds as if there is a fire or something'" MIELITZ replied 'Oh, don't you know? a clipper has crashed.'[40]
16. MARTINS has agreed to bring along any future letters for our examination and he has been invited (by MIELITZ) to visit the property at Vale de Gatos.

Our representative has instructed him to accept and to keep his eyes open and that he should continue to act in all ways just as before. MARTINS was also asked to keep an eye on MIELITZ's contacts if and when the occasion arises.[41]

GOING NOWHERE

Captain M. Lloyd of Section Vx, SIS's section dealing with double-cross agents, sent an interesting communication to Tar on 19 November in which he stated that a telegram they had received from Lisbon appeared to have been sent either by or in agreement with Wilson:

> Contents as follows:-
> 'The proprietor of SOUSA E. CAMPOS Ltd. has confessed through a cut-out that he has been acting as a post-box.
> He has named GELATINE as having received payments through him and has quoted BALLOON's recent cable from Montreal including his name.
> On Wednesday (I take this to be Wednesday 17th Nov.) he is to see Waite. Waite will interrogate him thoroughly as if we had no previous knowledge of these matters.
> We propose that ARTIST should be asked to try to arrange that the agents mentioned should be warned off the relevant cover addresses and that new methods of payment should be adopted. Do you agree?
> Meanwhile BALLOON and GELATINE must not communicate with the addresses in the Rua da Roja.'[42]

ARTIST (Jebsen) was in Madrid so no urgent reply was required, but Lloyd requested that anything to be sent should be passed on to him in due course. He followed this up with another CX to Tar on 23 November clarifying that it was Pacheco who was to be interrogated by Waite on 17 November, not Mario Martins.[43]

Tar wrote to Mills on 25 November saying that

> There is a certain amount of difficulty at the Lisbon end as a cut out has approached SIS Lisbon coming from the cover address Barroso dos Santos, 162A-164A Rua Rosa, Lisbon, to give the information that a telegram has been received from BALLOON originating in Canada and that he has been responsible also for making payments to GELATINE in the UK. The whole matter is extremely tricky but fortunately both Ian Wilson and Foley are at the moment in Lisbon dealing with the TRICYCLE case and we are hoping, by a compromise, to avert a disaster in this direction. We are in fact advising them to approach the owner of the Cover Address direct and virtually turn him into a double agent, telling him that he has done good work so far as the British are concerned and at the same time instructing him virtually to act as a double agent in the matter of passing on correspondence. It is undoubtedly a dangerous technique but there seems to be no other way round the difficulty.[44]

A further CX from Lloyd on 28 November pointed out that if BALLOON and GELATINE were blown then TRICYCLE would be compromised and SIS could not see how ARTIST could pull it off without drawing suspicion on himself or causing the Germans to investigate Martins. He suggested that Martins be interviewed in person and told to continue as normal, but sworn to secrecy: 'He should be both complimented and frightened but should be promised a reward if he carried out our instructions. The Germans should be encouraged to warn BALLOON and GELATINE to lay off the addresses.' However, this would depend on Martins' reliability and whether he was willing to help.

Referring to his CX of 19 November, Lloyd confirmed that SIS had heard from Wilson that the addresses Rua Bartolomeu da Costa 43-1, Floor Right, and Rua Do Embaixador 158 First Floor, were also involved. Wilson advised that those addresses not be used until he could send SIS further details. The next day Lloyd reported that Martins had been interviewed but 'cannot be trusted to keep his mouth shut indefinitely if he continues to receive correspondence, which after a time he must guess is controlled'.

***

BALLOON was becoming frustrated that his long anticipated visit to Canada was getting unnecessarily prolonged, telling Astor on 2 December that by this time he should have completed 'all the notional business with the sale of his sub-machine gun to the Canadians'. Astor agreed with the suggestion that he should write a letter *en clair* and echoed what Wilson had said earlier about its contents, adding that BALLOON should ask the Germans to pay him the money that was long overdue:

> In view of the possibility that BALLOON may in reality visit Canada in the near future, I suggested to him that it might be prudent for his astral body to remain in Canada until joined by his material body, when they can return to this country together. BALLOON argues that it would be most plausible for him to have already completed his visit, and that if the sale of his sub-machine gun proved successful in Canada, it would be natural for him to return there and that this visit could co-incide with the visit of his material body. The way would then be open for us to arrange for BALLOON to return to this country via Lisbon. The wisdom of this action must, of course, be considered in conjunction with Wilson, and in any event the matter is not urgent.[45]

Marriott told Tar that he didn't entirely agree with Astor's reasoning, or that Wilson be reminded 'of the fact which must in the circumstances be constantly on his mind'. Any cable sent should simply say that BALLOON was ready to return from Canada and ask Wilson for directions.

Tar informed Lloyd on 4 December that Censorship had intercepted a telegram dated 15 November sent from Francisco Santos in Lisbon to Santos c/o Ferostallo, Schaffhausen:

We have received telegrams 12/14 Government protested arbitrary attitude we are putting through action proposed. We are transferring money requested but I draw your attention total remitted 22000 francs (? on an average) 5500 a month which we consider excessive judging by reports received on cost of living at your end. Kindly cut down expenses in the necessary way as (your) stay will probably be prolonged for the duration of the war. MANUEL asked VASCO to get THIEL to give you work so as to avoid idleness and to earn at least enough to cover expenses.

COPIED
I.R.B.d.
1.12.43[46]

He noted that 'Francisco Santos is of course the resident of 162-164 Rua da Rosa, Lisbon, and is ... one of the cover addresses used by BALLOON and GELATINE.' MI5 had carried a look-up on the other names mentioned in the telegram but failed to come up with any 'identifiable traces'. Astor followed up his consultation with Lloyd by contacting Wilson in Lisbon the same day, seeking his views:

1. BALLOON is of the opinion that his visit to Canada is becoming unnaturally prolonged. He feels that it would be more plausible for him to make two short journeys to Canada in connection with the sale of his gun, rather than one long visit.
2. BALLOON may actually make this second visit if it is considered desirable from our point of view or if his own business necessitates it.
3. The question of BALLOON returning via Lisbon would remain optional.
4. BALLOON suggests that he should write a letter to the Germans which would contain no secret ink but the open text of which would indicate
   a) That he has returned to this country.
   b) That he has much information for transmission.
   c) A demand for new secret ink and cover addresses.
   d) A demand for payment.

Lloyd had informed him that there was currently a backlog in the cable traffic to Lisbon; therefore they agreed that the message should go by fast bag aimed at reaching Wilson on 7 December.[47] But by the time Wilson left Lisbon on 12 December he had not received Astor's communication. Lloyd and Tar agreed that BALLOON

> should write an open letter indicating that he had returned to London and received the instructions not to use his existing secret ink any

longer, and that therefore he could do nothing more until he got new ink. As TRICYCLE will avoid bringing a new ink if he can decline without incurring suspicion, the BALLOON case will be dormant until, if ever, the Germans succeed in getting him a new ink.[48]

SIS Lisbon's CX of 20 December reported that, according to ARTIST, BALLOON was not highly thought of in Berlin or Lisbon. While the Germans didn't think he was double-crossing them, he wasn't much use but 'This might be cured by a personal visit'. Those thoughts were echoed in a further discussion about his case two days later, an extract of which appears in both TRICYCLE's and BALLOON's files:

> ARTIST was asked whether it would be a good thing for BALLOON to visit Lisbon and he said that if BALLOON could play his part very well it would be advantageous. On the other hand Lisbon did not regard BALLOON in the extremely favourable light in which they regarded TRICYCLE, and therefore BALLOON would have a much more difficult reception than TRICYCLE ever had. Both in Lisbon and Berlin they did not think BALLOON was working under British control but the Germans were continually reminding themselves that BALLOON was, after all, an Englishman. They were inclined to think that he was lazy and had no judgement, and further, that although he was prepared to sell them information for money it was unlikely that he, as an Englishman, would let them have really vital information which would be detrimental to this country.
>
> In view of this it seems to me that there is little advantage in continuing the case of BALLOON. His arrangements for making contact in Lisbon involve his calling upon MARTINS, and for this reason a meeting in Lisbon is undesirable, quite apart from the fact that it would seem to be rather an unnecessary risk to send him to face what would be rather a hostile reception. Even if he succeeded, the only advantage would be that he would be more likely to be believed if subsequently we wished to put over deceptive information through him.
>
> As he is only a letter writer, and as there is no reason why TRICYCLE and other agents should not put across such deceptive material as BALLOON could be used for in the future, it seemed hardly worth while [sic] to continue with the case, particularly if we could make it appear that the Germans themselves had brought the case to an end. They had gone a long way towards this by prohibiting him from writing until they send him a new secret ink. They might suggest that TRICYCLE should bring the new ink to London for him, but TRICYCLE was instructed to refuse to do this provided he could do so without prejudicing his own position. Although at

first sight it s[ee]ms rather paradoxical that TRICYCLE should agree to bring material for GELATINE but should decline to bring material for BALLOON, he thought he could probably do this without arousing suspicion, particularly as he had, some time ago, been advised not to have anything to do with BALLOON, and later he informed the Germans that he had met BALLOON accidentally and had left BALLOON with the impression that he was no longer interested in the business. It was expected that KARSTHOFF would support TRICYCLE in his reluctance to become involved again in the BALLOON case. They would not feel the same about the case of GELATINE, whom they regard as a good German who would not do anything to give TRICYCLE away. It was therefore agreed that BALLOON should, as soon as possible, write an open letter stating that on his return from Canada he had found the last letter to him, and in view of the letter he could do nothing further until he heard again from the Germans. He should then do nothing more until there were further developments.[49]

Masterman was unhappy about the BALLOON proposals, but 'otherwise it all sounds very satisfactory'.

Chapter 26

'He continues to provide such information ...'

The New Year arrived, with still no sign of an end to the war, and many of BALLOON's creditors still baying at the door for outstanding debts. Wilson met with him on 13 January 1944 to discuss the current status of his case. BALLOON informed him that things were moving ahead favourably with the production of the gun so he was not as busy as before and asked how he could assist MI5. Wilson told Marriott that the information BALLOON provided could be used as traffic for other agents. Marriott agreed with Wilson's suggestion that there might be occasions when they could submit incoming questions to BALLOON to which he could provide answers. The following day B1a reported that

> While TRICYCLE was still in Lisbon BALLOON's open letter was received. They discussed asking TRICYCLE to take new ink and money to BALLOON in the same way as he was to take them for GELATINE, but they decided that it would be useless to sent [sic] him a new ink without satisfying him financially, as it was obvious from his disgruntled letters that he would not work properly unless he were fully paid.

But when TRICYCLE left Lisbon the Germans were still waiting for the necessary authority from Berlin to pay BALLOON, and for a decision on the future of his case. TRICYCLE thought it quite likely that when he next visited Lisbon he would be asked to bring back both money and a new ink for BALLOON.[1]

BALLOON had learnt from Major Hodgson of BSA that Straussler had got himself into hot water for shooting his mouth off about amphibious tanks and self-propelled guns, and forewarned them that Hodgson was contemplating getting in touch with MI5 about it.

> Some of BALLOON's information to us has in fact come from Straussler, and BALLOON was worried in case Straussler's difficulties arose from this fact. I was able to assure him that this was not the case and that therefore any accusations that might be outstanding against Straussler were no concern of this part of the department.[2]

'HE CONTINUES TO PROVIDE SUCH INFORMATION ...'

The following day, in response to TRICYCLE's questions about gas, Tar reported to Lieutenant Colonel Harold L. Petavel[3] who worked under Bevan at the War Cabinet Office:

1. As regards the parachute mines. BALLOON reported to the Germans on 28.5.43 that the British had many big gas parachute mines and the bursting container was replacing former ideas of spray. On 3.7.43 BALLOON gave headings of a lengthy report he could make if the enemy provided him with better facilities for communication, and included in the heading under 'Weapons' was a reference to aerial containers. The Germans have failed to give BALLOON adequate facilities so he has not in fact amplified this statement. The actual proposed answer as far as mines are concern [sic] is adapted by me from some suggestions which BALLOON himself put up and which were not at the time finally approved by the author of Plan LANGTOFT, who did however suggest that they might be re-written as a follow-up.

   As far as the gas rockets are concerned, BALLOON reported on 28.5.43 that the British had developed a rocket carrying gas which was far better than any weapons they had had before. It carried about 30 lbs of gas and had a very long range, 4 miles had been mentioned. On 3.7.43 in the headings of the report which has never been made, BALLOON referred to rocket guns firing 50 lbs drums with persistent or non-persistent gases.[4]

At the end of the month Tar wrote to Marriott attaching a 'lengthy and somewhat illegible note by BALLOON on the subject of industrial diamonds':

The alleged facts about the production of these diamonds by a special process by one NUSSBAUM are set out in BALLOON's own note.[5] Whether what BALLOON claims for these diamonds is justified I have no idea, but he is quite confident that commercially he is on to a big thing. This is of no concern of ours and we have only to consider whether, assuming these diamonds do exist or can be made, any use can be made of the fact by B.1.A.[6]

Austrian Leon Nussbaum had been involved with Richard Markus, a German interned in Britain under DR.18B, for dealing in industrial diamonds thought to be fraudulent, and Pilot Officer Robert William Liversidge, RAFVR @ Jacob Perlzweig, an intelligence officer with Fighter Control at Stanmore, also interned under DR.18B,[7] who 'was associated until the obtaining of his commission with NUSSBAUM, who is held by the Diamond Trade to be a notorious swindler'. Lieutenant Colonel Robin Stephens' (of Camp 020) account in Liversidge's file refers to Markus as 'a known swindler'.[8] Liversidge's file mentions that Nussbaum had come into contact with Paul Markus [sic] in 1934. Together they had formed the Cardimond Industrial Diamond Company (also known as the Hardimond Company) of 39 St James's Street, London SW1:

> NUSSBAUM poses as a scientist of great erudition and gives out that his process was the hardening of diamonds by fusion under controlled heat with graphite. The Diamond Trade however found this to be false and that the process is, in fact, merely a fusion of aluminium dust with diamonds of poor quality. Profits are considerable as a low grade diamond fetches 5/6d per carat and the spurious diamond is sold at £3 per carat.[9]

ARTIST had revealed that the Germans were suffering from a shortage of industrial diamonds, due largely to the manufacturers hiding their stocks, saving them for peace-time manufacture, 'and while all manufacturers are continually stressing to the German controllers of stocks of diamonds that they are in urgent need of more, their claims are exaggerated'. As far as BALLOON's case was concerned, Wilson declared, 'I do not think there is much in the plan, as the present position of his case seems to me to be absolutely clear cut and will be decided one way or another when TRICYCLE goes to Lisbon. At the moment he is precluded from acting because he has no ink. He is in effect also precluded from making personal contact for two reasons':

> 1) His scheme for making contact has ceased to be practicable ... owing to its involving a call upon the cover addressee MARTINS, who has spilled the beans to us. MARTINS knows BALLOON real name [sic] because he has made payments to BALLOON and has received a cable from Canada in BALLOON's own name. If therefore BALLOON called upon MARTINS in order to make contact with KARSTHOFF, MARTINS would presumably become aware of the fact that this was done with our knowledge, and he is too unreliable a man to trust in Lisbon with the knowledge that BALLOON is a controlled agent.
> 2) There are excessive complications and risks in BALLOON and TRICYCLE both being in Lisbon at the same time.

Wilson reiterated what had been said earlier in the 22 December 1943 report about BALLOON not being trusted to provide the Germans with vital evidence. He presumed that by the time TRICYCLE returned to Lisbon the Abwehr in Berlin would have decided how they wanted to induce BALLOON to work more energetically for them, as well as providing him with a new ink via TRICYCLE, 'or it will be clear that the Abwehr have decided that it is not worth their while to continue with BALLOON'.

Both Wilson and BALLOON had doubts as to what advantages the plan would have towards his case. BALLOON thought that perhaps there might be a way in which misleading information about the diamonds could be passed to the Germans, even if he were not involved, but Wilson was sceptical and doubted whether any capital could be made out of it. Besides, they had other channels available for passing misleading information when they needed to.[10] Nor was he enthusiastic about giving the Germans samples of the diamonds, but thought that 'Tommy [Tomás Harris] or some of our more inventive minds might be able to work something out'. He felt that nothing would be achieved other than to confirm that BALLOON was 'willing to commit crimes for money' and 'The fact that he is willing to sell diamonds for a price is no proof that military information of real value will follow, and it will appear to the Germans that the diamonds are being built up by him as a means of making money.' If the intent was to 'test the corruptibility of the German agents in Lisbon', it was redundant as they already knew how they operated. They also knew that the Germans were anxious to get their hands on industrial diamonds, but whoever BALLOON contacted in Lisbon was unlikely to let slip any important information.

Marriott was in general agreement with Wilson's arguments against allowing BALLOON to become involved in it and thought that Harris's 'ingenious mind may make something of it'; however, Harris was also unimpressed:

> I do not know the Tricycle-Balloon set up but if Tricycle wants to re-establish Balloon – this story might be used by the former, allowing Tricycle to take out a sample of the diamond with him to prove Balloons [sic] willingness to collaborate. I should imagine that any other story would be just as good without the need to give away samples of material which they probably need.[11]

***

A note about TRICYCLE extracted from a report by ARTIST dated 14 February 1944 reads:

> IWAN II
> In a way HANSEN would have liked IWAN II to continue working. I have, however succeeded in convincing KARSTHOF that it is not in the interest of IWAN I's security to get him to influence IWAN II in this respect. I have also sent a report along these lines to Berlin in which KARTHOF [sic] is backing me. WIEGAND also by radio has promised to support my opinion in Berlin.[12]

Oberst Georg Alexander Hansen replaced Admiral Canaris as interim head of the Abwehr in February 1944 following Canaris's resignation, and served as Walter Schellenberg's deputy from May 1944 until the Abwehr was subsumed by the RSHA. He was hanged on 8 September 1944 at Plötzensee prison for his part in the 20 July Plot to assassinate Hitler. Canaris was arrested following his involvement in the Plot and executed in Flossenberg concentration camp on 9 April 1945.[13]

B1a reported on 26 February 1944 that 'If they ask him [TRICYCLE] to carry material to BALLOON or GELATINE he will accept it so long as it is understood that he is to deliver it without revealing his identity as the courier. He will not agree to work in conjunction with either of them.'[14] However, a report on his visit to Lisbon (26 February - 13 April 1944) stated, 'No official mention was made to TRICYCLE of BALLOON, METEOR, or THE WORM, nor was there on this occasion any suggestion of his bringing anything for anyone else.'[15]

The Royal Marines Small Arms School at Browndown, Gosport, wrote to BALLOON informing him that they were still trying to persuade the Marine Office to take on the VAP gun without waiting for the results of the Pendine trials. The RMO wanted to know where it was going to be produced, 'but if it is going to be produced for General B. [Browning], I see no reason why we should not get it from the same source.'

On 21 April 1944 Lord Birkenhead of the Foreign Office Political Intelligence Department, based at Bush House, wrote to BALLOON about the gun, saying: 'I will let you know as soon as I hear of anything. So far I have not struck out as everyone is so damned busy and boring, but have not forgotten.'

Ever the optimist, during his interview with General Browning BALLOON asked him about the possibility of obtaining an operational job with airborne troops. Browning quite firmly insisted that he was 'too old and too fat' but hinted that there might be a commissioned job connected with small arms and weapons used by airborne troops, which would release a younger, fitter man for operational duties and would write to the Director, Air, suggesting that he consider him. That BALLOON had been forced to resign his commission wasn't considered an obstacle to now being commissioned.

When asked what he'd been doing during the war so far BALLOON informed him, for his information and that of the Director, Air only, that he'd been working under the direction of MI5, although not actually in it. But it was not until 5 May 1944 that Tar met with the Director, Air, Major General Kenneth N. Crawford, at the War Office about BALLOON. Crawford's PA, Lieutenant C.M. Cogger, wrote to BALLOON on 9 May 1944 regarding his possible employment with AFDC (Air Force Department Constabulary) informing him that 'this matter was receiving attention'.

On 13 May when BALLOON and MI5 were about to part company, he wrote to Tar thanking him for his help and expressing 'how very much I have enjoyed working for you'. As well as having been associated with Duško Popov whom he held in high esteem, Tar's 'thoughtful bonus' was also much appreciated, and he hoped he might still be offered a job with MI5, and put himself at their disposal. Tar replied that he wished it 'would have been possible for you to play a more active part, as I was always certain that you would have done some great work'. He reassured him he was 'doing all that I can to try and get you back your commission and I have taken certain active steps in this direction which I hope will prove successful', and hoped that they would keep in touch.[16]

On 15 August Wilson informed Dick White that he had spoken to BALLOON who had contacted Cogger. The general was busy but still wanted to see him. BALLOON told Wilson that BSA were doing well in making up models of the gun and that, 'subject to certain tests which will take place shortly, big orders for it are expected soon'. He was going to leave Postnikow and go into business with Mackenzie at Brassert's if his commission didn't come through.[17] By early September MI5 cancelled the Home Office warrants on BALLOON's home address and British Graphitised Metals Co. Ltd.

Since BALLOON was now not working for MI5, the Ministry of Labour contacted him saying that he was de-restricted from call-up. He sought Marriott's advice about whether he should go into business as a consulting engineer, 'since … [it] probably means that the MOL are proposing to direct him into some form of National Service'. He had become resigned to the fact that nothing would come of the negotiations between himself, MI5 and D.Air, particularly as Browning had advised him to drop the matter since '(a) he was too old and fat for active service, and (b) the war was going so well that there would be little demand for his services in a section dealing with research and design.'

Both Marriott and Malcolm Cumming (ADA) felt that it would be inappropriate for MI5 to intervene in de-restricting BALLOON from call-up and didn't think they could justify seeking an exemption for him, but were keeping their options open: 'His new business will have no direct or even indirect, bearing on the war effort, and … if it is successful it might put BALLOON into a position where in the post-war world he might gain access to information which would be of interest to this Office,' namely, the arms trade.[18] Cumming suggested that BALLOON should go to the Ministry and explain that he had been exempted at the request of the War Office and seek their advice. He was due to sign a lease at Imperial House so he didn't want to incur unnecessary office expenses if the Ministry had other plans for him.

There were also difficulties in persuading the Germans to revive his case, given the difficulties of corresponding with the Iberian Peninsula, but also because of their doubts in him, according to TRICYCLE and ARTIST. Therefore, the only thing remaining was for MI5 to provide him with some financial remuneration for his services, and pay him a lump sum when they ceased to employ him. To that end Marriott suggested

1. We ought as far as possible to ensure that he leaves our service free from debt.
2. The sudden cutting off of a source's income will be bound in the case of a man of BALLOON's temperament and mode of life to cause him immediate financial embarrassment.
3. Although through no fault of his own, he has not had an opportunity of exploiting his case in the way which has been possible with TRICYCLE, he would nevertheless have been perfectly willing to

undertake any task we asked him, and in the work which he has been able to do he has operated willingly and efficiently.

4. It is not impossible that had he not undertaken this work he would before now have succeeded in satisfying his great ambition of regaining his commission in the Army. It will be remembered that he started his career as a regular soldier and lost his commission through irregularities over cheques.[19]

Everyone at MI5 who had dealt with BALLOON considered him very loyal and intelligent. They had also profited from him financially to the tune of nearly £1,700. Marriott therefore requested that they make him a payment of £250 upon leaving their employ, but felt that MI5 owed him much more – getting him reinstated in HM Forces, as well as trying to find him a job. He arranged an appointment for him on 22 September with Mr Toogood, the Assistant Regional Controller, Appointments Department at the Ministry of Labour at Alexandra House, Kingsway. Toogood had been informed that for the past three years BALLOON had been involved part-time in 'certain special work'. Marriott warned BALLOON to be frank with him in discussing his business position, and to take his advice, saying that 'the M of L will not look with too sympathetic an eye upon the starting up of a new business'. BALLOON's medical examination had placed him in Grade II, which he imagined would result in his being left alone.

Chapter 27

'A man of intelligence and resource'

At the end of November 1944 moves were being made to reinstate BALLOON's commission. Lennox and Tar met with Colonel G.H. Batty of the Military Secretary's office at the War Office to give him an overview of BALLOON's case.[1] Batty recommended that they should speak to Brigadier O'Donnell in the Adjutant-General's branch of the War Office 'who could probably give us the best advice', as there was nothing he could do. O'Donnell recommended that BALLOON provide them with a summary of his court martial and his activities since that date, mentioning that he had been employed by MI5 in work of a highly secret nature, and a reference from 'some reputable person' attesting to his good conduct since being discharged from the Army. He should state that he was seeking a Royal Pardon and having his commission reinstated. MI5 then needed to provide a brief outline of what he had been doing for them. Someone, either the DG or Lennox, should submit all this documentation to the VCIGS, Lieutenant General Nye: 'If the Pardon is granted then he will be secretly gazetted (this is a point which should be made in our note to the VCIGS) and immediately after this he will be transferred to the Non-Active List.'[2]

BALLOON duly obliged by writing to the DG, Sir David Petrie, on 12 December, outlining his Army career, the circumstances of his court martial, his subsequent position as an ARP officer, his approach to Lennox, a brief account of his dealings with Browning and Vesely and how proud he was to have served MI5 'even in a modest capacity'. He enclosed references from Lieutenant Colonel Desmond MacManus, RAMC – who had known him and his family for many years and had been both his medical adviser and friend – attesting to his good character. Petrie stated that 'In February 1941 circumstances arose in which we required the services of a man of intelligence and resource for secret work'.[3]

On 28 February 1945 he wrote to the Under-Secretary of State for War, Lord Nathan, giving an account of his career to date and his involvement with MI5, concluding:

> I shall be deeply grateful and I do humbly request that you may see fit to intercede with His Majesty on my behalf, so that he may see fit to grant me a Royal Pardon and the restoration of my commission, and I sincerely trust that my recent services may be adjudged to be such as to warrant this act of clemency.[4]

He also petitioned the Army Council. Shortly afterwards, Lennox made discreet enquiries of one of Nye's staff about what was happening and was told that it was still circulating around the Army Council. Further informal enquiries would be made and 'If it does not produce a satisfactory answer then I think we ought to ask the DG to send a formal reminder', which Petrie did on 24 March. The War Office replied that 'The case has not yet been finally disposed of.' Luke recounted:

> BALLOON seemed most grateful for the treatment he had received at the hands of this Office, and told me that General Nye was interesting himself in the proposal that he should get back his Commission in the Army. He made it clear, however, that he had no intention of resigning for [sic] Tarlair Ltd if this should transpire; the idea being that he should be commissioned and then immediately be placed on the unemployed list.[5]

Tarlair Ltd had been set up by Popov and Mackenzie who had also provided most of the capital as Metcalfe, working as its London manager, was unable to do so. The name had been devised by Tar Robertson, presumably using his initials as part of the name. While lunching with Luke on 2 April 1945, Metcalfe told him that he, Murdo Mackenzie, A.C. Maxwell [sic] and Popov had become its directors. Currently, it was running at a loss, but Popov had recently received a lucrative order from the French government to provide rubber hose, meaning that the company – described as 'Engineering Advisers and General Merchants' – would now be able to pay its way. Luke observed, 'I gather they propose to buy and sell anything in any market, but that since both BALLOON and Mackenzie are more interested in engineering, the firm will probably do more business of this type than any other.' Indeed, in 1945 Brassert's transferred their Turkish business to Tarlair.[6]

Correspondence between Gisela Ashley, Tar's secretary, and MI5 regarding Popov's Certificate of Identity, revealed that in 1946 she was working for Tarlair at 193 Imperial House, Regent Street, W1. She was 'thoughtfully provided by MI5, as was his manager, Mrs Brander, and although Popov never spotted it, he was kept under constant surveillance and his apartment on Park Street was fitted with hidden listening devices.'[7]

But it was not until mid-August 1945 before any progress was made, and only at the beginning of March 1946 when the War Office finally reinstated Metcalfe's commission, backdated to when he 'retired' in March 1935, placing him on the Retired List as of the date of his employment by MI5 in May 1940, with the rank of captain. He wrote to MI5 thanking all those instrumental in helping him to achieve this. But, contrary to the request for no publicity, a notice appeared in the *London Gazette*.[8] Luke, who had left MI5 and returned to business at The Linen Thread Co., Ltd, Glasgow, wrote to Masterman, now back at Christ Church, Oxford, giving him the news. Petrie also sent him a copy of the letter BALLOON had received from the War Office, which he requested be destroyed afterwards. It seems that, as in a duel, honour was satisfied.

Epilogue

There was a new gun in which Metcalfe was interested, and models were being produced by BSA from his firm's blueprints.[1] The Russians had expressed interest, and the Ministry of Supply had offered to give them four guns free of charge for testing purposes, but Metcalfe had protested as the Russians would almost certainly copy them, thereby depriving his company of any payment. He informed the War Office that, should this happen, he reserved the right to institute legal action against the government for loss of profit. This so alarmed the War Office that they withheld the guns. In the meantime, he'd approached the Russians offering to sell them the patents for £35,000, which they'd rejected.

He commented to Luke about the attitude of the Allied Control Commission to Germany towards Germany how

> at the end of hostilities German Government officials would be treated quite well, and that the peace from their point of view would be a soft one. He also thought that the Russians would probably overrun Czechoslovakia very quickly and would obtain the armament factories intact. He pointed out that the best guns in the world were produced by Czech designers, and that these factories were probably the most efficient in the world. His idea is that while the United States and Great Britain and others are busy organising different countries for peace and occupying their attention with matters such as future disarmament and economic problems, the Russians would be producing armaments on an enormous scale in Czechoslovakia, and would be able to bully the Allies into adopting a post-war policy favourable to the Russians simply by the power of their ability to fight.[2]

While Luke thought this to be 'rather far-fetched', he agreed that Russia's current position was hard to understand. He unofficially encouraged dealings with Russia over armaments, confiding that 'it would be a very good thing if he continued, even improved, his contacts with an eye to the future', the idea being that BALLOON might penetrate the Russian Intelligence Service for MI5 as he had done with the Germans. A note in the margin said, 'I doubt it!'

On 24 May Wilson went to see Lord Farrer at the Department of Overseas Trade[3] extolling MI5's praises for the work TRICYCLE had done for them, and also spoke favourably about THE WORM. Without seeking any particular favours from the DoT, 'we were satisfied that, in so far as it was in accord with their general policy to assist a firm of this type, it would be a good thing to do so.' Wilson reported on 27 May 1945 that it was Farrer's hope that Tarlair would be able to do export business in Yugoslavia since two other firms he knew of which had the same intention 'seemed to him altogether desirable'.[4] Metcalfe had entered into discussions with Farrer on that possibility. Farrer, who knew and trusted Mackenzie, showed some interest and intended to make some enquiries about Popov. Once things settled down in Yugoslavia either he or Metcalfe would be able to go there on business backed by the DoT. Farrer agreed to send out business letters on behalf of Tarlair through the commercial attaché to various contacts of TRICYCLE in Yugoslavia.

Some time prior to November 1945 DREADNOUGHT (Ivo Popov) and Metcalfe visited Italy trying to establish a connection with Signor Caproni – possibly Giovanni Battista Caproni, the aeronautical engineer – and proposing to form a company called 'Britali' which would import and export goods to and from Italy and Great Britain.[5] Their trip was unsuccessful owing to problems with export laws and the need to retain capital in Italy as it was not permitted to have a company half-owned in Britain and the other half in Italy. Metcalfe intended to discuss the issue with Ernest Holford-Strevens at the DoT. [6]

A report produced by HQ Intelligence Division, 70 HQ, CCG, BAOR 15 in Herford, Germany, dated 3 November 1947 stated that they had just learned of Tarlair operating in Krefeld and had approached T Force for more information. It said that Tarlair was being supplied with rations by the Cheshire Regiment and T Force, which were also providing their premises. Furthermore, all foreign business representatives had to live in T Force hotels, although Popov had apparently refused to do so because he claimed his briefcase had been rifled while staying in one. Towards the end of the war T Force, a joint British-US Army unit, was formed tasked with retrieving German scientific and technical equipment and personnel before it could be destroyed or fall into Russian hands.

HQ Intelligence Division sought confirmation whether it was true that all members of Tarlair had worked for MI5 – Popov, Major Cole, Colonel Maxwell and Tedd, 'a naturalised Yugoslav'. There were also a Colonel Page, claiming to work for MI5, 'who operates in the AACHEN Area as the representative of a Belgian textile firm, address BANQUE SOCIETE GENERAL, AIX-LA-CHAPELLE'; Colonel Marshbank, who represented the SHAEF Trading Company;[7] and Florian Brann, a German-born British subject, ex-captain in the Intelligence Corps, and son of Paul Brann, 'the celebrated MUNICH Marionette Exhibitor, who represents a firm LE GRAND of LONDON, also dealing in textiles'.[8]

An intercept revealed that Tarlair was offering a cholera serum to the Egyptian government, through Maxwell, of Maxwell and Co., Cairo, who had recently visited Germany. This, the report observed, was peculiar since Tarlair and Maxwell were

EPILOGUE

textile dealers: 'The only place from which POPOV could obtain Cholera serum would be via BAYER, I.G. Farben, LEVERKUSEN, and it is questionable whether such a deal would be legal.'

Tar's response about the activities of Tarlair in Krefeld provided some information on others connected with the company, such as Maxwell, a regular soldier who had served with SOE in the Middle East and was well-known in commercial circles.[9] Given the Cairo connection, this was most likely Arthur Terence Maxwell CBE, of the King's Royal Rifle Corps, who had served as SOE's Head of Mission in Cairo (A/DH), 1941-42, and as AD/H, Stations VIIA and VIIB, Radio Communications, married to Beatrice Diane Chamberlain, the daughter of Sir Austen Chamberlain. Unfortunately, his SOE file gives no indication of his post-war activities.

Tar thought it 'extremely unlikely that POPOV would have represented himself as having been connected with M.I.5'. Tedd was a regular soldier who had never been employed by MI5;[10] nor had Colonel Page, Colonel Marshbank or Florian Brann, who were unknown to them. The unnamed representative of Tarlair to whom he had spoken stated that there was no T Force hotel in Krefeld, and mentioned that Popov had been in touch with Bayer and I.G. Farben. Major Frederick Levens Cole, he said, had never been with MI5, but had served in North Africa with the 6th Battalion, Durham Light Infantry.[11]

A Top Secret note to MI5 from HQ Intelligence Division reported that Tarlair had been communicating with three telephone numbers in London which MI5 confirmed were for Tarlair Ltd, 8 Duke Street, Manchester Square; Mrs Charles W. Wilson, 51 Hertford St., W1; and British Overseas Manufacturers of Regent Street.[12]

A letter from 'FGB' on 20 November 1947 to Brigadier E.A. Howard at HQ Intelligence Division added to what Tar had said earlier, that

> some group or individual has been trying to denounce TARLAIR at Krefeld to the authorities and cause them as much trouble as possible. The name of a certain Kurt ENGLANDER has been mentioned in this connection. The TARLAIR undertaking in Krefeld is, we understand, sponsored by the Board of Trade here and is believed to be doing good and useful work in this country's cause in connection with manufactures and the import and export trade.[13]

The letter also provided information on Florian Oskar Paul Brann, born in Munich on 22 October 1915, who had served with the Intelligence Corps and had been attached to 21st Army Group.[14] However, the Military Intelligence Museum has him listed as MI9/MI19: 'After the war, around 1946, one of his jobs was the de-Nazification of schools and universities.' He is also listed as a lieutenant on the staff of the 'London Cage', MI19's wartime interrogation centre in Kensington Palace Gardens.[15]

On 10 December B1a noted that 'I have been led to believe that Mackenzie is rather fed up with BALLOON at the present time because the latter is devoting too much time to the affairs of the Hardwick-Dreadnought-Maxwell group and too little time to his own business, namely Tarlair Ltd ... .' It 'would be very unfortunate if Mackenzie should fall out with BALLOON who is absolutely dependent on Tarlair for his livelihood.'[16] Further remarks about Tarlair were provided by Brigadier Howard on 19 December 1947 when he wrote to MI5 about their investigations:

> It would seem that certain members of the firm are, to some extent, using their background to obtain privileges in the way of rations and accommodation which are denied to others. It has, however, been confirmed by 'T' Force here that TARLAIR Ltd and in particular the branch in GERMANY, is well thought of in industrial circles.[17]

On 3 February 1949 Dicky Metcalfe married Evelyn Katherine Johnson, daughter of Sir Robert Arthur Johnson and Kathleen Eyre Greenwell, widow of Commander Julian Liddell RN.

Later in the year there were indications that SIS was considering employing him. On 7 November Marriott wrote that he had a hard job trying to figure out what to say about it but 'On the whole I should say that he would be exceedingly useful to them and that they would be quite safe in taking him on'. However, he thought it would be unwise to make him permanent as he was 'more ... of the knockabout business man that there is of a civil servant'.[sic] They would be wise to consult Ian Wilson, who had worked with him the most and after the war had acted as his solicitor.[18] Tar was 'very much opposed' to SIS taking him on 'at any rate as a Headquarters officer':

> Apart from further underlinging [sic] BALLOON's unsuitability as a desk officer, Colonel Robertson agrees with the general terms of my letter to SIS. As regards the final paragraph, he suggests that we should discuss the position with Commander Burt, Special Branch, who when in B.5. is believed already to have studied be familiar with BALLOON's file in CRO.[19]

Liddell noted in his diary that, on behalf of Malcolm Cumming, he had asked Leonard Burt to check whether Metcalfe had a criminal record.[20] Burt's only trace of Metcalfe was 'some incident when he gave assistance to the Police.' This may relate to information about the Mauser deal passed to Special Branch in 1938. A request for information on Metcalfe from SIS, dated 23 October 1951, has been totally redacted from the file. There is no further information available on whether they decided to employ him.

Interestingly, a letter from D.H. Whyte in B2a (counter-subversion), dated 15 November 1950, indicates that MI5 had also been 'exploring the possibility of using him as a line to the Soviet Trade Delegation or Embassy', an echo of what Luke had commented on earlier, but

EPILOGUE

BALLOON told us that he had not recently been in touch with any Soviet officials over here, and the older trade delegates whom he had known in the past had left the UK and been replaced by younger men who were less approachable ... . Mr Marriott and I got the impression that BALLOON had now settled down and would not readily agree to any 'disreputable' line of action, such as would be involved if he represented himself to the Soviets as a man with a grievance against the British Government who would be ready to help them, although in fact we had not bluntly put any such proposition to him.[21]

Afterword

Had it not been for a family connection with Sir Vernon Kell, the first Director of MI5, Dicky Metcalfe would doubtless have continued to work as an ARP instructor and expert on gas warfare and not been recruited by MI5, but may still have appeared on their radar as an arms dealer. Unlike many of those who became part of the Double Cross system, he was not coerced as he had volunteered his services to them and had a relatively 'good war'. But how useful was he as a double agent?

From the Abwehr's point of view, they hadn't been overly impressed with his performance and the quality of his information. They considered that he wasn't taking his role seriously enough, and only providing them with chickenfeed.

Overall, MI5 appears to have had mixed feelings. Sir David Petrie, the wartime Director General of MI5, regarded him as 'an important link in the organisation which we built up, which can ... claim to have ultimately put us in the position ... of controlling substantially the whole of the German espionage network in this country'. But some were less sanguine. Tar Robertson had referred to him as 'an old and trusted friend', and William Luke, writing in April 1940, said of him that while they believed he was a loyal subject, 'his history and background suggest that he is in certain ways somewhat unreliable and ... an unavoidable risk'. John Marriott was even more critical, asserting that much of his information was very vague and containing 'practically no facts at all', with a tendency to produce 'gossipy material which is of interest to the English as opposed to the Germans,' largely due to the fact that he wasn't a real spy.

As sub-agents in TRICYCLE's Yugoslav Ring neither BALLOON nor GELATINE were ranked as highly as the larger-than-life TRICYCLE, and largely remained a footnote in his more illustrious career. Yet there were times when he was suspected of being under British control, but BALLOON had helped to ensure that he wasn't blown. Whether any of BALLOON's titbits of information were ever acted upon by either the Germans or the British is not recorded. But as he stated in his letter of 11 May 1942 to Ian Wilson:

> I can say that I am definitely of the opinion that we have sent the Boche some very poor material for several months past. I am sure that if you compare what we are sending now against that which we were

AFTERWORD

sending 9 month[s] ago, you will find a marked difference .... After all the greater part of what I do collect is not passed and presumably the Germans are entitled to expect a standard of information which in point of fact they would actually be receiving if I was a spy.

A continuing major bone of contention with MI5 had been his finances and his seemingly unavoidable habit of falling into debt. Even when they tried to keep him on the straight-and-narrow whenever this occurred, he always refused their help.

And while MI5 was supportive of his venture with Vesely and the development of the V-42 sub-machine gun, that project was largely thwarted by the Ministry of Supply and internal bickering, mostly brought about by Vesely who demanded more recompense to which he believed he was entitled. Ultimately, the project came to naught and the gun was not adopted by British forces during or after the war, and remains a largely forgotten weapon and a museum curiosity. The Sten, already in service, was able to do the job for a cheaper price; in 1953 it was supplanted by the Sterling sub-machine gun. But without MI5's lobbying, it is doubtful whether Metcalfe would have succeeded in having his Army commission reinstated at the end of the war.

Double agent BALLOON was, in his own way, a colourful character, but pales in comparison to TRICYCLE. Together they succeeded in deceiving the Germans in the 'great game' of double-cross. Dickie Metcalfe passed away in Westminster on 1 March 1988.

Bibliography

Primary sources (The National Archives = TNA)

TNA FO1004/250
TNA FO 1093/219
TNA HO144/19151
TNA HO144/20664
TNA HO144/20664
TNA HO214/1
TNA HO334/134/4380
TNA HO334/181/27603
TNA HO334/226/301
TNA HO382/180
TNA HO382/180/1
TNA HO396/3/200
TNA HS9/563/1
TNA HS9/949/5
TNA WO 339/43444
TNA WO 373/73/859
TNA KV2/1070-83 (BALLOON)
TNA KV2/1275-80 (GELATINE)
TNA KV2/1280 (GERTLER/HOWARD of EFFINGHAM)
TNA KV2/1182 (KRAATZ)
TNA KV2/1740 (PROTZE)
TNA KV2/61-62 (TATE)
TNA KV2/616-8; KV2/2266 (TESTER)
TNA KV2/845-866 (TRICYCLE)
TNA KV2/2769 (WEISBLAT)
TNA KV4/5

Secondary Sources

Andrew, Christopher, *The Defence of the Realm* (Viking Canada, Toronto, 2009).
Anon, *SOE in Denmark. An Official History* (Frontline Books, Barnsley, 2021).

BIBLIOGRAPHY

Atkin, Malcolm, *Section D for Destruction* (Pen & Sword, Barnsley, 2017).
Bendeck, Whitney T., *'A' Force: The Origins of British Deception During the Second World War* (Naval Institute Press, Annapolis, MD, 2013).
Booth, Nicholas, *ZigZag* (Portrait Books, London, 2007).
Boyce, Frederic & Douglas Everett, *SOE the Scientific Secrets* (Sutton Publishing, Stroud, 2003).
Brown, Paul & Edwin Herbert (eds), *The Secrets of Q Central* (The History Press, Stroud, 2015).
Chapman, Betty, *Mrs ZIGZAG*, (History Press, Stroud, 2013).
Chapman, Eddie, *The Real Eddie Chapman Story* (Library 33, London, 1956).
Clark, Freddie, *Agents by Moonlight* (Tempus Publishing, Stroud, 1999).
Cole, Howard N., *Heraldry in War: Formation Badges, 1939-1945* (Wellington Press, Aldershot, 1950).
Cunard, Nancy, *Negro Anthology* (Wishart, London, 1934).
Curry, John C., *The Security Service 1908-1945* (Public Record Office, London, 1999).
Delattre, Lucas, *A Spy at the Heart of the Third Reich* (Grove Press, New York, 2003).
Delattre, Lucas, *Betraying Hitler: The Story of Fritz Kolbe* (Grove Press, New York, 2005).
Draper, Christopher, *The Mad Major* (Air Review, Letchworth, 1962).
Farago, Ladislas, *The Game of the Foxes* (David McKay, New York, 1971).
Fort, Adrian, *Prof: The Life of Frederick Lindemann* (Jonathan Cape, London, 2003).
Fry, Helen, *The London Cage* (Yale University Press, New Haven & London, 2017).
Garby-Czerniawski, Roman, *The Big Network* (George Ronald, London, 1961).
Glanville, John & William M. Wolmuth, *Clockmaking in England and Wales in the Twentieth Century* (Crowood Press, Marlborough, 2015).
Griswold, John, *Ian Fleming's James Bond: Annotations & Chronologies for Ian Fleming's Bond Stories* (Authorhouse, Bloomington, IN & Milton Keynes, 2006).
Hastings, Max, *Das Reich* (Zenith Press, Minneapolis, 1981), paperback edition.
Haufler, Hervie, *The Spies Who Never Were* (NAL Caliber, New York, 2006), paperback edition.
Hinsley, F.H. & C.A.G. Simkins, *British Intelligence in the Second World War* (HMSO, London, 1990) Vol.4.
Holt, Thaddeus, *The Deceivers* (Weidenfeld & Nicolson, London, 2004).
Howard, Joshua H., *Workers at War: Labor in China's Arsenals, 1937-1953* (Stanford University Press, Stanford, CA, 2004).
Jeffrey, Keith, *The Secret History of MI6* (Penguin Press, New York, 2010).
Jonasson, Tommy & Simon Olsson, *Agent Tate* (Amberley, Stroud, 2011).
Loftis, Larry, *Into the Lion's Mouth* (Berkley Caliber, New York, 2016).
Macintyre, Ben, *Agent Zigzag* (Bloomsbury, London, 2009).
Macintyre, Ben, *Double Cross* (Bloomsbury, London, 2012).
Mackenzie, William, *The Secret History of SOE 1940-1945* (St Ermin's Press, London, 2000).

Masterman, J.C., *The Double-Cross System* (Yale University Press, New Haven & London,1972; republished by Vintage Books, London, 2013), paperback edition.
Masterman, J.C., *On the Chariot Wheel* (Oxford University Press, Oxford, 1975).
Masters, Anthony, *The Man Who Was M*, (Basil Blackwell, Oxford, 1984).
Middlebrook, Martin, *The Peenemunde Raid* (Pen & Sword, Barnsley, 2006).
Middlebrook, Martin & Chris Everitt, *The Bomber Command War Diaries* (Midland Publishing, Hersham, 2011).
Miller, Joan, *One Girl's War* (Brandon, Dingle, Co.Kerry, 1986).
Miller, Russell, *Codename Tricycle* (Secker & Warburg, London, 2004).
Moen, Jan, *John Moe, Double Agent* (Aschehoug, Oslo, 1986).
Montagu, Ewen, *Beyond Top Secret U* (Peter Davies, London, 1977).
O'Connor, Bernard, *Agent Fifi and the Wartime Honeytrap Spies* (Amberley, Stroud, 2016).
Olsson, Simon & Tommy Jonason, *Gosta Caroli – Double Agent SUMMER* (Stockholm: 2003).
Owen, Frank, *The Eddie Chapman Story* (William Messner, New York, 1954);
Popov, Dusko, *Spy CounterSpy* (Weidenfeld & Nicolson, London, 1973); (Fawcett Crest, Greenwich, CT, 1975), paperback edition.
Pujol, Juan, *GARBO* (Weidenfeld & Nicolson, London, 1985).
Rankin, Nicholas, *Ian Fleming's Commandos* (Faber & Faber, London, 2011).
Rankin, Nicholas, Defending the Rock (Faber & Faber, London, 2017)
Riis, Ib, *Gagnnjosnari Breta a Islandi* (Reykjavik, 1991).
Roberts, Madoc, *SNOW* (Biteback, London, 2011).
Sergueiev, Lily, *Secret Service Rendered* by (William Kimber, London, 1968).
Simmons, Mark, *Ian Fleming's War* (The History Press, Cheltenham, 2020), pp.213, 234-5;.
Simpson, A.W. Brian, *In The Highest Degree Odious* (Clarendon Press, Oxford, 1994).
Smith, Edward Abel, *Ian Fleming's Inspiration* (Pen & Sword History, Barnsley, 2020
Stephens, Robin & Oliver Hoare (eds), *Camp 020.MI5 and the Nazi Spies* (Public Record Office, London, 2000).
Stevenson, William, *A Man Called Intrepid* (Ballantine Books, New York, 1981), paperback edition.
Tremain, David, *The Beautiful Spy* (The History Press, Stroud, 2019).
Turner, Des, *Aston House, Station 12. SOE's Secret Centre* (Sutton Publishing, Stroud, 2006).
War Office, *The Abyssinian Campaigns: The Official Story of the Conquest of Italian East Africa* (HM Stationery Office, 1 January 1942).
Weinberg, Gerhard L., *A World At Arms: A Global History of World War II* (Cambridge University Press, Cambridge, 2005).
West, Nigel, *MI5: British Security Service Operations 1909–1945* (Bodley Head, London, 1981; republished by Pen & Sword, Barnsley, 2019).

BIBLIOGRAPHY

West, Nigel, *Seven Spies Who Changed the World* (Secker & Warburg, London, 1991).

West Nigel (ed.), *The Guy Liddell Diaries, Vol.1, 1939-1942* (Routledge, London & New York, 2005).

West, Nigel (ed.), *The Guy Liddell Diaries, Vol. 2, 1942–1945* (Routledge, London & New York, 2005).

West, Nigel, *Historical Dictionary of British Intelligence* (Scarecrow Press, Lanham, MD, 2005).

West, Nigel (ed.), *Historical Dictionary of World War II Intelligence* (The Scarecrow Press, Lanham, MD, 2008).

West, Nigel, *Double Cross in Cairo*, (Biteback, London, 2015).

West, Nigel, *Churchill's Spy Files* (History Press, Stroud, 2018).

West, Nigel, *Secret War* (Pen & Sword, Barnsley, 2019).

West, Nigel (ed), *Guy Liddell's Cold War MI5 Diaries, Volume 2, January 1948–December 1950* (Amazon, 2019).

West, Nigel & Oleg Tsarev, *Triplex: Secrets of the Cambridge Spies* (Yale University Press, 2009).

Witt, Carolinda, *Double Agent CELERY* (Pen & Sword, Barnsley, 2007).

Young, Commander Robert Travers, *The House That Jack Built. The Story of H.M.S. Excellent* (Gale & Polden, Aldershot, 1955).

Notes

Foreword

1. Farago, *The Game of the Foxes* (David McKay, New York, 1971).
2. Masterman, *The Double Cross System of the War of 1939-45*.
3. TNA KV4/5.
4. Draper, *The Mad Major*.
5. Owen, *The Eddie Chapman Story*; Chapman, *The Real Eddie Chapman Story*.
6. Sergueiev, *Secret Service Rendered*.
7. Garby-Czerniawski, *The Big Network*.
8. Popov, *Spy CounterSpy*.
9. Moen, *John Moe, Double Agent*.
10. Pujol, *GARBO*.
11. Riis, *Gagnnjosnari Breta a Islandi*.
12. Roberts, *SNOW*.
13. Witt, *Double Agent CELERY*.
14. Olsson & Jonason, *Gosta Caroli – Double Agent SUMMER*.
15. Jonason & Olsson, *Agent TATE*.
16. Grosjean, François, 'FIDO: French Pilot and Security Double Agent', *International Journal of Intelligence and Counterintelligence*, Vol 18, No. 3, 2010).
17. West, *Double Cross in Cairo*.
18. Macintyre, *Agent Zigzag*; Booth, *ZigZag*; Chapman, Betty *Mrs ZIGZAG*.

Introduction

1. Popov, Duško, *Spy/Counterspy*, paperback edition.
2. Ibid., p.5.
3. Op.cit., p.126.

NOTES

Chapter 1. Arms and the Man

1. See: Marquis of Ruvigny and Raineval, *The Plantagenet Roll of the Blood Royal. The Mortimer-Percy Volume* (Heritage Books, Inc., Maryland, 2001, originally published 1911), p. 419. See also: https://www.greatwarforum.org/topic/213265-lt-col-herbert-charles-metcalfe/
2. Hannah Dale, Archivist, Cheltenham College, 24 January 2021.
3. It became the Royal Military Academy Sandhurst in 1947.
4. TNA KV2/1073.
5. Richard Aldwyn Pulliblank, (b. 25 April 1911). Loyal Regiment, 2nd Lt 28/1/32; Lt 28/1/36; listed as Captain, 2nd Battalion, The Loyal Regiment, killed in action in Singapore on 28 February 1942, see: Commonwealth War Graves Commission; John Percy Delabene Underwood, DSO (b. 25 January 1882) became a Brigadier and Regimental Colonel of The Loyal Regiment, 1945-9.
6. TNA KV2/1073, serial 148a.
7. Not found in TNA KV2/1073; a petition from the War Office to the King can be found in KV2/1080, but this is dated February 1946.
8. Walter Pitts Hendy Hill CMG DSO (1877-1942), CO of the 2nd Bn The Loyal Regiment, 1922-28; probably William Green, who was Brevet Lieutenant Colonel of The Loyal Regiment on 2 January 1928; promoted to Major General on 1 March 1935.
9. General Sir John Theodosius Burnett-Stuart GCB KBE CMG DSO DL (1875-1958), appointed GOC-in-C Southern Command 1934; retired 1938.
10. TNA KV2/1073, serial 146. Extracted from Army Papers P/36714/8. Metcalfe's name was redacted from the original document. The MGO at that time (April 1934-January 1938) was Lieutenant General Sir Hugh Jamieson Elles KCB KCMG KCVO DSO (1880-1945).
11. *Motor Sport* magazine, March 1981, p.50: https://www.motorsportmagazine.com/archive/article/march-1981/50/around-and-about
    https://www.goodwood.com/grr/event-coverage/members-meeting/2017/3/members-meeting-history-part-2--motor-racing-for-weekend-warriors/
    https://www.motorsportmagazine.com/archive/article/september-2001/97/le-strange-but-true
    See also: Gardiner, Tony, *Motor Racing at Goodwood in the Sixties* (Veloce Publishing, Poundbury, 2003), p.92.
12. TNA KV2/1077.
13. William Vincent Ltd, known as Vincents of Reading, a coach builder founded in 1805 which made its first car body in 1899. See: https://en.wikipedia.org/wiki/William_Vincent_Ltd.
14. TNA KV2/1077, serial 419a; https://patents.google.com/patent/FR859582A/en
15. TNA KV2/1082, serial 2A. Now the tri-service Defence Nuclear, Biological and Chemical Centre. *Army List*, February 1937, p. 926. Captain Albert S.

Smedley also served as Secretary to Air Vice-Marshal Andrew Macgregor CB CBE DFC, Commandant of Taymouth Castle Civil Defence Technical Training School (1950-60). Awarded the MBE (Civil Division) in the Coronation Honours, 1953.

16. Dame Beryl Carnegy Joseph, Lady Oliver GBE RRC (1882-1972).
17. TNA KV2/1077, serial 419. 'a special oil carrying in suspension colloidal graphite prepared under a special process discovered by Dr E. G. Acheson, and manufactured and marketed by E. G. Acheson, Ltd, 40, Wood Street, London S.W.1.': http://archive.commercialmotor.com/article/31st-march-1933/56/colloidal-graphite-in-lubrication
18. TNA KV2/1082, serial 11b.
19. Shown as A.A. Postnikow and Postnikoff in the files. See: TNA HO334/226/301: Alexander Alexandrovich Postnikow, Naturalisation certificate, wife's name Anna Mikhailovna Postnikow, issued 14 February 1934; TNA HO144/19151: Nationality and Naturalisation, closed until 1 January 2035.
20. TNA KV2/1082, serial 3a.
21. TNA KV2/1082, serial 3A: Nita Stoddart, 9 Store Street, WC1, off Tottenham Court Road. An advertisement appeared in *The Times* on 31 January 1939: 'Expert by inexpensive dressmaking. Original designs or French models copied.'
22. TNA KV2/1082, serial 4A.
23. TNA KV2/1082, serial 11b.
24. *Westender*, July-August 2014, p.5; Edith Mary Cubitt, b.1888, shown as living in Winchester in 1921 Census.
25. TNA KV2/1082, serial 8A; see also TNA KV2/1280, serial 73 (Manci Gertler, Lady Howard of Effingham), and KV2/2769, serial 200B (Wiesblat).
26. TNA KV2/1082, serial 4A.
27. TNA KV2/1082, serial 5a.
28. TNA KV2/1082, serial 11A.
29. Frederick J. Peters, of the Winchester Repeating Arms Company, of which the London Armoury was a subsidiary.
30. TNA KV2/1082, serial 1B.
31. TNA KV2/1082, serial 12a.
32. TNA KV2/1082, serial 1c.
33. TNA KV2/3158, serial 167B. Georg Frank is mentioned in a US Senate report on the munitions industry: *Munitions Industry: Hearings Before the Special Committee Investigating the Munitions Industry, United States Senate, Seventy-third [-Seventy-fourth] Congress, Pursuant to S. Res. 206, a Resolution to Make Certain Investigations Concerning the Manufacture and Sale of Arms and Other War Munitions* ...US Government Printing Office, January 1937: 'Sedgley writes Georg Frank, 5 Monckebergester, Calidoniahaus, Hamburg, Germany. Still looking for Hotchkiss parts and he (Sedgley) has large quantity of *new barrels* for Colt-Marlin, 1914, also about 8,000 *new barrels* for Browning rifle, 1918.' (p.13596)

NOTES

34. TNA KV2/1082, serial 1C.
35. TNA KV2/3157, Minute Sheet. Weil was associated with Hugo Junkers and worked in the US during the Second World War with General Motors. See: https://www.nytimes.com/1992/01/08/obituaries/kurt-weil-96-dies-professor-at-stevens.html
Much of Weil's file has been destroyed, but a letter from the US Embassy in London, dated 21 February 1944 provides further information on him and his involvement with the German aircraft industry (KV2/3158, serials 280a, 281).
36. TNA FO 1093/219. Baron Wolfgang Gans zu Putlitz (1899-1975) was a German diplomat, and First Secretary (Consular) at the German Embassy, London, recruited by British Intelligence in 1934.
37. TNA KV2/3157, serial 9a. Born Breslau, 8/7/1879. See: 'Internees at Liberty in UK, As-Ba', TNA HO396/3/200, and Naturalisation Certificate, 14 June 1947, HO334/181/27603; listed in *London Gazette* 18 July 1947 as Banker's Agent and Company Director, 11 Dalkeith Grove, Stanmore, Middlesex. A Second Lieutenant R.R.M. Channel of the Queen's Regiment is listed in the *London Gazette* as resigning his commission on 6 April 1932 (*London Gazette*, 5 April 1932, p.2216).
38. TNA KV2/3158, serial 173a.
39. TNA KV2/3158, serial 193A.
40. See: http://acluleaks.com/uploads/Vol_1.pdf
Stevenson, *A Man Called Intrepid*, paperback edition, pp. 318-21, 325-6, 330; Farago, op.cit., p.388 (death). Both notoriously unreliable books. No books on Stephenson mention any connection to Davis's death.
41. TNA KV2/3165, Minute Sheet; KV2/3154, Minute Sheet.
42. TNA KV2/3158, serial 277 (destroyed), note on Minute Sheet, Max Aufrichtig.
43. TNA FO1004/250, closed until 2039; HO334/134/4380, naturalisation certificate; HO144/20664, supplementary papers.
44. Tremain, *The Beautiful Spy*, pp.147-8, 164, n.8-11. Quoted from TNA KV2/357, serial 47a.
45. *Hansard*, Trade and Commerce (China), HC Deb 06 June 1939 vol 348 cc209-11.
46. TNA KV2/1082, serial 14a.
47. TNA KV2/3165, serial 30ay. Cooper is also mentioned in TNA BT31/33583/298499, Norman A. Cooper (Issues) Limited, incorporated in 1935. Cooper's file, PF.49530, is not available from Kew.
48. TNA KV2/1082, serial 14a. Lovinfosse Hardy François and Lovinfosse Hardy François & Fils are listed in Daubress, Alain, *Belgian Liege Gunmakers*, L-M, vol.4, and at 74, Rue Hayeneux, Herstal: https://mallorquina.pagesperso-orange.fr/source/pageL.htm
49. Major P.E.C. Tuckey, Middlesex Regiment, Department of the Chief of Imperial General Staff (CIGS).
50. TNA KV2/1077, serial 419.

Chapter 2. 'The man's keen!'

1. TNA KV2/1082.
2. TNA KV2/1082, serial 17a.
3. Possibly Second Lieutenant Charles James Wright, Machine Gun Corps; see: TNA WO 339/43444. The 104th joined 35th Division, April 1916; moved into 35 Bn MGC, February 1918.
4. TNA KV2/1082, serial 21a.
5. TNA KV2/1082, Minute Sheet.
6. TNA KV2/1082, serial 21b.
7. Also mentioned as J.H. Weil (TNA KV2/3165, serial 1A) and Pierre Weil in serial 5A. See: KV2/3157-8 (Weil).
8. TNA KV2/3165, serial 2a.
9. de Zheng, Henry L. & Douglas G. Stankey, *Career Summaries - Luftwaffe Officers 1935-1945, Section S-Z*, VELTJENS, Joseph 'Seppl', version 01 April 2013; Leitz, Christian, *Economic Relations Between Nazi Germany and Franco's Spain, 1936-1945* (Clarendon Press, Oxford, 1996) p.38.
10. *Records of the External Assets Investigation Section of the Property Division, OMGUS, 1945-49.* Report No.B.68 (J.Veltjens, Waffen und Munition). https://www.archives.gov/files/research/microfilm/m1922.pdf
11. TNA KV2/3165, serials 73a and 74a.
12. TNA KV2/3165.
13. TNA KV2/3165, Minute Sheet.

Chapter 3. Going Dutch

1. TNA KV2/1082, serial 22B.
2. Lieutenant Colonel W.S. Outram, Directorate General of Production, Director of Aeroplane Production.
3. TNA KV2/1082, serial 22B.
4. TNA KV2/1082, serial 22D.
5. Pujol & West, *Operation GARBO*, p.80.
6. Count Johan Gabriel Oxenstierna af Korsholm och Wasa (1899-1995) won a gold medal at the 1932 Summer Olympics in Los Angeles in the modern pentathlon. See: TNA FO/188/412.
7. Delattre, *A Spy at the Heart of the Third Reich*, p.129; Bradsher, Greg, *A Time to Act: The Beginning of the Fritz Kolbe Story 1900-1943*, Spring 2002, Vol. 34, No.1: https://www.archives.gov/publications/prologue/2002/spring/fritz-kolbe-1.html
8. Paterson, Tony, *The Independent*, Saturday 25 September 2004. See also: https://www.archives.gov/publications/prologue/2002/spring/fritz-kolbe-1.html https://www.cia.gov/library/center-for-the-study-of-intelligence/kent-csi/vol10no1/html/v10i1a06p_0001.htm

NOTES

9. Delattre, *Betraying Hitler: The Story of Fritz Kolbe*, paperback edition.
10. TRIPLEX: Intelligence derived from the interception and opening of diplomatic bags. The operation was headed by David Boyle of SIS, but Anthony Blunt reviewed its activities in 1941. See: West, *Historical Dictionary of British Intelligence*, 1st edition, pp.550-1, and West & Tsarev, *Triplex: Secrets of the Cambridge Spies*.
11. West, Nigel, 'Fritz Kolbe and Allen Dulles: Masterspies?' in *International Journal of Intelligence and Counterintelligence*, 23 Nov 2006, pp. 756-61.
12. Delattre, *A Spy*, pp.200-1.
13. This small group was most likely CS5 – Cornelie Straat 5, the address of Jan Kanada Boissevain, nephew of Bob Boissevain – 'a paramilitary group, well supplied with ammunition. CS5 lasted long after the Communist Resistance in Holland was wiped out'. John Tepper Marlin. Personal communication to the author, 12 August 2019. Jan Kanada Boissevain died in Buchenwald concentration camp on 30 January 1945.
14. TNA KV2/1082, serial 27a.
15. May refer to Hans Schultz of Schultz and Larsen, a Danish rifle and silencer manufacturer founded in 1919. They were relatively inactive during the Second World War since Nazi Germany was controlling the factory, which closed down in 1943.
16. Patent granted 19 December 1939; see: https://patents.google.com/patent/US2183674A/en and: https://www.joiscientific.com/taming-hydrogen-the-road-to-practical-hydrogen-applications/ and: Stolten, Detlef (ed), *Hydrogen and Fuel Cells: Fundamentals, Technologies and Applications* (Weinheim: Wiley WCH-Verlag GmbH & CO, 2010), p.812.
17. TNA KV2/1082, serial 24a.
18. See: TNA HO214/1; HO382/180; HO382/180/1; ancestry.co,uk. He applied for naturalisation in 1946. See: TNA FO 1032/227.
19. TNA KV2/1082, serial 25a.
20. Jessurum was also involved with helping Greek Jews to escape from Greece: Berry, Burton Y., 'The Jews in Greece 1941-1944, in: *Journal of the Hellenic Diaspora*, Fall 1985, vol.XII, no.3, pp.24-6.
21. This is likely Hermanus Hendrik Willem Schrameier Verbrugge of Gravenhage, in connection with an advertisement for a BSA Scout Roadster car for sale for 2,000 florins in *Der Massbode van Zondag*, for 25 June 1939: https://www.delpher.nl/nl/kranten/view?identifier=MMKB04:000193599:mpeg21:a0116&objectsearch=Schrameier+Verbrugge+&coll=ddd
22. TNA KV2/1082, serial 30x.
23. Dr Heinz Gruner was a German scientist. Listed in: https://www.archives.gov/files/iwg/declassified-records/rg-65-fbi/fbi-disclosure-act-files.pdf
Probably KLOSE, Gustav. From OSS Secret Intelligence Special Funds Record 2801-2850: Hisma Ltda. Lawyer. Address: Alameda del Puerto 21, Neguri, Bilbao. Born Hannover-Waldhausen, 16 April, 1898. Passport No 191R/1269/37 issued Berlin 14.12.1937. Member of NSDAP and NSRB and formerly SA (1933-1937).

24. TNA KV2/1082, serials 36a, 37a.
25. Blog by John Tepper Marlin, Adjunct Professor of Business Ethics at the Stern School of Business at New York University, and currently Senior Economist at the US Congress Joint Economic Committee: http://warriors-families.blogspot.com/2014/12/the-dutch-resistance-goldberg-family.html
From a draft chapter of John Tepper Marlin's book, *How Holland Defied Hitler: The Boissevains and van Halls* (currently on hold).
26. TNA KV2/1082, serials 36a, 37a.
27. TNA KV2/1082, serial 33a.
28. Joods Monument also lists a son, Mozes (1919-43), but no daughter: https://www.joodsmonument.nl/en/page/113421?utm_source=OpenArchieven&utm_medium=browser&utm_campaign=OpenData
https://www.genealogieonline.nl/en/genealogie-van-raam/I46089.php
29. http://db.yadvashem.org/righteous/family.html?language=en&itemId=4043088
30. Robert Boissevain (1895-1945) died on 12 April 1945 at the Langenstein-Zweiberg concentration camp, a sub-camp of KZ Buchenwald, Halberstadt, Saxony-Anhalt, Germany. See: http://warriors-families.blogspot.com/2014/12/the-dutch-resistance-goldberg-family.html
https://cityeconomist.blogspot.com/2015/01/the-boissevains-and-dutch-resistance.html
31. http://db.yadvashem.org/righteous/family.html?language=en&itemId=4043088

Chapter 4. BALLOON's Report on Holland

1. TNA KV2/1082.
2. Otto Wolff AG founded in Cologne in 1904 by Wolff and Ottmar E. Strauss as a steel trading and steel wrecking company. Woolf died in 1941. His son Otto Woolf von Amerongen succeeded the business. During the war they produced armaments for the Wehrmacht. See: http://www.rheinische-geschichte.lvr.de/Persoenlichkeiten/otto-wolff/DE-2086/lido/5d0a11427ff2b3.47089066
3. Pastor Frederich Gustav Emil Martin Niermöller (1892-1984), a German anti-Nazi theologian and a founder of the Confessing Church who was arrested by the Gestapo on 1 July 1937 and tried by a Special Court on 2 March 1938. Having been fined 2,000 Reichmarks and sentenced to seven months' imprisonment he spent from 1938 until 1945 in Dachau and Sachsenhausen concentration camps in 'protective custody' because Rudolph Hess thought the sentence too lenient.
4. Captain John Buxton Pelham, 8th Earl of Chichester (1912-44), Third Secretary and Press Attaché at The Hague, married Ursula von Pannwitz (1911-89), daughter of Walter von Pannwitz and Catalina Roth, in 1940;

NOTES

he was killed in a road accident while serving with the Scots Guards on 21 February 1944.
5. TNA KV2/1082.
6. TNA KV2/1082, serial 39a. W.A. Burton OBE was an Assistant Secretary (Temporary) and head of the Enemy Resources Department II (E.I.6) at the MEW.

Chapter 5. The Air Ministry Leaks

1. Marshal of the Royal Air Force Cyril Norton Lewis Newall GCB OM GCMG CBE AM (1886-1963) had a distinguished career in both the Army and Royal Air Force, was appointed Chief of the Air Staff in 1937, and Governor-General of New Zealand in 1941; Sir Arthur William Street KCB KBE CMG CIE MC (1892-1951), Permanent Under-Secretary of State for Air; Air Chief Marshal Sir Wilfred Rhodes Freeman Bt GCB DSO MC FRAeS (1888-1953), Vice Chief of the Air Staff, 1940-42, Air Member for Research and Development, 1936; E.J.H. Lemon is listed as being Department of the Air Member for Development and Production, Director-General of Production, September 1939: http://www.niehorster.org/017_britain/39_raf/_air_ministry/am_air_development.html
2. TNA KV2/1083, serials 52c, 53x. See also: Imperial War Museum, catalogue number Documents 11293. Major Christopher John Galpin DSO served in the Royal Naval Air Service from 1914 to 1919, seeing action in Gallipoli and in the North Sea Patrol. After the war he worked in the Air Ministry as financial adviser to the RAF in Palestine, Egypt and Sudan (1922-25); private secretary to Lord Londonderry (1931-5) and Sir Phillip Cunliffe-Lister, Secretary of State for Air (1935-8).
3. TNA KV2/1083, serials 52c, 53x.
4. He should not be confused with Obersturmbannführer Wilhelm Wanneck @ Warneck, *Leiter* of Amt VI-E of the RSHA.
5. TNA KV2/1083, serial 43w.
6. The information related to Fighter Command's approach to their night-fighters and the fitting of searchlights to the American Douglas A-20 Havoc twin-engined night-fighters. In the RAF the bomber version was known as the Boston. TNA KV2/1072, serial 111b.
7. TNA KV2/1072, serial 111b. BY and JB were Bill Younger and John Bingham who worked under Maxwell Knight in B5b.
8. TNA KV2/1072, serial 119B.
9. TNA KV2/1072, serial 122A.
10. TNA KV2/1072, serial 123A.
11. TNA KV2/1074, serial 255A.
12. TNA KV2/1074, serial 263a.

Chapter 6. 'A man of intelligence and resource'

1. TNA KV2/1080, serial 15a.
2. TNA KV2/1080, serial 17a.
3. TNA KV2/1070.
4. TNA KV2/1083, serial 47a.
5. https://en.wikipedia.org/wiki/Charles_Howard,_20th_Earl_of_Suffolk
   https://www.telegraph.co.uk/history/world-war-two/7849612/The-scruffy-earl-who-swung-the-war.html
6. TNA KV2/1077, serial 419a.
7. TNA KV2/1083, serial 47a. AVM Sir Patrick Playfair, AOC Advanced Air Striking Force; AM Sir Arthur Sheridan Barrett, AOC-in-C, British Air Forces in France; Flying Officer John Adolphus de László, RAFVR, son of painter Philip de László. The squadron involved was likely 271 Squadron, RAF which evacuated RAF units in France.
8. TNA KV2/1083, serial 57a.
9. TNA KV2/845, serial 1a.
10. TNA KV2/1070, serial 3a; also in TNA KV2/846.
11. West, *The Guy Liddell Diaries, Vol.1, 1939-1942*, p.135.
12. TNA KV2/846, serial 76a.
13. Notes prepared by BALLOON on 13 May 1941 (?) described Irsay de Irsa as 'that old rogue'. George Irsay de Irsa and his wife Hélène became naturalised in Britain 12 February 1948. See: TNA HO334/203/38694. He is recorded as arriving in New York on the *Queen Elizabeth* on 29 November 1946: https://www.ancestry.ca/search/?name=_irsay&pg=4
    https://www.ancestry.co.uk/search/collections/60882/?name=_irso&viewMode=category&qh=6YOqcAvMfxOqoLOjfGjJaw3D3D
14. TNA KV2/1070.
15. TNA KV2/1083, serial 70a. This may be György Irsay, a first lieutenant of the hussar unit in the Imperial Hungarian Army: http://www.yellowstarhouses.org/historical_background/publications/yad_vashem
    The *London Gazette* for 19 March 1948, p.1946, described him as a Manager of 69 High Street, Marlow, Buckinghamshire. A passenger list on Ancestry.co.uk shows that he departed Southampton for New York on 14 July 1951 on the Cunard White Star liner *Georgic*. The entry was handwritten as opposed to the others suggesting this may have been a last minute entry. His address concurs with the one above. Further entries show that he arrived in New York on the *Queen Elizabeth* on 20 August 1951, and arriving in Southampton on 13 December 1956 on the *Queen Elizabeth*. This time his address was given as 51 Little Marlow Road, Marlow. Also the author of an outline of *Der Tod des Kronprinzen Rudolf von Oesterreich* (*The Death of Crown Prince Rudolph of Austria*), of Mayerling fame: Writers Guild of Great Britain, 4 November 1952.

NOTES

16. https://patents.google.com/patent/CA452588A/un
    https://patents.google.com/patent/GB9218518D0/en
17. There is no one listed by that name in 'List of Cases Investigated by Camp 020' (TNA KV2/2593) or in the official history of Camp 020: Stephens & Hoare (eds), *Camp 020.MI5 and the Nazi Spies*. A Hauptman (Captain) Schirnick is listed in Army Corps D in Hanover, as of 3 January 1939. There is also a Major Schirnick listed as a general staff officer in *Order of Battle of the German Army* October 1942, Military Intelligence Service, Washington DC, p.198.
18. TNA KV2/1070, serial 12b.

Chapter 7. A Network Evolves

1. TNA KV2/845, serials 1a, 2a.
2. West, *Historical Dictionary of British Intelligence*, 1st edition, pp.594-5; Masters, *The Man Who Was M*, p.61.
3. Miller, *One Girl's War*, p.88.
4. TNA KV2/845, serial 6a. RAF Leighton Buzzard, also known as RAF Stanbridge, during the war was the main Central Exchange and Wireless telegraph station for the RAF, handling the national landline teleprinter communications and a large part of the private speech telephone system. See: https://www.leightonbuzzardonline.co.uk/lifestyle/unveiled-the-secret-base-at-the-heart-of-mi5-1-6410952; https://en.wikipedia.org/wiki/RAF_Stanbridge; https://www.bbc.com/news/uk-england-beds-bucks-herts-18519369; Brown & Herbert (eds), *The Secrets of Q Central*. A Vermondo Frederick Valli (1917-2000) was living in Leighton Buzzard in 1942.
5. Popov refers to him as a major in the Transport Division: Popov, op.cit., p.65; http://www.thepeerage.com/p3679.htm#i36784
6. TNA KV2/1280; Miller, op.cit., p.138; O'Connor, *Agent Fifi and the Wartime Honeytrap Spies*, p.138; paperback edition, refers to it as at Worplesdon, near Guildford.
7. TNA KV2/1276, serial 46a.
8. TNA KV2/845, serial 43a.
9. Miller, Russell, *Codename Tricycle*, pp.7-8; Loftis, Larry, *Into the Lion's Mouth*, pp.42-3, 52-3
10. TNA KV2/1080, serial 113.
11. Miller, Russell, op.cit., pp.7-8.
12. TNA KV2/1280, serial 6.
13. TNA KV2/1280, serials 30 & 32. Wheatley served as a Flight Lieutenant, later Wing Commander, in the RAFVR.
14. George Graf (GIRAFFE) was a Czech former member of the French Foreign Legion who had parachuted into England with Kurt Goose (GANDER) in

September 1940, after previously being talent-spotted by the Abwehr in Lisbon in the summer of 1940. Their MI5 files have not been released to the National Archives at Kew.
15. TNA KV2/846, serial 77a.
16. Luke wrote to BALLOON to that effect on 26 March and his particulars were sent to ADS (A) on 1 April; a reply dated 9 April indicated that this had been arranged until 31 December 1941.
17. TNA KV2/1070, serial 3a; also in TNA KV2/846.
18. West, *Liddell*, op.cit., p.135.
19. TNA KV2/1070, serial 15b.
20. TNA KV2/1070, serial 23a.
21. TNA KV2/1070.
22. TNA KV2/1072, serial 106c.
23. IVAN I is also referred to as Joe Kessler working with IVAN II in New York, in Kammler's file: TNA KV2/1962, Interrogation Report of KURRER, Otto on JEBSEN, Johann.
24. TNA KV2/1072, serial 106c.
25. KV2/849, serial 201b (TRICYCLE). The last two paragraphs are not included in TRICYCLE's file; point (c) is not included in BALLOON's file.
26. TNA KV2/1275, serial 5A.
27. TNA KV2/849, serial 177b, pp.8-9.
28. Friedl's report of 28 August 1939 mentions a Fraulein von Ahlefeld who had been instructed in August to transfer all DAF and Party records from Cleveland Terrace to the German embassy.
29. TNA KV2/849, serial 177b, pp.8-9. The CIA described him as 'a typical member of the "CANARIS Familie GmbH", a regular offr, conscientious but completely unthinking, with no conception of 'the work he was supposed to do; even at this stage, he is without any clear idea of why he was unsuccessful in SPAIN': https://www.cia.gov/library/readingroom/docs/OSS20-20SSU20-20CIG20EARLY20CIA20DOCUMENTS202020VOL.202_0001.pdf
https://www.cia.gov/readingroom/docs/GERMANINTELLIGENCESERVICE28WWII2C2020VOL.203_0001.pdf
30. TNA KV2/1275, serial 8A.
31. Major Albert Ludovico von Karsthoff, *Leiter* III, Abwehr KO Lisbon, real name Kremer von Auenrode.
32. TNA KV2/1075, serial 5a.

Chapter 8. Plan MIDAS

1. Macintyre, *Double Cross*, p.88.
2. TNA KV2/848, serial 132k; His name is spelled Erich in the file. Glass's own MI5 file PF48710 is currently not available from the National Archives at Kew.

NOTES

He and his wife Blanche did not become naturalised Britons until 26 August 1946. TNA HO334/164/19218.
3. West, (ed.), *Historical Dictionary of World War II Intelligence*, pp.15, 149.
4. https://www.thestage.co.uk/features/obituaries/2018/agent-janet-glass/ See also her obituary in *The Times*: https://www.legacy.com/obituaries/thetimes-uk/obituary.aspx?n=janet-ruth-glass-crowley&pid=190250874
5. https://www.marshlibrary.ie/catalogue/Record/BI28262
6. TNA KV2/848, serial 132k.
7. TNA KV2/848, serial 138b. See also Miller, op.cit., Ch.5, pp.67-89.
8. An investment bank established in 1876, now at 277 Park Avenue, 26th floor, New York.
9. TNA KV2/849, serial 184a.
10. Sir Edward James Reid, Bt. (1901-72), recruited to MI5 by Guy Liddell and wrote a report for MI5 on the German production of fake British bank notes – *Report on the Operation of B1B (Sir Edward Reid) in Connection with Financial and Currency During the War 1939–1945* (KV4/465). See: Curry, *The Security Service 1908–1945*, pp.259, 262; West, *MI5, British Security Service Operations 1909–1945*, pp.180-1.
11. TNA KV2/848, serial 136b.
12. TNA KV2/849, serial 186c.
13. TNA KV2/849, serial 175a.
14. TNA KV2/849, serial 177c.
15. West, op.cit., p.149. See also: TNA KV2/856, serial 753a: 'Deputy Leiter of the Sonderstab of the 4 Years Plan and as such close collaborator of KOERNER, Secretary of State in the Reichswirtschaftsministerium. He was formerly Leiter ZF (= Finances) of the Abwehr.'
16. West, *Liddell,* op.cit., p.161.
17. TNA KV2/849, serial 179a.
18. TNA KV2/849, serial 181b.
19. TNA KV2/849, serial 182a.
20. TNA KV2/849, serial 186d.
21. TNA KV2/849, serial 187a.
22. TNA KV2/849, serial 187k.
23. 14th Prime Minister of Yugoslavia, 27 March 1941-12 June 1942. Possibly Lieutenant Colonel Vasilije Matic, Chief of Staff to General of Division Milorad Bozic, CO of the Unska division.
24. TNA KV2/849, serial 188a.
25. West, *Liddell,* op.cit., p.165.
26. TNA KV2/61, serial 149a.
27. TNA KV2/849, Minute Sheet.
28. TNA KV2/849, serial 191a.
29. TNA KV2/849, serial 191a.
30. TNA KV2/849, serial 187k.

31. TNA KV2/849, serial 195a; KV2/1072, serial 110a.
32. TNA KV2/849, serial 199a.
33. West, *Liddell*, op.cit., p.168. Agents TATE and DRAGONFLY were Wulf Schmidt and Hans George respectively (see: TNA KV2/3650).
34. TNA KV2/849, serial 206a.

Chapter 9. BALLOON's Reports

1. Major General Clifford Cecil Malden, late of Royal Sussex Regiment, GOC 47th London Division, killed on 25 March 1941 while inspecting coastal defences at Shoreham.
2. This must have been RAF Ashford.
3. TNA KV2/1070.
4. TNA KV2/1071, serial 46a.
5. TNA KV2/1070
6. TNA KV2/1071.
7. TNA KV2/1071, serial 52b.
8. TNA KV2/1071.
9. TNA KV2/1071, serial 57a.
10. TNA KV2/1071, serial 57a.
11. TNA KV2/1071, serial 73a.
12. The Imperial War Museum lists it as the formation badge of the 56th (London) Infantry and 1st (London) Infantry Division; Cole, *Heraldry in War: Formation Badges, 1939-1945*, 3rd ed., p.47.
13. According to 45 LAA battery was based at Crewe.
14. TNA KV2/1071, serial 63a.
15. General Sir Archibald Wavell was replaced by General Sir Claude Auchinleck on 11 July 1941.
16. Curtiss P-40 Warhawk, known as the Tomahawk by British and Commonwealth air forces.
17. TNA KV2/1071, serial 75a; see also KV2/1073.
18. Hector McNeil (1907-55) was the Scottish Labour MP for Greenock. After the war he was Minister of State at the Foreign Office (1946) and employed Guy Burgess as his confidential secretary.
19. William Francis Forbes-Sempill, 19th Lord Sempill (1893-1965) @ Lord Sempill @ Master of Sempill. Eugen Olgen Kronisch was born in Berlin on 17 October 1907 and died in Fredericksburg, Spotsylvania, Virginia on 10 September 1980, having lived in Garden City, Nassau County, New York. His ex-wife was Edith Kronisch *née* Daniel born in Berlin on 9 August 1910 who died in Wandsworth, London on 2 February 2002. See also note 48.
20. TNA KV2/1071, serial 58k.
21. TNA KV2/1071, serial 55a.

NOTES

22. TNA KV2/1071, serial 72a. Also mentioned as being vice-consul, Hanover, Germany, US Department of Commerce, *Commerce Reports, July, August, September*, nos. 154-230, vol.3, 1916, p.783; see also: Gray, Robert Lee, vice-consul, Hanover, 1914, Rotterdam February 3, 1917, Zurich October 25, 1917, and Lucerne, November 7, 1917, in: *Register of the Department of State, December 23, 1918* (Government Printing Office, Washington DC, 1919), p.115.
23. G.A. Petzold and his son G.E.C. Petzold, two Croydon chemists.
24. TNA KV2/1083, serial 69a.
25. TNA KV2/1071, serial 72a.
26. Catomance Processing Company Ltd. was a 'company who developed waterproofing of textiles': https://www.ourwelwyngardencity.org.uk/content/history-of-welwyn-garden-city/where_do_you_think_we_worked/audio_recordings-2/catomance_processing_company_ltd
It is still at the same address.
27. *Register of the Department of State* gives his date of birth as 28 June 1888 at Winchester, Virginia.
28. TNA KV2/1073.
29. TNA KV2/1073.
30. TNA KV2/1083, serial 70a: 'In view of the fact that no outside enquiries have been made, it has not been possible to identify MYER (mentioned in my previous report) as one of KRONISCH's associates attempting to travel to the USA.'
31. TNA KV2/871-4.
32. TNA KV2/1083, serial 70a; see also: HO334/217/45595 on Friedmann. Eyssen's MI5 file is not available from the National Archives at Kew. West, Nigel, *MI5*, op.cit., p.55. Rösel was suspected by MI5 of being a Gestapo agent and deported in April: Simpson, *In The Highest Degree Odious*, p.52.
33. TNA KV2/1280, serial 56.
34. Chief Inspector of Arms.
35. MI4, the Geographical Survey, General Staff (GSGS) *was* ordered to transfer to Cheltenham in September 1939 to make room for other departments. HMSO Ch.1, pp.2, 3 & 5: https://library.mcmaster.ca/maps/ww2/HMSO_chapter01.pdf
The War Office also requisitioned Cheltenham Ladies' College.
36. Queen Victoria's Rifles, 9th (County of London) Regiment, was a Territorial Army infantry battalion of the British Army, which became 7th Bn King's Royal Rifle Corps on 1 April 1941.
37. The Projector, 2.5 inch – more commonly known as the Northover Projector – was an *ad hoc* anti-tank weapon used by the British Army and Home Guard during the Second World War, designed by Home Guard officer Robert Harry Northover, and was put into production in 1940 following a demonstration to the Prime Minister, Winston Churchill.
38. Russian ambassador to Britain (1932-43).

39. Possibly refers to William Stephenson, head of British Security Coordination (BSC).
40. Sir Frank Nelson, KCMG (1883-1966), first head of SOE (1940-42).
41. TNA KV2/1071, serial 78a.
42. TNA KV2/1071, serial 57J.
43. TNA KV2/1071, serial 57b.
44. TNA KV2/1072, serials 80k, 81a
45. TNA KV2/1072, serial 85a.

Chapter 10. Plan STENCH

1. West, *Liddell*, op.cit., p.182.
2. TNA KV2/1073, serial 165B.
3. A document in the Wellcome Library, Western Manuscripts lists Williams as being at the CDRD (Chemical Defence Research Department) at Porton Down 1941-2: Chemical warfare agents research: general correspondence, SA/SRL/M.1/1/1/2, Box 29; he is also listed as being at the Ministry of Supply and the author of 'Interrogation of Professor Ferdinand Flury and Doctor Wolfgang Wirth on the Toxicology of Chemical Warfare Agents' in: Verdon, Rachel (ed.), *Lyme Disease and the SS Elbrus. Collaboration between the Nazis and Communists in Chemical and Biological Warfare* (Elderberry Press LLC, Oakland, OR, 2011), p.173, n.6.
4. https://erenow.net/ww/british-military-respirators-anti-gas-equipment-two-world-wars/3.php
   See: Schmidt U. (2017) 'Preparing for Poison Warfare: The Ethics and Politics of Britain's Chemical Weapons Program, 1915–1945', in: Friedrich B., Hoffmann D., Renn J., Schmaltz F., Wolf M. (eds) *One Hundred Years of Chemical Warfare: Research, Deployment, Consequences.* Springer, Cham: https://link.springer.com/chapter/10.1007/978-3-319-51664-6_6#citeas
5. James Davidson-Pratt was an industrial chemist who was Controller of Chemical Defence Research and Development at the Ministry of Supply, who had worked at the Ministry of Munitions during the First World War. See: Hartcup, Guy, & B. Lovell, 'Unacceptable Weapons: Gas and Bacteria', in: *The Effect of Science on the Second World War* (Palgrave Macmillan, Basingstoke, 2000), p.143.
6. TNA KV2/1073, serials, 165c, 167C.
7. Skatole is also known as 3-methylindole, with a chemical formula of C_9H_9N, produced by the decomposition of tryptophan in the digestive tract of mammals.
8. https://www.jpost.com/diaspora/britains-secret-wwii-plan-stink-bomb-hitler-467593
   https://www.thetimes.co.uk/article/secret-plan-to-stink-bomb-the-nazis-gfwm5fdvx

NOTES

Chapter 11. The 'mythical Christmas card'

1. TNA KV2/1074, serial 216. Not in the file.
2. TNA KV2/1074, serial 201L.
3. TNA KV2/1074, serial 206.
4. TNA KV2/1074, serial 210A.
5. TNA KV2/1074, serial 223A.
6. TNA KV2/1074, serial 220A. BALLOON's answers are not included in the file.

Chapter 12. 'Gardiner is all right'

1. TNA KV2/1073, serial 177A.
2. TNA KV2/1073, serial 190b.
3. After the war he became the first Courtauld Professor of Chemical Engineering at Imperial College, London (1945-61) and President of the Institution of Chemical Engineers.
4. Most likely Wing Commander Thomas R. Bird in DSR.
5. Listed as E/D.1 (Devices) and E/D.1C (Devices). Source: Alan 'Fred' Judge, Military Intelligence Museum, Chicksands.
6. Charles Howard 'Dick' Ellis was an Australian who joined SIS in Paris in 1923 and became deputy head of British Security Coordination (BSC) in New York under William Stephenson; after the war he served as the SIS Controller Far East, and Controller Western Hemisphere; later he helped to establish the Australian Secret Intelligence Service (ASIS). He was first married to 17 year-old White Russian Elizabeth (Lilia) Zelensky (Zelinski) at the British High Commission in Constantinople (now Istanbul) on 12 April 1923.
7. Major (later Lieutenant Colonel) Francis Thomas Davies, PA to Sir Frank Nelson, and later Director of Service & Supplies (A/DZ). See: Mackenzie, *The Secret History of SOE 1940-1945*, p.81. TNA HS9/949/5. Information supplied by Alan 'Fred' Judge; West, *Secret War*, pp.9, 18, 51, 79, 256, 259, 261 & 263.
8. TNA KV2/1073, serial 187A. Alexander Michailovich Prigorowsky, born in Russia on 12 November 1886, who arrived in Britain from Germany in 1917 and a shareholder in British Graphitised Metals Ltd., owned by Postnikow. Prigorowsky, and his wife Katarina *née* Jakovleva (1897-1964) became naturalised Britons in 1948: TNA HO334/216/45015.
9. TNA KV2/1073, serial 189A.
10. TNA HS9/563/1. P.T.C. = 'put through the cards' – the vetting process by Special Branch & MI5.
11. TNA HS9/563/1.
12. Turner, *Aston House, Station 12. SOE's Secret Centre*, p.51; however, Turner's information is almost certainly a typo. Steven Kippax, personal communication to the author, 27 May 2020. Listed in the *Supplement to the London Gazette*

20 September 1945 (p.4671), as 'Robert Drummond GARDINER (175244), Corps of Royal Engineers (St Leonards-on-Sea). Major (Temporary)'; and later in the *Supplement to the London Gazette* 4 March 1949 (p.1119) in the Supplementary Reserve of Officers, as CORPS OF ROYAL ENGINEERS. Transportation. Lt (War Subs. Maj.) Robert Drummond GARDINER, MBE (175244), from Emerg. Commn, to be Maj., 11th Jan. 1949, with seniority 13th June 1946. Lt (War Subs. Capt.)' He is also listed as serving in Italy between 1943 and 1945, according to Forces War Records and TNA WO 373/73/859.
13. Boyce & Everett, *SOE the Scientific Secrets* (Sutton Publishing, Stroud, 2003), pp. 12, 25, 28, 30, 42, 133-5, 151, 154, 202, 224 & 265; Mackenzie, op.cit., p.333 & n.*, pp.722, 724. See also: http://dudleynewitt.weebly.com/
14. TNA KV2/1073, serial 191k.
15. TNA KV2/1074, serial 209b.

Chapter 13. The Scandinavian Connection

1. Extract from a Home Office file in TNA KV2/1074, serial 242b.
2. The Geni.com website states born Akershus, Norway, 1 February 1898, died Oslo, 28 April 1956.
3. Fertik, Ted, 'Packaging Industrialization and Selling It: State-Guaranteed Export Financing and Nationalist Industrialization, 1920-1940', Paper for the History Project "Institutions, Credit, and the State" Conference, September 2014, p.22, and note 44.
4. Perin & Marshall of New York were consulting engineers to the Tata Iron and Steel Company (TISCO) Ltd., of Jamshedpur, India.
   Hermann Alexander Brassert (1875-1961) was a German-American iron and steel entrepreneur who founded the company in Chicago in 1925. He left Germany in October 1939. See: https://de.m.wikipedia.org/wiki/Hermann_Alexander_Brassert
   Knute Lund is also mentioned in: Howard, *Workers at War: Labor in China's Arsenals, 1937-1953*, n.47, p.381; and in: US Department of State, *Foreign Relations of the United States: Diplomatic Papers 1944, Volume VI China*, (US Government Printing Office, Washington, 1967), n.21, pp.1051-2.
5. Extract from a Home Office file (L.3055) in TNA KV2/1074, serial 242k; b. Akershus, Norway 1 February 1898; died Oslo, 28 April 1956; married to Beatrice Helen Bengston Lund, b.1906; she later married David Fortune 'Taffy' Landale (1905-70) in 1956.
6. TNA HS9/949/5.
7. TNA KV2/1074, serial 242b.
8. TNA HS9/949/5.
9. TNA KV2/1074, serial 242b.

NOTES

10. TNA HS9/949/5.
11. TNA HS9/949/5.
12. TNA HS9/949/5.
13. TNA KV2/1074, serial 242b. Political Intelligence Department of the Foreign Office (1939-43); Sir Reginald 'Rex' Wildig Allen Leeper, GBE, KCMG (1888-1968), British diplomat who worked in the PID – Political Intelligence Department – during the First World War.
14. TNA KV2/1074, serial 221y.
15. TNA KV2/1074, serial 242b.
16. TNA KV2/1075, serial 331a.
17. TNA AIR27/956, 138 Squadron Operations Record Book, p.133: 'Halifax P627 took off on operation TABLELAMP/TABLEGOSSIP captained by F/O POLKOWSKI. Target DENMARK. Operation completed ...'; Clark, *Agents by Moonlight*, p.153: 'Finding the target flashing 'Q' it took four minutes to parachute in from 800 feet, Kai Lund, four containers and one package'; Anon, *SOE in Denmark. An Official History*, p.64.
18. Major (later Major General) Sir Kenneth William Dobson Strong, Royal Scots Fusiliers. DSO in Gibraltar (1935); assistant military attaché, Berlin (1938): Rankin, Nicholas, *Defending the Rock*, p.146. Became Director of the Joint Intelligence Bureau (JIB) in 1946.
19. TNA HS9/949/5.
20. http://modstand.natmus.dk/Person.aspx?85063

Chapter 14. 'A sub-machine gun of outstanding design'

1. TNA KV2/1076: *Chronological Diary of Events re: V.A.P. Sub-Machine Carbine 9 m/m Type V.-A2. 1941-1942*. Josef Vesely, b.1905/6, TNA HO405/57319, closed until 2052; HO334/350/17535; the Vesely Machine Carbine (aka V-41, V-42, and V-43).
2. Major R.V. Shepherd OBE, Inspector of Armaments in the Ministry of Supply, Design Department at the Royal Arsenal, Woolwich.
3. (Sir) Claude Dixon Gibb CBE ME MIMechE (c.1898-1959), awarded the KBE in 1945. Chairman of the Tank Board in 1945 and also Director General of the Armoured Fighting Vehicles Division of the Ministry of Supply. See: *Hansard*, 14 February 1945, vol.408. Also Director General of Weapon & Instrument Production, Ministry of Supply; *Graces Guide*: https://www.gracesguide.co.uk/Claude_Dixon_Gibb
http://adb.anu.edu.au/biography/gibb-sir-claude-10294
4. TNA KV2/1070, serial 19a.
5. TNA KV2/1070, serial 14a.
6. Captain (temporary Major) Samuel George Maddox Shallard MBE, Royal Artillery.
7. TNA KV2/1070, serial 16c.

8. TNA KV2/1070, serial 19a; see also serial 16c.
9. TNA KV2/1070, serial 16c.
10. TNA KV2/1070.
11. Hastings, *Das Reich*, paperback edition, p.237.
12. Firearms Act (1937), Section 17, 1(a): '1) It shall not be lawful for any person without the authority of the Admiralty, the Army Council or the Air Council to manufacture, sell, transfer, purchase, acquire, or have in his possession – (a) any firearm which is so designed or adapted that, if pressure is applied to the trigger, missiles continue to be discharged until pressure is removed from the trigger or the magazine containing the missiles is empty;' https://www.legislation.gov.uk/ukpga/1937/12/section/17/enacted
13. Colonel J.H.T. Icke, Deputy Assistant Director (Small Arms), Department of the Master-General of the Ordnance in 1937; Chief Inspector of Small Arms (CISA), 1942.
14. TNA KV2/1076, serial 380b.
15. Gerald Austin Gardiner CH QC PC (1900-90), later Lord Gardiner and Lord High Chancellor (1964-70); Dr James Mould QC (1893-1958), whose career was built around patents and design cases.
16. TNA KV2/1076, serial 374a.
17. TNA KV2/1076, serial 379k.
18. Listed in the *Army List* 1939 as Major E.R. Hooper, an Inspector in the Small Arms Inspection Department, of the Inspection and Experimental Staff, Armaments Inspection Department, Royal Arsenal, Woolwich, and a member of the Loyal Regiment, Metcalfe's former regiment.
19. Sir Charles Northrup McLaren (c.1899-1955).
20. TNA KV2/1077, serial 430a. 'Brief report on the activities of the writer in connection with the advancement of the above mentioned weapon' (the V-42 Submachine Carbine 9 mm).
21. TNA KV2/1077, serial 448b.
22. TNA KV2/1077, serial 453a.
23. Freshfields, Leese & Munns (1921-45); now Freshfield Bruckhaus Deringer LLP.
24. Young, *The House That Jack Built. The Story of H.M.S. Excellent.*
25. TNA KV2/1077, serial 463A.
26. TNA KV2/1077, serial 463A.
27. Colonel G. Rutledge RM (ret'd), Naval Ordnance Department.
28. TNA KV2/1078, serial 476a.
29. Quoted from Ben Pimlott's review in the *Guardian* 25 October 2003 of Fort's biography of Lindemann, *Prof: The Life of Frederick Lindemann*.
30. Cherwell attended the Third Washington Conference (12-25 May 1943) on 25 May 1943 prior to going on to Quebec City (14-24 August), and met with Harry Hopkins, Roosevelt's foreign policy advisor, and Vannevar Bush, who headed the US Office of Scientific Research & Development.
31. TNA KV2/1078, serial 505a. One website mentions that the gun was tested at Valcartier, Quebec.

32. Major E.J.T. Goudie, permanent secretary of the Inter-Services Security Board, Military Secretary's Office, War Office, recommendation for award; see: TNA WO373/147/682.
33. PIAT (Projector, Infantry, Anti-Tank) Mk1 entered service in the British Army in mid-1943. The Dome trainer was an anti-aircraft gunnery trainer. See: https://langhamdome.org/about-raf-langham/the-dome-dome-training/
See also: TNA WO291/2034
34. TNA KV2/1078, serial 539a.
35. TNA KV2/1079, serial 578a.
36. TNA KV2/1079, serial 573k.

Chapter 15. A thorn in BALLOON's side

1. TNA KV2/1079. See Ch. 14, n.3.
2. TNA KV2/1079, serial 551a.
3. TNA KV2/1079, serial 550a.
4. Major Brian Ashford-Russell, OBE (1907-2003), formerly of 7 Commando, recruited by SIS in 1943 to penetrate Italy after having been wounded in North Africa and repatriated under the Geneva Convention. His wife, Elizabeth Catherine Todd (1921-2009) worked at SIS as Dansey's secretary.
5. Jeffrey, *The Secret History of MI6*, pp.501 & 557.
6. Major Aeneas John Martin Perkins RE: https://www.pegasusarchive.org/arnhem/war_4parasqn.htm
Perkins later commanded 4 Para Squadron, Royal Engineers during Operation MARKET GARDEN, part of Brigadier 'Shan' Hackett's 4 Para Brigade. He dislocated his shoulder on landing at Arnhem and was captured. See also: https://www.unithistories.com/officers/1AirbDiv_officersP.htm and TNA WO311/870, Correspondence relating to 'Q' forms (MI9 form, information supplied by ex-POWs).
7. https://www.paradata.org.uk/unit/airborne-forces-development-centre Now JATEU, the Joint Air Delivery Test and Evaluation Unit at RAF Brize Norton.
8. Lieutenant General Sir Frederick 'Boy' Browning (1896-1965), Commander, HQ Airborne Troops (later known as I British Airborne Corps).
9. Middlebrook & Everitt, *The Bomber Command War Diaries*, pp.422-4; Middlebrook, *The Peenemunde Raid*; TNA AIR20/4040.
10. TNA KV2/1079, serial 555a.
11. Possibly Louis de Saumarez Tufnell (1908-81), described as a company director: *London Gazette*, 18 October 1966, p.11302.

Chapter 16. The Grand, Cliveley and Postnikow Affair

1. TNA KV2/1075, serial 283f.
2. TNA HS9/328/4.

3. 'Major Richard Constantine CLIVELY, MC (108306), from Army Officers' Emergency Reserve, to be Lt 2nd Sept. 1939 (Substituted for the notifn in the Gazette of 5th Sept. 1939.)': *Supplement to The London Gazette*, 26 January, 1940, p.524; SUPPLEMENT TO THE LONDON GAZETTE, 21 MARCH, 1941, p.1652: 'PIONEER CORPS. War Subs. Capt. R. C. Clively, MC (108306), from Spec. List (T.A.R.O.) [Territorial Army Reserve of Officers], to be War Subs. Capt. 13th Feb. 1941, retaining his present seniority.' Richard Constantine Clively (1892 – 1960), Atkin, *Section D for Destruction*, Appendix 2, p.18; pp.30, 129, 145, 146 & 210, and personal communication to the author, 24 January 2021.
An organisational chart for the Ministry of Economic Warfare in 1942-43 shows an F.F. Clively in that position.
4. For more information on Section D and Grand, see Mackenzie, op.cit. Ch.II, pp.12-37; Atkin, op.cit. In 1943 W/S Colonel, Temporary Brigadier Grand was recommended by General George Giffard, GOC-in-C 11th Army Group in India and Burma, for a CBE while serving at HQ IV Corps in Burma as Chief Engineer (Works) (awarded 16.12.43), see: TNA WO 373/79 Pt.2.
5. 'The Russo-British Grain Export Company was specially formed to assist in the sale of Soviet grain produce in Great Britain. The composition of this company is as follows: on the Soviet side (1) Centrosoyus – the Soviet Consumers' Co-operative Organisation; (2) Arcos ...' Krassin, Leonid, 'Future of Soviet Trade Relations II', in: *Russian Information and Review*, April 5, 1924, Vol. III, no.1, p.213.
6. TNA KV2/1075, serial 269b.
7. TNA KV2/1075, serial 286c.
8. Atkin, op.cit., pp.129-30; TNA HS8/255.

Chapter 17. 'It is clear that B is in debt'

1. TNA KV2/1074, serial 224A.
2. TNA KV2/1074, serial 224D.
3. TNA KV2/1074, serial 263B.
4. TNA KV2/1074, serial 263B.
5. TNA KV2/1075, serial 274b.
6. TNA KV2/1075, serial 274b.
7. TNA KV2/1075, serial 282a.

Chapter 18. Correspondence

1. TNA KV2/1079, serial 641A.
2. TNA KV2/1074, serial 233A.

NOTES

3. TNA KV2/1075, serial 276a.
4. TNA KV2/1075, serial 276b.
5. TNA KV2/1075, serial 277d.
6. TNA KV2/1075, serial 286a. This bank was also responsible for sending Rosina Anna Schmidt a cheque for £50 in June 1940 (KV4/465).
7. TNA KV2/1075, serial 285a.
8. TNA KV2/1075, serial 286b.
9. The company, now Sousa, Campos & Pereira Lda, according to the Dun & Bradstreet Business Directory, 'is located in MAIA, Portugal and is part of the Solid Waste Services & Recycling Industry. SOUSA, CAMPOS & PEREIRA, LDA has 11 employees at this location and generates $1.97 million in sales (USD)': https://www.dnb.com/business-directory/company-profiles.sousa_campos__pereira_lda.e3fa523873b8bb9d287804dcde071c6a.html
It is described as an importer of canned, preserved foods in *International Commerce*, July 4, 1966, Vol.72, No.27, p.33.
10. TNA KV2/1075, serial 287c.
11. TNA KV2/1075, serial 287b.
12. TNA KV2/1172; Paul Fidrmuc, TNA KV2/197, serial 174b.
13. TNA KV2/854, serial 619k.
14. TNA KV2/1075, serial 293a.
15. Theresa Rachel 'Tess' Clay (1911-95) was an English entomologist who worked with Victor Rothschild in B1c during the Second World War and until 1948. She was suspected of being involved in the scientific frauds perpetrated by Richard Meinertzhagen. She was acknowledged by SIS and GC&CS as the 'expert on the sabotage aspects of ISOS and by her knowledge of the technicalities played an important part in elucidating the texts': Curry, op.cit., pp.241-2.
16. This may be (unconfirmed) Charles Herbert Schatz, son of clockmaker Carl Schatz of C.H. Schatz GmbH ('GUFA') and Hilda Fleming. See: Glanville, John & William M. Wolmuth, *Clockmaking in England and Wales in the Twentieth Century*.
17. TNA KV2/1073, serial 192a. Mentioned on p.69 of US Group Control Council: Directives (April 1945-June 1945): '722/66 Charles Herbert Schatz, Zürich (Vervaltung für das inländisch Vermögen)', US National Archives, Records of the Foreign Exchange Depository, Group of the Office of the Finance Advisor OMGUS, 1944-1950.
18. TNA KV2/1075, serial 290A; KV2/1276, serial 76a (GELATINE).
19. TNA KV2/285, serial 3a; KV2/850, serial 351c.
20. TNA KV2/1075, serial 290B.
21. Chiang Kai Shek (1887-1975) was the leader of the Republic of China (1928-75) and later President of Taiwan (1949-75) to which his nationalist forces fled in 1949, driven out by Mao Tse-tung.
22. TNA KV2/1075, serial 294a.
23. TNA KV2/1075, serials 298a (5.4.42) and 304a (12.4.42).

Chapter 19. The BALLOON Traffic (Part 1)

1. TNA KV2/1075, serial 305a.
2. TNA KV2/1075, serial 306a.
3. TNA KV2/1079, serial 572b.
4. TNA KV2/849, serial 242A.
5. TNA KV2/849 (TRICYCLE), serial 242b.
6. TNA KV2/1075, serial 312a.
7. TNA KV2/1075, serial 313B.
8. Not available in the file.
9. TNA KV2/1075, serial 313B.
10. TNA KV2/1075, serial 313bc. The last paragraph of the report is included as serial 289b in TNA KV2/61 (TATE).
11. TNA KV2/1075, serial 314b; the original is in KV2/849, serial 248a (TRICYCLE).
12. TNA KV2/1075, serial 315A.
13. TNA KV2/1076, serial 322A.
14. TNA KV2/1076, serial 323A.
15. TNA KV2/1076, serial 317a.
16. TNA KV2/1076, serial 317b.
17. TNA KV2/1076, serial 317b.
18. TNA KV2/1076, serial 318A.
19. TNA KV2/1076, serial 318A.
20. TNA KV2/1076, serial 320A.
21. TNA KV2/845, serial 21b.
22. TNA KV2/1276, serial 90k.
23. TNA KV2/1172, serial 24a, CSDIC report on Kraatz, p.iv. Ponal, also known as pyramidon, was the second-to-last secure secret ink available to Abw I/g.
24. TNA KV2/1962, serial 162b.
25. TNA KV2/1962, serial 162b.
26. TNA KV2/3568, serial 4a, a report produced by Headquarters, Military Intelligence Service Center, United States Forces European Theater, APO757, 29 August 1946.
27. The *Air Force List*, September 1941, p.851; *London Gazette*, 15 August 1941, p.4734.
28. The *London Gazette* (p.4734) shows him as a corporal as of 15 August 1941; the *Air Force List* for May 1942 (p.711) shows him as a pilot officer in the Administrative & Special Duties Branch as of 18 September 1941.
29. Air Vice-Marshal Ronald Graham CB CBE DSO DSC* DFC (1896-1967). In 1941 he was AOA, HQ Bomber Command.
30. Marshal of the RAF Sir John ('Jack') Cotesworth Slessor GCB DSO MC (1897-1979) was the son of Arthur Kerr Slessor and Adelaide Slessor *née* Cotesworth; Chief of Air Staff (1950-3).

NOTES

31. TNA KV2/1076, serial 322B.
32. Star Bonifacio Echeverria, S.A., in the Basque region of Spain, established c.1905-97.
33. TNA KV2/1076, serial 324a.
34. TNA KV2/1076, serial 325a.
35. TNA KV2/1076, serial 320B.
36. TNA KV2/1076, serial 320B. Colonel H.M. Allan of the GPO should not be confused with Colonel (later Brigadier) Harry L. Allen, Director of MI5's C and D Divisions (DC&D).
37. TNA KV2/1076, serial 329a.
38. TNA KV2/1076, serial 325b (BALLOON); KV2/849, serial 261a (TRICYCLE).
39. TNA KV2/849, serial 183a: pp.11-12 re: BALLOON.
40. TNA KV2/1076, serial 325b (BALLOON); KV2/849, serial 261a (TRICYCLE).
41. Banco Espírito Santo e Comeciale de Lisboa was founded in 1869 as the Banco Espírito Santo (BES); in 1937 the BES merged with the Banco Commercial de Lisboa to form the Banco Espírito Santo e Comeciale de Lisboa (BESCL). See: https://en.wikipedia.org/wiki/Banco_Esp%C3%ADrito_Santo#cite_note-2
42. TNA KV2/1076, serial 330a (BALLOON); KV2/849, serial 263a (TRICYCLE).
43. Commander Edward Reignier Conder DSO DSC MBE (1901-70), Operations Division, Admiralty, HMS *President*; Commander Frank Reginald Woodbine Parish DSO RNVR (1903-73), Local Defence Division, Admiralty, HMS *President*.
44. TNA KV2/1076, serial 338A. The ADNI is likely Major General R. Neville RM, in charge of Security, or Colonel Caulfield RM.
45. Possibly Major General Joseph Charles Haydon CB DSO* OBE MiD, Vice Chief of Combined Operations 1942-3.
46. Lieutenant General Sir Giffard Le Quesne Martel KCB KBE DSO MC MIMechE (1889-1958), Commander of the Royal Armoured Corps (1940-42).
47. Oliver Lucas (1892-1948), Director, Research and Development at the Ministry of Supply, involved with tank design.
48. TNA KV2/1076, serial 338b.
49. https://en.wikipedia.org/wiki/Nicholas_Straussler
   PF.39788, not available from the National Archives, Kew. A Canadian patent was issued to him on 1 December 1942, 'Means of Imparting Buoyancy to Vehicles', CA408921.
50. TNA KV2/1076, serial 342a. Rothschild's letter is not included in the file.
51. TNA KV2/1076, serial 337k.

Chapter 20. The TRIBAGE Organisation

1. TNA KV2/1076, serial 318k (BALLOON); KV2/849, serial 254b (TRICYCLE); KV2/176, serial 90c (GELATINE).
2. TNA KV2/1076, serial 318k. 3. Masterman, op.cit., pp.83-6; Holt, Thaddeus, *The Deceivers*, p.151; Montagu, *Beyond Top Secret U*, p.71 (MIDAS); see also: https://codenames.info/operation/machiavelli/
3. TNA KV2/845, serial 14c.
4. Masterman, *On the Chariot Wheel*, pp.212-13.
5. TNA KV2/845, serials 30a, 40a. Montagu was assigned to Hull as Assistant Staff Officer Intelligence in 1938. See: Montagu, op.cit., pp.58-9.
6. West, *Churchill's Spy Files*, p.132.

Chapter 21. The BALLOON Traffic (Part 2)

1. West, *Liddell*, op.cit., 10 October 1941, p.183.
2. TNA KV2/1074, serial 242c.
3. Hinsley & Simkins, *British Intelligence in the Second World War*, Vol.4, p.127.
4. TNA KV2/1076, serial 374b.
5. TNA KV2/1076, serial 374b.
6. Possibly Otto Karl Wilhelm Neurath (1882-1945), philosopher, philosopher of science, sociologist and political economist, who was interned in Onchan Camp on the Isle of Man. It could also refer to Wilhelm Theodor 'Willy' Neurath von Neudenegg, born in Vienna on 14 March 1900 and died early 1960s.
7. The original handwritten note mentions 'Commander R-M' which would suggest Commander Alan David James Robertson-MacDonald, listed as in NID (Naval Intelligence Division); see: the *Navy List*, February 1942, p.116, and HMS *President* (1939-42): https://www.unithistories.com/officers/rn_officersr2.html
8. Brigadier General Stuart Milligan Anderson DSO (1879-1954), married to Alexandra Helen Anderson *née* Janesco (1895-?), born Sinaia, Prahova, Romania. https://www.wikitree.com/wiki/Anderson-38192
9. Sir Miles Wedderburn Lampson, 1st Baron Killearn (1880-1964), Ambassador to Egypt and High Commissioner for the Sudan (1934-46).
10. According to American historian Gerhard L. Weinberg, Farouk wrote to Hitler promising him that when the Wehrmacht entered the Nile river valley, he would bring Egypt into the war on the Axis side: Weinberg, *A World At Arms: A Global History of World War II*, 2nd ed., p.223.
11. He took pickpocketing lessons and once stole a pocket watch from Winston Churchill, and the Shah of Iran's ceremonial sword.
12. TNA KV2/1076, serial 348a.

NOTES

13. TNA KV2/1076, serial 342b. First published in 1844; final issue 1961. Cunard, *Negro Anthology*. There was also lawyer, journalist, politician and diplomat Augusto de Castro Sampaio Corte-Real (1883-1971), a supporter of Salazar. It has not been possible to verify his identity.
14. TNA KV2/1076, serial 343a. Presumably George VI, but unclear what this information was supposed to be.
15. TNA KV2/1075, serial 314A.
16. TNA KV2/1076, serial 384a.
17. This must actually be 66 Westminster Gardens, Marsham Street, London SW1.
18. TNA KV2/1076, serial 366A.
19. Major Bernard Lancelot Pavey MBE (1893-1966) who served in the Bedfordshire Regiment during the First World War is listed as having papers deposited with the Imperial War Museum; listed on Geneanet as living at the address cited: https://en.geneanet.org/fonds/bibliotheque/go1&lang=en&nom=pavey&page=51size=20
And in the *London Gazette*, 21 December 1934 (p.8321) had been appointed as Liquidator to Factory Holding Limited whose business was being wound up. He is also shown as being an occasional student at King's College, London, 1930-1.
20. Geoffrey Harry Langdon (1887-1971).
21. TNA KV2/1076, serial 388a.
22. TNA FO9/2667.
23. TNA KV2/1076, serial 387b. Trooper Maclennan's (7944768) address was B Squadron, 52nd Training Regiment RAC, Bovington Camp, Wareham, Dorset.
24. TNA KV2/1076, serial 387b.

Chapter 22. 'Plan A'

1. Lieutenant General Laurence Carr CB DSO OBE (1886-1954), Senior Military Advisor, Ministry of Supply (29 April 1942 – 6 October 1944).
2. TNA KV2/1076, serial 381k.
3. FAS = 'Free alongside ship' (named port of shipment) means that the seller fulfils his obligation to deliver when the goods have been placed alongside the vessel on the quay or in lighters at the named port of shipment. This means that the buyer has to bear all costs and risks of loss of or damage to the goods from that moment: http://www.worldclassshipping.com/incoterm_fas.html;
FOB = 'Free on Board' or 'Freight on Board', means that the seller fulfils his obligation to deliver when the goods have passed over the ship's rail at the named port of shipment. This means that the buyer has to bear all costs and risks of loss of or damage to the goods from that point: http://www.worldclassshipping.com/incoterm_fob.html
4. TNA KV2/1076, serial 381k.

Chapter 23. 'I regard this as very naughty of BALLOON'

1. TNA KV2/1079, serial 576a. Raymond Mortimer (1895-1980) who became its literary editor (1935-47).
2. Some sources vary. See: http://www.v2rocket.com/start/makeup/design.html http://www.v2platform.nl/book/technical.html
3. TNA KV2/1079, serial 582a. Crowe is most likely Dr D.A. Crow, Chief Superintendent, Projectile Development, Ministry of Supply.
4. Fernando Eduardo da Silva Pais (1905-81), listed as an Army officer and engineer and one of the most famous technocrats in the repression of the Estado Novo regime (Second Republic, 1933-74). Linked to the PSP (Polícia de Segurança Pública, the civil preventive police force (est. 1867) from 1937 to 1944; Inspector general of economic activities in the years of the war economy; Director of PIDE and DGS, from 1962 to 1964, succeeding Homero de Matos. In 1974, during the so-called 'Carnation Revolution', he was captured and imprisoned. The PIDE (Polícia Internacionale e de Defensa do Estado) (1933-69) and DGS (Direcção-Geral de Segurança) (1969-74) were the Portuguese secret police. See:
http://www.politipedia.pt/pais-fernando-eduardo-da-silva-1905-1981/
http://portohojeesempre.blogspot.com/2010/10/falando-do-antigamente-e-tirando.html
5. War Office, *The Abyssinian Campaigns: The Official Story of the Conquest of Italian East Africa*. For list of countries where the publication was sent see: TNA KV2/1077, serial 438a.
6. TNA KV2/1077, serial 430b; see also serial 427k.
7. TNA KV2/1077, serial 431b.
8. TNA KV2/1077, serial 435a.

Chapter 24. Cover Addresses

1. TNA KV2/1077, serial 441b; the original is in KV2/1444, serial 428b (CARELESS). Federico Knappe @ Friederich Knappe-Ratey @ Fritz Knappe-Ratey. See: TNA KV2/101; https://fsu.digital.flvc.org/islandora/object/fsu:175857/datastream/PDF/view
2. TNA KV2/1077, serial 441b (BALLOON); KV2/1444, serial 428b (CARELESS).
3. TNA KV2/1442, serial 314a.
4. TNA KV2/1077, serial 445a.
5. TNA KV2/1077, serial 446a.
6. TNA KV2/1077, serial 446a.
7. The winery building is on the Praça David Leandro da Silva 4-5-6, 1950-064, Lisbon. A counter-jumper is a shop assistant (Oxford English-Spanish

NOTES

Dictionary). See: https://www.orientre.pt/marvila/sociedade-comercial-abel-pereira-da-fonseca-empresa-frente-do-tempo/
https://restosdecoleccao.blogspot.com/2011/10/abel-pereira-da-fonseca-era-no-inicio.html

8. TNA KV2/1078, serial 491a.
9. TNA KV2/1078, 493a.
10. TNA KV2/1078, serial 494a.
11. TNA KV2/1078, serials 500a, 501a.
12. TNA KV2/1078, serial 473k.
13. TNA KV2/1079, serial 574a.
14. TNA KV2/1277, serial 149a.
15. TNA KV2/1078, serial 469a.
16. Holt, op.cit., pp.500-1, 836; TNA CAB154/68; https://codenames.info/operation/shotgun/
17. TNA KV2/1078, serial 499a.
18. TNA KV2/1078, serial 504a.
19. TNA KV2/1078, serial 520a.
20. TNA KV2/1079, serial 578b.
21. TNA KV2/854, serial 627A; KV2/1078, serial 499a; see also CAB 154/68 for the actual document on SHOTGUN.
22. TNA KV2/1078, serial 504B, Extract from Weekly Traffic Summary No.119.
23. TNA KV2/1078, serial 509a.
24. Eugn Šoštarić-Pisarcic. See: West, Nigel, *Historical Dictionary of World War II Intelligence*, p.232. He became a naturalised British Subject on 5 November 1948 and lived at Cranbrook, Kent. See: TNA HO334/222/48480.
25. TNA KV2/1078, serial 511a.
26. TNA KV2/1078, serial 530a.
27. Possibly Emygdia Rosa de Aguiar, born São José dos Matões, Portugal, 1893.
28. Tiago José Garcia Vieira Neto, *The Violin in Portugal, c.1875-1950*, PhD Thesis, University of Sheffield, 2009, pp.345, 381. See also: http://ric.slhi.pt/Seara_Nova/visualizador/?id=09913.020.003&pag=24
29. TNA KV2/1078, serial 507B.

Chapter 25. Going nowhere

1. TNA KV2/1079, serial 555a.
2. TNA KV2/1079, serial 555a.
3. TNA KV2/1079, serial 572b. IVAN II = BALLOON; HOEFLINGER = Muntzinger, *Leiter* I H Ost (Army Intelligence East); PALAIS = OKW Abwehr, Berlin; HIOB = Heer I Ost Berlin;
HERIBERT = Hauptmann Otto Kurrer @ Kammler. See: TNA KV2/1172 (Kraatz)
4. TNA KV2/1079, serial 555a.

5. TNA KV2/1079, serial 556a.
6. There is no information available on which armoured car this was.
7. TNA KV2/1079, serial 558k.
8. TNA KV2/1079, serial 558k.
9. TNA KV2/1079, serial 565B, extracted from TNA KV2/854, serial 619k, page 1 (verso), report on TRICYCLE's latest visit to Lisbon.
10. J.J.W. Herbertson, Air Civil Administration, Air Group.
11. TNA KV2/1079, serial 655B
12. TNA KV2/1079, serial 568a.
13. Major General (later Lieutenant General) Sir John Fullerton Evetts CB CBE MC (1891-1988), ACIGS, 1942-4, and Senior Military Advisor to the Ministry of Supply, 1944; Sir Desmond Morton KCB CMG MC (1891-1971), Principal Assistant Secretary, Ministry of Economic Warfare, 1939, and Churchill's Personal Assistant, 1940.
14. TNA KV2/1079, serial 569a.
15. TNA KV2/1079, serial 569a.
16. TNA KV2/1079, serial 571a.
17. TNA KV2/3568.
18. TNA KV2/1079, serial 580a.
19. TNA KV2/1079, serial 572a.
20. TNA KV2/1079, serial 573L.
21. TNA KV2/1172.
22. TNA KV2/1079, serial 581a.
23. TNA KV2/1079, serial 589a.
24. TNA KV2/1079, serial 591B.
25. West, *British Intelligence*, p.263; TNA KV2/1079, serial 583a. See Ch.23, n.53.
26. Hinsley & Simkins, op.cit., p.247. Also mentioned as Major E.P. Combe MC, MI11 in TNA KV2/853, serial 582a.
27. Holt, op.cit.; Bendeck, *'A' Force: The Origins of British Deception During the Second World War*.
28. TNA KV2/1079, serial 593a. Clarence Decatur 'C.D.' Howe, Minister throughout the war.
29. TNA KV2/1079, serial 585a.
30. TNA KV2/1079, serial 587a.
31. GARBO's network was used 'on a large scale to support Operation STARKEY'. https://history.army.mil/documents/cossac/Cossac.htm
    See also: Holt, op.cit., p. 479, *passim*; https://codenames.info/operation/starkey/
    https://fas.org/irp/doddir/army/fm90-2/90-2ch1.htm
    https://www.combinedops.com/Operation%20Starkey.htm
    TNA CAB79/63/24; CAB79/63/26; CAB79/64/3; CAB79/64/6; FO954/32B/268.

32. TNA KV2/1079, serial 587a.
33. TNA KV2/1079, serial 588a.
34. TNA KV2/1079, serial 590x: 'Portuguese Acting As International Post Office', 12 November 1943. The copy appears to be incomplete (i.e. redacted). Lieutenant (later Lieutenant Commander) J.A.C. John Anthony (Tony) Hugill DSC RNVR (b.1916), assistant naval attaché, Lisbon, 1942-3. Later served in Ian Fleming's 30 Assault Unit, and managing director of Tate & Lyle (1956-65). Mentioned in Fleming's *The Man with the Golden Gun*: 'The top man at Frome is a man called Tony Hugill. Ex-navy. Nice man. Nice wife. Nice children. Does a good job... .' Cited in Simmons, *Ian Fleming's War*, pp.213, 234-5; Smith, *Ian Fleming's Inspiration*, pp.92, 96-7; Rankin, *Ian Fleming's Commandos, passim*; Griswold, *Ian Fleming's James Bond: Annotations & Chronologies for Ian Fleming's Bond Stories* p.431. The previous assistant naval attaché Lisbon was Francis Bartholomew Stillwell (1916-93) in 1942.
35. TNA KV2/1079, serial 590x.
36. TNA KV2/1079, serial 590x.
37. TNA KV2/856.
38. Michaela Keyserlingk: Personal communication to the author, 31 March 2021.
39. https://www.sabado.pt/vida/detalhe/o-carteiro-bissexual-dos-nazis-em-lisboa
40. The crash occurred on 22 February 1943. *New York Times*, 23 February 1943, p.1. Four were killed and twenty missing.
41. TNA KV2/856.
42. TNA KV2/1079, serial 589B.
43. TNA KV2/1079, serial 590x.
44. TNA KV2/1079, serial 590a.
45. TNA KV2/1079, serial 593B.
46. TNA KV2/1079, serial 594a. Schaffhausen is in eastern Switzerland. MANUEL is possibly (unconfirmed) Manuel Álvaro Marques de Aguiar. THIEL may be Hans Walter Ritter @ Hans Richter @ Horst Reinhardt @ H.W. Renken @ Fritz Thiele who had been working in KO Spain for Abt. II (Sabotage) since 1941. See: KV2/2130.
47. TNA KV2/1079, serial 595a.
48. TNA KV2/1079, serial 599a.
49. TNA KV2/856, serial 727a; KV2/1079, serial 601a, respectively.

Chapter 26. 'He continues to provide such information ...'

1. TNA KV2/1079, serial 604a, and KV2/856.
2. TNA KV2/1079, serial 606B.
3. Holt, op.cit., pp.193-4, 195, 196, 197, 199, 200, 203, 204, 272, 325. Harold Leonard Petavel (1900-77).
4. TNA KV2/856, serial 774a.

5. The process involved fusing bort (also spelled boart or boort), dark, imperfectly formed crystals to create industrial diamonds.
6. TNA KV2/1079, serial 608a. BALLOON's note is not in the file.
7. Simpson, op.cit., pp.337-41. The Home Office files on Robert William Liversidge (1904-94) are closed until 1 January 2065: HO382/410; HO382/410/1; HO382/410/2, but see: KV2/3717-18; TS27/501; TS36/261; HO45/25994. Liversidge's association with Nussbaum is mentioned in KV2/3717, serials 51x, 74a, 75a.
8. TNA KV2/3717, serial 51x.
9. TNA KV2/3717, serial 51x.
10. TNA KV2/1079, serial 608a.
11. TNA KV2/1079.
12. TNA KV2/1079, serial 613ab (extract); KV2/856, serial 801b (full report).
13. Jefferson, *op.cit.*, p.162, and see: TNA KV2/560 (Wrede).
14. TNA KV2/1079, serial 613c; KV2/857, serial 833b.
15. TNA KV2/857, serial 871a; KV2/1079, serial 618z.
16. TNA KV2/1079, serial 628a.
17. TNA KV2/1079, serial 630a.
18. TNA KV2/1079, serial 632a.
19. TNA KV2/1079, Minute Sheet, serial 616.

Chapter 27. 'A man of intelligence and resource'

1. Listed as Major (Brevet Lieutenant Colonel), Quarter-Master, on the Extra Regimentally Employed list, *Army List*, October 1938, pp.171-4. The Military Secretary's office was responsible for appointments, promotions, postings and discipline. At that time (1942-6) the Military Secretary was General Sir H. Colville Wemyss KCB KBE DSO MC.
2. TNA KV2/1079, serial 639A.
3. The MI5 reference can be found in TNA KV2/1079, serial 640a. The various drafts and correspondence can be found in KV2/1080.
4. TNA KV2/1079.
5. TNA KV2/1079, serial 643A.
6. Supplement to the *London Gazette*, 26 February 1946, p.1126: *Loyal R.*
The notifns regarding Lt C. le S. METCALFE (36714) in *Gazette* (Supplement) dated 5th Apr. 1935 and 20th Aug. 1935 are cancelled. Lt C. le S. METCALFE (36714) retires 7th May 1940, and is granted the rank of Capt.'
7. TNA FO371/48802. There is some discussion about Tarlair in TRICYCLE's file, KV2/862.
8. West, *Historical Dictionary of World War II Intelligence*, pp.181-2; West, *Churchill*, op.cit., p.132.

Epilogue

1. This may refer to the BSA 28P assault rifle being considered to replace the Lee-Enfield .303. However, there were issues with it and it was outdated compared with the EM2 and L1A1 SLR rifles, so never went into production. Alternatively, it might have been the 9x19mm BSA machine carbine (BSA EMC) unveiled in 1945.
2. Probably Nigel Sutton, Secretary-General of the Inter-Allied Separations Agency. https://history.state.gov/historicaldocuments/frus1945v03/pg_1316 https://history.state.gov/historicaldocuments/frus1945v03/pg_1317 TNA KV2/1079, serial 643A.
3. Cecil Claude Farrer OBE, 3rd Lord Farrer (1893-1948).
4. TNA KV2/1079, serial 645a.
5. TNA KV2/1079, serial 649a. Philip Grantham Yorke, 9th Earl of Hardwicke (1906-74); Giovanni Battista Caproni (1886-1957), Italian aeronautical engineer.
6. Ernest Jack Holford-Strevens, listed in 1932 as an intelligence officer with the DoT. Awarded the CBE (Civil Division) in the 1954 New Year's Honours List, as Joint Controller for the Board of Trade and the Ministry of Supply, North Western Region.
7. Possibly Major Donald Stuart Gore Marshbanks, Commanding 19 Army Troops Coy, New Zealand Engineers, responsible for all major docks in Benghazi, February to May 1943. Recommended for MBE; awarded 6 January 1944. TNA WO373/77/526.
8. TNA KV2/862, serial 1219a.
9. TNA HS1009/7. Information supplied by Alan 'Fred' Judge, Military Intelligence Museum, Chicksands. See also: Mackenzie, op.cit., pp.145, 164, 165, 178, 182-4, 186-7, 375, 376, 387.
10. The letter in TRICYCLE's file from H.K. Stocks of HQ Intelligence Division, 70 HQ, CCG, BAOR 15, states that Tedd, Flodorovic, held British Passport No. C.602683 '(Passport gives Christian name as John, British by naturalisation. Born YUKOYAR or YUKOVAR 19.9.16).' TNA KV2/862, serial 1228A.
11. Listed as Captain, Frederick Levens Cole MC, Headquarters 37 Military Mission, Mediterranean Special Operations; recommendation for MC, TNA WO373/59/386. He is also listed as Cole, F.L., Maj., Yugoslavia, ME66 in information supplied by Alan 'Fred' Judge, Military Intelligence Museum, Chicksands.
12. TNA KV2/862, serial 1221b.
13. TNA KV2/862, serial 1225a. Kurt Englander most likely was connected with Vereinigte Seidenwebereien GmbH of Krefeld, founded in 1920. See: *Administration and Operation of Customs and Tariff Laws and the Trade Agreements Program*, US Congress, House Committee on Ways and Means, 4th Congress, 2nd Sitting, 1956, p.1966.

14. Died 18 March 2000; son of Paul Brann (1873-1955) and Gabrielle Brann (1924-2015) *née* Biermer; married Rosemary Hewitt. Ancestry.com shows him as a major in the Intelligence Corps on their wedding day. He became a naturalised Briton on 5 February 1945; see: TNA HO334/160/17180; HO405/2275. The *London Gazette* for 19 March 1943 (p.1320) notes that his naturalisation had been granted on 6 February 1943 and that he was serving with HM Forces and gives his address as Hill House, Hill Road, Watlington, Oxfordshire. The *Supplement to the London Gazette* for 7 July 1944 lists him as Intelligence Corps (p.3175).
15. Fry, *The London Cage*, Appendix, p.222.
16. TNA KV2/1079, serial 650a.
17. TNA KV2/862, serial 1230A.
18. TNA KV2/1080, serial 658.
19. TNA KV2/1080, serial 673.
20. West, (ed), *Guy Liddell's Cold War MI5 Diaries, Volume 2, January 1948–December 1950*, p.286; KV4/471, p.212.
21. TNA KV2/1080, serial 677a.

Index

A

Abwehr, xiv, 17, 31, 36, 40, 46, 50, 52, 134, 147, 151, 189–90, 200, 216–17
   KO Portugal, 17, 47, 117–18, 134, 172, 216
   KO Spain, 44, 235
Admiralty, 62, 64, 66, 100, 126, 137, 143–4, 224, 229
Agent M/G, 6
Aguiar, 164–65, 233, 235
Aguiar, Herberto, 164–5
Aguiar, Veronica, 164–5
Ahlefeld, Fraulein von, 44–5, 216
Airborne Forces Development Centre (AFDC), 103, 191
Air Ministry, 9, 18, 22, 25–6, 66, 68, 104, 124, 135, 144, 147, 158, 169, 213
Allan, Col H.M., 40, 78–9, 136, 148, 156, 162, 229
Allen, Harry L., 14, 229
Allied Control Commission, 196
Almeida, Manoel, 160
Anderson, Brig. Gen. Stewart M., 146
Anderson, Sir John, 163
Anglo-German Fellowship (AGF), 36
Arents, Henri, 158
Arnold, S/Ldr Henry, 26–7
ARP, 4, 12–13, 194, 200
ARTIST. *See* Jebsen
Ashford-Russell, Maj. Brian, 225
Ashley, Gisela, 195
Astor, Hugh, 169, 177, 183–4
Auenrode, Maj. Albrecht, 17, 47, 118, 216
Aufrichtig, 9–10, 209
Azavada, Francisco, 78

B

Babington Smith, F/O Constance, 104
BALLOON, 2–14, 18, 20, 24, 26, 30, 32, 36, 38, 40, 42, 44, 48–74, 80, 82, 86–106, 110, 112, 114, 116, 118, 122–32, 136, 138, 142, 146–56, 160, 162, 164, 168–92, 198, 201, 204, 208–46
   allegations, 145
   arrest, 128
   brother-in-law, 96
   career, 100
   character, 112
   claims, 188
   communications, 141
   company, 150
   connection, 168
   contacts, 144, 146
   controlled, 129
   correspondence, 32, 141
   cousin, 146
   creditors, 187
   debt, 111
   double-cross, xvi–xvii
   files, 6, 84, 114, 184, 199, 216
   gas mask, 76–77
   and GELATINE, 118, 121, 128, 140–2, 175–76, 182, 184
   and GELATINE's arrest, 142
   home address and British Graphitised Metals Co., 192
   information, 75, 187
   letters, 108, 115, 129, 137, 158, 160–1, 169–70, 173, 195
   letter to TRICYCLE, 137
   messages, 78
   motor racing activities, 4

name, 41, 169, 173
notional voyage, 174
outgoing letters, 117, 136
and Postnikow, 94
questionnaires, 129
recruited, 137
reports, 22–3, 60–75, 212, 218
salary, 40
secret ink, 132, 137, 170
secret letter, 80
services, 39
set-up, 137
status, 135, 144
temperament and mode of life, 192
titbits of information, 200
traffic, 120–39, 144–5, 147, 149, 174, 228, 230
and TRICYCLE, 39, 158, 189
unsuitability, 199
vagueness, 128
and War Office, 102
Balloon Trust, 108
Banco Espírito Santo e Commerciale de Lisboa (BES), 137, 149, 229
Barra, Col Alfonso, 60–1, 63–4, 114
Barroso, 116, 147, 178
Barroso, Francisco, 114, 116, 146, 171, 180
Barton, Susan, 55, 146
Batty, Col G.H., 194
Bayswater Security Section of SOE, 87
Beaverbrook, Lord, 67
Bennett, Sir Peter, 96
Bevan, Col John, 36, 188
Bingham, John, 26, 34, 213
Bird, Roland, 81, 160, 162, 164
Birkenhead, Lord, 101, 191
Blackford, A/Cdr Douglas Leslie 'Gerry', 27
Blunt, Anthony, 211
Blyth, W.H., 126
Boher Jessurum, 19
Boissevain, Charles Ernest Henri, 20
Boissevain, Robert, 19–21, 25–6, 156, 211–12
Bond, James, xvi
Boothby, Robert, 10, 15
Bowlby, Cuthbert, 103
Boyle, A/Cdr Archie, 9

Brann, Florian Oskar Paul, 197–8
Brann, Gabrielle, 238
Brann, Paul, 197, 238
Brassert, 84–5, 88, 98, 192, 195, 222
British Army, 162–3, 219
British Graphitised Metals, 4–5, 10, 12, 18, 41, 86, 103, 110, 192, 221
British Intelligence, 17, 19, 31, 46, 128, 142, 145, 149–50, 164, 168, 203, 205, 209, 211, 215, 230, 234
British Red Cross Society (BRCS), 4
British Security Coordination (BSC), 9, 137, 168, 220–1
British Small Arms (BSA), 7, 13, 63, 138, 187, 192, 196, 237
Brønderslev, 84, 87–8
Brooman-White, Dick, 60
Browning, Gen. Sir Frederick, 104, 191–2, 194, 225
Brust, Erik Nikita Wilhelm, 70, 72
Burma Defence Bureau, 6–7
Burnett-Stewart, Sir John, 3
Burnett-Stuart, Gen. Sir John Theodosius, 207
Burnett-Stuart, Sir John, 2–3
Burt, Supt Leonard, 109, 199

C
Cahan, J.F., 156
Canada, 18, 102, 119, 169–74, 176, 182–4, 186, 189
Canaris, Adm. Wilhelm, 134, 190
Canaris's resignation, following, 190
Captain Jarvis, 53
Caroli, Gosta, 204, 206
Carr, Lt Gen. Laurence, 151, 231
CELERY, xv, 205–6
Central Security War Black List, 20
Chamberlain, Sir Austen, 198
Chapman, Eddie, xv, 179, 203, 206
CHEESE, xv
Chemical Defence Experimental Station, 27
Chemical Defence Research Department, 220
Cherwell, Lord, 101
Chiang Kai Shek, 118, 227
Chichester, Lord, 23

INDEX

Chief Inspector of Small Arms (CISA), 90, 93–6, 101, 224
Chief of Imperial General Staff (CIGS), 11, 66, 209
Cholmondeley, Charles, 27, 74, 116, 140
Churchill, 101, 170, 236
Churchill, Winston, 219, 230
Clarke, Gen. D.M.C., 85, 98
Clay, Theresa, 117
Cliveley, Maj. Richard Constantine, 105–7, 225–6
Cliveley and Postnikow Affair, 107
COBWEB, xv
Cogger, Lt C.M. , 191–2
Cole, Maj. Frederick Levens, 198
Colville, Jock, 101
Combe, 27
Combe, Gp Capt Gerard , 27, 234
Combes, Colonel Edmund, 174
Combined Operations, 95–8, 102, 138, 229
Conder, Cdr Reignier , 137–9, 229
Cooper, Norman, 11, 22, 152, 209
Corey, Lt Gen Sir George, 4
Cotesworth, F/O William Lethbridge, 135–6, 228
Cowgill, Felix, 49, 53, 56, 61, 68–9, 115, 117–18, 120–2, 125, 131
Craufurd, John, 9, 70, 156
Crawford, Major General Kenneth N., 191
Cunard, Nancy, 146
Cunliffe-Lister, Sir Phillip, 213

D

Dale, Jim, 47
Dansey, Claude, 17
Davidson-Pratt, James, 76, 220
Davies, Lt Col Tommy, 82
Davis, Maj. Francis Thomas, 9, 82
Davis, William Rhodes, 9
De Azevedo, Maria Gonzalves, 52, 115, 122
Delattre, 203, 210–11
Denmark, 22, 84, 87–8, 161, 202, 223
Derbyshire, Capt.F.C. , 11, 16
Deutsche Arbeitsfront, 36, 73
diamonds, industrial, 188–90, 236
Dicky Metcalfe, xvi, 199–201
Director of Scientific Research (DSR), 28, 82, 94, 98, 221

Dos Santos, Francisco Barroso , 118, 130, 177
double agents, xiv–xv, xvii, 28, 36, 39, 44, 61–2, 100, 120, 123, 182, 200
Double Cross, 140, 203, 205–6, 216
Double Cross Committee, 34, 123, 162
Double Cross System, xiv–xv, 200, 204, 206
DRAGONFLY, 59, 218
DREADNOUGHT, 31, 197
Drew, John, 162
Dulles, Allen, 17, 211

E

Elles, Lt Gen Sir Hugh Jamieson , 2, 207
Ellis, Charles Howard 'Dick', 81
Englander, Kurt, 198, 237
Erren, Rudolf Arnold, 18
Evetts , Sir John Fullerton, 170, 234

F

Farrer, Lord, 196, 237
FBI, 9, 58, 97, 99, 118, 128, 133, 141–2, 167–8, 172
FEDERICO, 158
Fidrmuc, Paul, 227
FIFI, 204, 215
Fleming, Ian, xvi, 203–4, 235
Foley, Frank, 32, 131, 133, 136–7, 148, 162, 182
Foster, Supt Albert, 148
Frau Gaertner, 37
Freeman, ACM Sir Wilfred Rhodes , 213

G

Gaertner, Friedl, xvi, 34–7, 40, 45, 178, 216
Galpin, Maj.Christopher John , 26, 213
GANDER, 215
GARBO, xv, 176–7, 204, 206, 234
Garby-Czerniawski, Roman, xv, 203, 206
Gardiner, 32, 81–4, 86–7, 105, 207
Gardiner, Lord, 94, 224
Gardiner, Robert Drummond, 82, 86, 222
GELATINE, xvi, 35–8, 43–4, 73, 115–18, 120–2, 128–33, 137, 140–2, 161–2, 174–8, 181–2, 184–5, 187, 191, 200, 202, 227, 230
German agents, 24, 28, 32, 99, 169, 190
German Army, 61, 215

German espionage, xv, 23, 28–9, 200
Gertler, Manci, 6, 208
Gibb, Bridges, 103
Gibb, Sir Claude Dixon, 90–1, 101, 103, 223
Gil, Antonio Valverde, 149
Glanville, 149, 195, 203, 227
Glass, Eric, 46, 52, 56–7
Gledhill, Cecil, 117, 179–80
Golding, Maj. Ardale Vautier, 30
Gonçalves, Maria, 37, 133
Göring, Hermann, 9, 15, 152
Goudie, Maj. E., 102, 174, 225
Grand, Col. Laurence Douglas, 105–7, 225–6
Gray, Robert Lee, 67–8, 71–2, 219
Grogan, Alan, 54, 58, 136, 147–8, 160
Gruner, Dr Heinz, 20, 23
Gwyer, John, 161

H

Hambro, Sir Charles, 85
Hansen, Obst Georg Alexander, 190
Harker, Brig. Oswald Allen 'Jasper', 29, 35
Harmer, Maj. Christopher Harmer, 123, 158, 162
Harris, Tomas 'Tommy', 176, 190
Hart, Herbert, 164
Harvey, 148–9, 156, 158
Harvey, Cyril, 146, 148, 156
Herbertson, Capt. J.J.W., 169, 234
Hill, Col Walter Pitts Hendy, 3
Hispanic Britannic Trading Corporation, 93, 149–50
Hitler, Adolf, 15, 23, 190, 230
Hodgson, Maj., 138, 187
Holford-Strevens, Ernest Jack, 197, 237
Hollingworth, Payr Lt Cmdr Ralph Cooper, 84
Home Defence Executive, 124, 163
Home Defence Security Executive, 144
Home Office, 8–9, 26, 32, 84–5, 102, 108, 114, 192, 222, 236
Hooper, Col Edward, 90–1, 95, 224
Hoover, J. Edgar, 168
Hope
    Capt. Clement, 31
    Maj. Peter, 93
Horsfall, 'Jock', 31
Howard, Brig. E.A., 198, 203, 214, 222

Howard, Charles Henry George, 30, 221
Hugill, Lt Cmdr Tony, 177–8, 235

I

Icke, Col J.H.T., 94, 96, 224
Indian Political Intelligence (IPI), 6
Inter-Services Research Bureau, 81, 98
Inter-Services Research Dept, 81
Inter-Services Security Board (ISSB), 174, 225
Irsay, George, 31–2, 72, 149, 214
ISOS, 122, 129, 133, 161–2, 167, 227
IVAN I, 31, 50, 59, 120–1, 130–1, 134–5, 151, 163, 190, 216
IVAN II, 40, 43, 58, 121, 134, 141, 167, 190, 216, 233

J

Jarvis, Ralph, 54, 161
Jebsen, Johann 'Johnny', 44, 166, 169, 178, 182, 184–5, 189–90, 192, 216
Jessurum, Boher, 211
Johnson, Sir Robert Arthur, 199
Joint Intelligence Bureau (JIB), 223
Joint Intelligence Committee (JIC), 174
José, Maria, 180–1
JOSEFINE, 17

K

Kammler, 169, 233
Karlinski, Serge, 10
Karsthoff, Ludovico von, 17, 43–4, 47, 50–1, 53, 57–8, 117–18, 134, 151, 153–4, 168, 172, 185, 189–90, 216
Kell, Maj.Gen. Sir Vernon, 4, 6, 9, 13, 200
Kellar, Alex, 81
Keyserlingk, 179
Knight, Maxwell, 1, 34–7
Kolbe, Fritz, 17, 203, 211
Korab, Clarc, 158
Kraatz, August, 117, 172
Kremer-Aurenrode, 134, 172
Kronisch, Eugen Olgen, 67–71, 218–19
Kurrer, Hpt. Otto, 134, 169, 179, 216, 233

L

Lampson, Sir Miles Wedderburn, 230
Lane, Lt Col A.P., 96–100, 181

INDEX

Leeper, Rex, 86, 223
Lemon, 25, 213
Lennox, Maj Gilbert, 11, 16–19, 25–6, 28, 30–2, 38, 47, 51, 54–5, 61, 91, 157, 194–5
Lenz, Gustav Wilhelm, 44
Leverhulme, Lord, 101
Liddell, Maj. Guy Maynard, 8, 29, 35, 37, 40, 49–50, 52, 56, 76, 86, 144, 199, 216–18, 220, 230
Lima, Paulo Pinta da, 38, 40, 62, 137, 147–9
Lindemann, Prof. Frederick, 101, 224
Liversidge, Robert William, 236
Lloyd, Capt. M., 181–2, 184
London Cage, 198, 203, 238
London Controlling Section (LCS), 36, 162, 174
Londonderry, Lord, 213
London Reception Centre (LRC), 31
Lovinfosse & Hardy, 11, 16, 29, 209
Loyal Regiment, 1–2, 96, 207, 224
Ludovico, Maj. Albert, 118, 216
Luke, William, 2, 27, 29, 31–2, 36, 39–41, 44, 48–9, 51–2, 54, 56–8, 61–2, 68–71, 74–5, 78–82, 84, 91, 93, 105–13, 115, 151, 195–6, 199–200, 216
Lund
  named, 82, 84
  Capt. Knute, 85
  Kaj Ronald, 84–5, 87–8, 223
  Knute, 83–8, 222
Lund and Gardiner, 86

M

MacDonald, Cdr Robert, 146
Mackenzie, Murdo, 98, 192, 195, 198, 203, 221–2, 226, 237
Maclennan, Duncan Shaw, 149–50
MacManus, Lt Col Desmond , 194
MacNeal, Sir Hector, 66–8, 73
MacNeil, Sir Hector, 66–7, 71
Madrid, 44, 61, 135, 158, 173, 182
Maisky, Ivan, 74
Mallet, Maj. J.E., 9, 14–15
Markus, Paul, 188–9
Marriott, John, 34, 39, 47–9, 51, 54, 56–7, 98, 116–18, 120, 122, 126–7, 131, 138, 145, 156, 167, 176, 183, 187–8, 190, 192–3, 199–200
Mars, Maj. W.S., 21
Marshbanks, Maj. Donald Stuart Gore, 197–8, 237
Martens, Lucilea, 133
Martinez, James, 61
Martins, Lucilia, 115, 178–9
Martins, Mario, 178–82, 185, 189, 204
Master General of the Ordnance (MGO), 2, 207
Masterman, J.C., xiv–xv, 34–5, 38, 56, 79, 98, 116–17, 120, 130–1, 143, 156, 167, 186, 195, 204, 206, 230
Masterman, Sir John, xiv, 143
Maude, John, 52
Maxwell, Arthur Terence, 195, 197–8
McLaren, Sir Charles Northrup, 96, 224
McNeil, Hector, 218
Menzies, Maj. Ian Graham, 35
Menzies, Sir Stewart, 35
Metcalfe, 2–3, 5–8, 11, 13–14, 16–31, 38, 41, 67–9, 86, 108, 138, 151–4, 156–7, 195–7, 199, 201, 224, 236
Metcalfe, Christopher Le Strange, 1
Metcalfe, Daphne Geraldine Dorothea, 1
Metcalfe, Dorothea Maude, 1
Metcalfe, Lt Col Herbert Charles , 1
Metcalfe, Violet Beatrice Armine, 1
METEOR, 164, 168, 174, 191
MI1c, 6–7, 14
MI4, 219
MI5, xiv–xvii, 4–9, 11–14, 16–20, 23, 25–6, 28–9, 31, 34, 38–41, 47, 49, 54, 57, 64, 76, 79, 81–4, 87, 89, 91, 97, 99, 102, 106–8, 120–1, 128, 131, 133, 135, 143, 146, 151, 156, 160, 165–8, 184, 187, 191–201, 204, 215, 217, 219, 229
MI6, 203, 225
MI9, 60
MI9/MI19, 198
MI10, 91
MI11, 74, 102, 234
Mielitz, Teodoro, 134, 178–81
Miller, 204, 215, 217
Miller, Joan, 34–5
Mills, Cyril, 168–9, 171, 173–4, 182
Milne, 164

Ministry of Economic Warfare (MEW), 20, 156, 213
Ministry of Supply and Director of Artillery, 91
Moe, John, xv, 204, 206
Montague, Lt Cmdr Ewen, xvi, 34, 100, 119, 122, 138, 142, 147, 204, 230
Mortimer, Raymond, 155, 232
Morton, Sir Desmond , 170, 234
Mountbatten, Lord Louis, 102
Mussolini, Benito, 15, 23
MUTT, xv

N
Nathan, Lord, 194
Naval Intelligence Division (NID), 34, 40, 137, 230
Nelson, Sir Frank, 74, 81, 86, 220–1
Newall, ACM Cyril Norton Lewis , 213
Newitt, Dudley Maurice, 82
Niemöller, Pastor Fredrich Gustav Emil Martin, 212
Noble, John, 70, 164
Nunes, Jose, 116–19, 146
Nussbaum, Leon, 188–9, 236
Nye, Gen. Sir Archibald, 28, 195

O
O'Donnell, Brig., 194
Oliver, Dame Beryl, 4
Oliver, Victor, 148
Operation CATAPULT, 62
Operation COCKADE, 176
Operation CROSSBOW, 104, 156
Operation CRUSADER, 63
Operation GARBO, 210
Operation HYDRA, 104
Operation MARKET GARDEN, 225
Operation OVERLORD, 139
Operation STARKEY, 176–7
Ordnance Board, 27, 89, 91, 95–7, 101, 103
Orr, Desmond, 156
OSTRO, 134
Oxenstierna, Count Johan Gabriel, 17, 210

P
Pacheco, Cesar, 177–80, 182
Page, Col, 197–8

Pais, Tenente Fernando Eduardo da Silva, 156
Parish, Cmdr Frank Reginald Woodbine, 137–8, 229
Passport Office, 16, 169
Peenemunde Raid, 104, 204, 225
Pelham, Capt. John Buxton , 212
Perkins, Maj. Aeneas John Martin, 103, 225
Perlzweig, Jacob, 188
Petavel, Harold Leonard, 188, 235
Peters, Frederick J., 7, 9, 208
Petrie, Brig. Sir David, 28, 30, 194–5, 200
Philby, H.A.R. 'Kim', 160, 164–5
Pinto
  Oreste, 34, 147
  Paulo, 38, 40, 62, 116, 137, 148, 180
Plan BIRD WATCHER, 140
Plan LANGTOFT, 188
Plan MACHIAVELLI, 140
Plan MIDAS, 41, 43–4, 46–59, 120, 140–1, 216, 230
Plan OMNIBUS, 140
Plan PISCATOR, 149
Plan SHOTGUN, 162–3
Plan STENCH, 76–7, 122, 220
Political Intelligence Department, 223
Political Warfare Executive (PWE), 101
Popov
  Duško, xv–xvi, 31, 34–6, 41–3, 126, 191, 195, 197–8, 204, 206, 215
  See also IVAN I
  Ivo, 197
  See also IVAN II
Postnikow, Alexander Alexandrovich, 4–6, 11, 14, 16, 18–19, 22, 24–6, 67, 69, 71, 82, 86–7, 93–8, 101–2, 105, 107, 138, 151, 153–54, 192, 198, 208, 221, 225
Prigorowsky, Alexander Michailovich, 221
Pulliblank, Richard Aldwyn, 1, 207
Putlitz, Baron Wolfgang Gans zu, 8, 209

R
RAF, 27, 62, 64–5, 73, 81, 104, 144, 213–15
RAF Ashford, 218
RAF Brize Norton, 225
RAF Duxford, 66
RAF Leighton Buzzard, 215

INDEX

RAF Medmenham, 104
RAF Stanbridge, 215
RAF Tempsford, 87
Reid, Sir Edward, 49, 57, 105, 109, 114–15, 217
Robertson, Maj. T.A., 4–5, 38, 43, 51, 62, 92, 111, 113, 195, 200
Robertson-MacDonald, Cdr Alan David James, 230
Rothschild, Victor, 76–7, 102, 138–9, 227
Royal Engineers, 82, 222, 225
Royal Victoria Patriotic School (RVPS), 31, 34
Russia, 10, 22–3, 74, 106, 196, 221
Rutledge, Col G., 224
Ryde, Michael, 21

S

Sadd, John A., 76
Sahrbach, Elizabeth, 117, 172
Sampson, 7
Sancho, Antonio M., 164, 168
Sand, Erik, 53–57
Santos, Francisco, 114, 116, 131, 146–7, 167, 171–3, 178–4, 229
Schallies, Gunther, 73
Schatz, Charles Herbert, 117, 227
Schellenberg, Walter, 190
Schmidt, Wulf, 220
secret ink, 37–41, 43, 58–9, 79, 100, 131, 134, 137, 141–2, 144, 148, 151–2, 173, 184, 228
  new, 167, 171, 175, 184–5
Secret Intelligence Service (*see also* SIS), 7–8, 10–11, 17, 20, 31–2, 35, 58, 61, 69, 71, 83, 85–6, 106, 120–1, 126, 128, 131–2, 146, 148, 156, 160, 162, 164, 168, 170, 179, 182, 199, 211, 221, 225, 227
Sempill, Lord, 67, 70–1, 218
Senter, Lt Cdr, 81–7
Shallard, Samuel George Maddox, 223
Sheppard, R.V., 89–90
Simmonds, Cyril F., 95
Simões, Paolo, 38, 142
Sinclair, Sir Hugh 'Quex', 106
SIS Controller Far East, 221
SIS Head of Station in Lisbon, 117

SIS in Germany, 83, 86
SIS in Madrid and Lisbon, 173
SIS Liaison, 82
SIS Lisbon, 182
SIS Mediterranean Section, 103
SKOOT, 31, 34, 40, 133, 142
Smedley, Capt. A.S., 4, 208
Smith, Frederick 'Freddie' Winston Furneaux, 78, 101, 204, 235
SO2, 106
Soares, Arthur, 40, 62, 147–8
SOE, Security Section, Bayswater, 87
Šoštarić, Eugn, 164, 233
Spain, 15, 61, 64, 66, 135, 149, 151–3, 165, 216, 229
Special Branch, 7–8, 14, 32, 54–5, 68–72, 147–8, 199, 221
Special Operations Executive (SOE), 9, 77, 81–2, 84–8, 98, 106, 198, 202–3, 220–3
Spencer, Wg Cdr, 26–7
Stephens, Lt Col Robin, 188
Stephenson, William, 9, 49, 52, 54, 125, 137, 168, 209, 220–1
Stewart, Capt. J.R., 95
Stilwell, Lt F., 178, 180
Stockinger Gaertner, Friedl, 35
Stoddard, Nita, 5–6, 208
Stottinger, Friedericka, 35
Straussler, Nicholas Peter Sorrel, 138–9, 174, 187, 229
Street, Sir Arthur William, 25, 213
Strong, Sir Kenneth William Dobson, 87, 223
STS 2 Bellasis, 84
Suffolk, Lord, 28
SUMMER, 204, 206
Swinton, Lord, 144

T

Tarlair Ltd, 195, 197–9, 236
TATE, xv, 50, 53, 56–7, 59, 99, 120, 123, 202–3, 206, 228
  and DRAGONFLY, 218
Tester, Arthur Albert, 202
Thorn, Capt. M., 2
Thornton, 74–5
Thurston, Arthur, 97, 99, 167–69
Töppen, Oberstleutnant Martin, 50, 57

245

TRIBAGE Organisation, xvi, 140–41, 143, 230
TRICYCLE, xv–xvi, 29, 31, 35–41, 43–59, 61–2, 78, 99, 113, 115–18, 120–2, 125–30, 132–4, 136–7, 139–42, 146–9, 156, 158–9, 166–9, 171–3, 175, 182, 184–7, 189–92, 197, 201–2, 216, 228–30, 234, 236–7
   and ARTIST, 192
   and BALLOON, 132, 140
   cable, 53
   in Estoril, 56
   larger-than-life, 200
   in Lisbon, 50, 55
   organisation, 40
   reports, 128
   traffic, 118, 120, 128, 132
   Yugoslav Ring, 200
TRICYCLE/BALLOON/GELATINE, 128
Triplex, 17, 205, 211
Truman, Harry S., 27
Tuckey, Maj. P.E.C., 11, 16, 209
Tufnell, F/O A.C., 98, 104
Turner, G.G., 95, 204, 221

U

Underwood, Col John Percy Delabene, 2–4, 207
Uzelai, Jose Maria, 114

V

VELOCIPEDE, 174
Veltjens, Josef 'Seppi', 14, 210
Vesely, Josef, 89–98, 100–1, 104, 176, 191, 194, 201, 223–4
   and agreement, 94
   and request for permission, 90
   and sub-machine gun, 90, 99, 168, 223
Vivian, 8, 19–20, 106

W

Waddington, 7, 9
Waddington, Richard, 7
Warden, Maj. R.H. 'Dick', 87
Warnecke, 26, 44–5, 213
War Office, 4, 6–7, 11, 13–16, 19, 73–4, 91, 95–7, 100, 123–4, 138, 156–7, 168, 174, 191–2, 194–6, 204, 207, 219, 225, 232
Webb, Bridges, 98
Weil, Kurt Hermann, 8, 14
Weisblat, Eduard Casimir, 6, 202
Wenninger, Lt Gen Ralph, 9
Wheatley, Dennis, 34, 36
Wheatley, Joan, 34
White, Dick, 14, 55–6
Whyte
   D.H., 199
   Jock, 6
Wiesblat, 208
Wilson, Charles W., 31, 113, 198
Wilson, D. Ian, 78, 87, 97–9, 101–2, 104, 110–11, 113–14, 116–18, 120, 122, 125–6, 128, 130–1, 133, 135–6, 139, 146–8, 150, 158–72, 174, 176–8, 181–4, 187, 189–90, 192, 197, 200
Wilson, Gwendoline K., 113
Woodward, Edward, 47
Wrede, Sdfr Dr Joachim, 236

Y

Young, Cdr Robert, 95, 98
Younger
   Kenneth, 7
   Wiiliam 'Bill', 26, 213

Z

ZIGZAG, xv, 179, 203, 206